IRAQ'S BURDENS

IRAQ'S BURDENS

Oil, Sanctions, and Underdevelopment

Abbas Alnasrawi

Contributions in Economics and Economic History, Number 229

GREENWOOD PRESS
Westport, Connecticut • London

Library of Congress Cataloging-in-Publication Data

Alnasrawi, Abbas.
    Iraq's burdens : oil, sanctions, and underdevelopment / Abbas Alnasrawi.
      p.   cm. — (Contributions in economics and economic history, ISSN 0084–9235 ; no. 229)
    Includes bibliographical references and index.
    ISBN 0–313–32459–X (alk. paper)
    1. Petroleum industry and trade—Iraq.   2. Economic sanctions—Iraq.   3. Iraq—Economic
conditions. I. Title. II. Series.
HD9576.I72 A6473   2002
338.2′7282′09567—dc21   2002070046

British Library Cataloguing in Publication Data is available.

Library of Congress Catalog Card Number: 2002070046
ISBN: 0–313–32459–X
ISSN: 0084–9235

First published in 2002

Greenwood Press, 88 Post Road West, Westport, CT 06881
An imprint of Greenwood Publishing Group, Inc.
www.greenwood.com

Printed in the United States of America

The paper used in this book complies with the
Permanent Paper Standard issued by the National
Information Standards Organization (Z39.48–1984).

10 9 8 7 6 5 4 3 2 1

To the victims of oppression and sanctions

Contents

Tables

Acknowledgments

It gives great pleasure to acknowledge with gratitude the support and help I received in the course of researching, writing, and publishing this book. In addition to a sabbatical leave from the University of Vermont, I was generously assisted by Dottie LaBrie, Michael Hermann, Sondra Blanchard, John Beck, and Ghanem Mouri.

The constant support and encouragement shown by my family is deeply appreciated. I alone, of course, am responsible for any errors that may remain.

CHAPTER 1

The International Context of the Iraqi Oil Industry

Looking at the world map of oil reserves, we find certain facts that have shaped the history of Iraq and its regional context and will continue to do so for a long time to come. At the end of 1999 world oil reserves amounted to 1,033 billion barrels of oil with two-thirds of these reserves found in five countries: Saudi Arabia, Iraq, Iran, Kuwait, and the United Arab Emirates (see Table 1.1). Similarly in that year these countries were responsible for nearly one-third of the world oil production of seventy-two million barrels per day (MBD) and over 40 percent of the world's oil exports of forty-one MBD. In relation to the Organization of Petroleum Exporting Countries (OPEC) these countries command more than four-fifths of the organization's reserves and two-thirds of its output and exports. Therefore, what happens to the oil industry in any one of these countries will affect the economic fortunes of its neighboring countries. Moreover, the high degree of concentration of oil reserves, output, and exports in these five countries make them a constant target of outside power machination and interference. It is a well-known fact that the oil sectors in these five countries have been, until recently, under the direct control of a handful of multinational oil corporations (BP, Exxon, Mobil, Shell, Texaco, Gulf, and Chevron).[1]

The exploitation of Iraq's oil resources began in the early part of the twentieth century but modest oil export did not begin to flow until 1934. Iraq's oil

Table 1.1
Proved Oil Reserves, 2000 (billions of barrels)

Region/Country	Reserves
World	1046
OPEC	814
Middle East	684
Saudi Arabia	262
Iraq	113
North America	64
South and Central America	95
Former Soviet Union	65
Africa	75
Asia Pacific	44
Europe	19

Source: BP, *Statistical Review of World Energy 2001* (London: BP, 2001), p. 4.

output and export and revenue increased significantly after 1950 when the world demand for oil made the accelerated development of the country's oil resources both necessary and profitable. This rise in oil exports increased the share of the oil sector in the country's gross domestic product (GDP) and made the economy more dependent on changes in the world economy. This dependency on the world economy became more pronounced after the OPEC-led oil price increases of the 1970s. The consequences of this dependency for the society and the economy have been keenly felt since 1980; both in the course of the Iraq–Iran War of 1980–1988, and since August 1990 in the course of the U.N. Security Council–imposed sanctions on Iraq in the aftermath of the latter's invasion of Kuwait.

In this chapter and the next an analysis of the rise of the oil industry, its contribution to the economy, and its decline will be undertaken.

IRAQ'S OIL IN THE ERA OF FOREIGN DOMINATION

Until the end of World War I Iraq was under the control of the Ottoman Empire. Although European capital sought investment in Iraq oil in the latter part of the nineteenth century, such attempts were not successful. But the defeat of the colonial Ottoman Empire removed whatever political and administrative difficulties the Ottomans may have placed in the path of European economic domination of Iraq and the rest of the Arab region in the Middle East. Following the defeat of the Ottoman Empire the League of Nations granted Britain mandatory power over Iraq, Palestine, and Transjordan while France was given mandate over Syria and Lebanon. The removal of the Ottoman influence enabled Britain and France to shape political institutions and economic relations to serve the needs of twentieth-century Europe. It was in this newly created political context that foreign capital—European and American—began to flow into the region to develop its oil resources.

In Iraq, the government, which had been installed by Britain in 1921, signed in 1925 a concession agreement with a consortium of multinational oil corporations for the purpose of developing the country's oil deposits. These companies were British Petroleum (BP), Exxon, Mobil, Shell, and Compagnie Francais des Petroles (CFP). The major features of the concession regime were the following: (1) the life of the concession extended over many decades—seventy-five years to be exact—from 1925–2000 in the case of Iraq; (2) the concession covered virtually the entire territory of the country, thus giving the companies monopoly power over the development of the country's oil resources; (3) the companies had the sole power to determine output and export levels and to set prices. This meant that the government was excluded from any participation in making decisions relating to the most important sector of the economy; and (4) the government of Iraq was confined to the passive role of a recipient of a fixed sum of money per unit of output (amounting to some twenty-four cents per barrel of oil). In commenting on this imbalance in company–government pattern of relationships, George W. Stocking was moved to state: "Never in modern times have governments granted so much to so few for so long" (Stocking 1970: 130).

The asymmetry in the respective positions of companies and governments derive from a number of historical facts. First, most governments in the oil producing countries of the Middle East were either installed or controlled by Britain at the time the concession agreements were signed in the early part of the twentieth century. The concessions in Iraq, for instance, were obtained when the country was under direct British rule. The situation was essentially the same in Kuwait, Qatar, and Abu Dhabi, since these sheikdoms were British protectorates.

A second factor was the sheer ignorance on the part of governments of the importance of oil and the oil industry. Thus in Saudi Arabia the concession was granted by a ruler who was described as a medieval man. And in Iran the concession was obtained from monarchy that was described as an old, long-mismanaged estate, ready to be knocked down at once to whatever foreign power bid highest or threatened most loudly its degenerate and defenseless rulers (Stocking 1970: 123–126). Even as late as 1951 Iraqi officials who were negotiating certain modifications in the concession with oil companies confessed their ignorance of the existence of posted prices—the prices at which oil was traded in open world markets (Al-Pachachi 1968: 2).

Third, the asymmetry in power relations between governments and companies was built into the concession system itself because every operating company, such as Iraq Petroleum Company (IPC) was owned by more than one multinational oil corporation. These multinationals, furthermore, had by 1928 entered into cartel arrangements to eliminate competitive pricing by fixing market shares, controlling output growth from various sources, exchanging oil to lessen transportation costs, and ultimately fixing prices of crude oil and products regardless of source or cost of production (Blair 1976: 54–56).

This long-term exclusive monopoly over the oil sector gave the concession holders the power to develop, accelerate, or decelerate the pace of development of the oil sector. No less important was the fact that in time the Iraqi economy had become dependent on the export of one raw material, the production and the price of which were determined by a few oil companies.

Following the end of World War II development of Iraq's oil resources was accelerated to accommodate the projected rise in the demand for oil as Europe and Japan embarked on the tasks of rebuilding their war-shattered economies. Moreover, under the impact of changing circumstances (the increase in Venezuela's per barrel oil revenue and Iran's nationalization of its oil concession) the companies agreed in the early 1950s to amend the fiscal terms of the concession so that the government would receive 50 percent of the difference between the cost of production and the posted price of oil. This change resulted in nearly quadrupling government per barrel revenue to $0.84 per barrel in 1952–1959 compared with $0.22 per barrel in 1950. Relative to GDP the contribution of the oil sector increased from 3 percent in 1950 to 16 percent in 1960. And following the oil price revolution of the early 1970s its contribution jumped to 50 percent in 1974. In absolute terms the revenue from oil increased from $19 million in 1950 to $182 million in 1960 and to $6.5 billion in 1974.

The change in fiscal terms and the rise in the demand for oil created new conditions which demanded the direct involvement of the government in oil sector developments. Since its revenue had become a function of costs and prices the government could no longer ignore what happened in the world economy or in the international oil industry. But the government was constrained by the terms of the concession regime which lodged price and output determination in the hands of the companies. Moreover, the fact that the international oil industry was dominated by few firms made it possible for them to engage in pricing behavior that would keep prices from fluctuating as happened during most of the decade of the 1950s when oil prices in the Middle East were stable. This stability reflected the ability of the few multinational oil companies to adjust oil output to meet the rising demand conditions in the world market.

A key explanation to this ability was the oligopolistic structure of the oil industry in the Middle East which allowed a small number of companies to form joint partnerships for the purpose of developing oil resources in several oil-producing countries in the region—Saudi Arabia, Iran, Kuwait, and the United Arab Emirates. But this oligopolistic stability could not be maintained indefinitely. Among the factors that eroded traditional oligopolistic control were the coal protectionism policies of European countries, the entry of new firms in the international oil industry, the oil protection policy in the United States which restricted oil imports, and the reentry of Soviet oil exports into the world market.

These developments led the companies between 1958 and 1960 to lower prices several times, resulting in lower per barrel revenue for the governments—26 percent in Iraq's case. As a reaction to the August 1960 price reductions five oil-producing countries (Iraq, Iran, Saudi Arabia, Kuwait, and Venezuela) decided to form the Organization of the Petroleum Exporting Countries in September of that year. One of OPEC's earliest resolutions was the demand that prices be restored to their pre-August level and that future price changes be effected in consultation with individual governments.

PRICING OF IRAQ CRUDE OIL PRIOR TO OPEC

Long before OPEC was formed, the international oil industry was dominated by seven vertically integrated major companies (the majors), which controlled over 90 percent of the world oil production outside the United States and the former Soviet Union (FSU) in addition to most transportation, refining, and marketing facilities. The American majors also controlled a sizable part of the American oil industry. In 1928, the dominant majors (Exxon, BP, and Shell) entered into cartel arrangements to eliminate competitive pricing by fixing market shares, controlling output growth from various sources, exchanging oil to lessen cross hauling, agreeing whether to exclude competitors or admit them into the cartel system, and ultimately agreeing to sell crude oil and products at a fixed price regardless of source or production cost. Prices at the U.S. Gulf (of Mexico) Coast terminals constituted the basis for price quotations throughout the world. Because of this single-point system consumers in Iraq, for instance, were charged prices based upon quotations at the U.S. Gulf Coast, despite the fact that (1) the crude oil was produced in Iraq, (2) it was produced at low cost, (3) it was refined in a nearby refinery, and (4) the products were marketed by a local company.

The majors, whose goal was an orderly development of oil production through market allocation and price stabilization, were able to solidify their control through the utilization of two important mechanisms. The first was the joint ownership of locally operating oil-producing companies in the Middle East and Venezuela. This technique went far toward helping the majors coordinate and direct output to meet corporate oil requirements and avoid excessive output. Second, in order to allow new oil to enter the world market through the majors' integrated channels, long-term contracts were concluded between certain majors. The provisions of these contracts, which specified where crude oil was to be marketed and the terms of its sale, had the effect of tightening the joint control of the majors over the international oil industry (Alnasrawi 1975: 370–372).

The functioning of this single-point system could have continued if the dominant position of the United States in the oil industry had remained unchallenged, but such was not the case, because the Middle East emerged as another major production center.

However, as the capacity of the Middle East oil industry expanded, an outlet for the increased output had to be found either in the adjacent markets or in markets closer to the United States. But in order to penetrate new markets, Middle East oil producers either had to engage in freight absorption or retain the U.S. Gulf price formula. The latter approach was resorted to by the Middle East oil producers to help them expand their markets in the direction of the United States. To achieve this they had to forfeit phantom freight on sales made in their vicinity by charging actual freight cost instead of a fictitious cost from the U.S. Gulf. They selected this pricing strategy for several reasons. First, the corporate structure of the oil industry was such that most of the international majors in the Middle East also had major interests in the Western Hemisphere oil industry. Thus it was possible for the industry to accommodate the expanding capacity of the Middle East by operating that source of oil as a nonbasing point, quoting as its free on-board prices those of the U.S. Gulf (Smithies 1949: 308–318).

Second, the military operations of World War II in the Mediterranean forced a shift in the geographical distribution of the oil exports (Federal Trade Commission 1952: 355). This shift resulted in the reduction of Middle East exports to Western Europe on the one hand and in the increase in these exports to other Eastern Hemisphere markets on the other hand, causing the latter market to become more dependent on the Middle East for its oil. The large-scale military operations in the Eastern Hemisphere that stepped up the demand for Middle East oil, together with a dependence on the Middle East to meet this demand, prompted the British government (as the major buyer of Middle East oil) to question the validity of basing the price of its oil supplies on the prevailing prices in the U.S. Gulf.

To solve these problems a solution was arrived at whereby the British government would pay the same price for the oil bought in the Middle East as for oil of comparable quality in the U.S. Gulf, plus the actual freight costs from the Middle East to the final destination. Obviously, this new arrangement reflected the fact that the Middle East was becoming an important production region with its own new basing point, making its own sales in adjacent as well as distant markets.

A number of developments in the world market in the postwar period dictated a series of changes in the oil-price structure. First, the United States was rapidly reversing its role from that of a major oil exporter to that of a major oil importer. Second, there was a considerable increase in the demand for oil and its products because of postwar reconstruction, the expansion of the industrial sectors in many countries, the mechanization of agriculture, the relatively high demand for oil for military purposes in peacetime, and the increase in the number of automobiles. Third was the continued expansion of Middle East production capacity. In 1940 the region's average production was 0.3 MBD, or only 4.8 percent of the world total production. By 1950 output rose to 1.8 MBD or18.4 percent of world total production.

As the Middle East capacity expanded, more markets had to be found to absorb the area's supply within the existing price structure. This was accomplished when delivered prices for oil exports from the Middle East were lowered to enable Middle East oil to penetrate first European markets and eventually the American market itself.

The ability of the oil industry to set prices under a single-basing point system and its ability to adjust prices downward to allow for Middle East oil to compete in various markets derives from the oligopolistic structure of the industry. As late as 1959 over 90 percent of Middle East oil was controlled by seven sellers, the major multinational oil firms. This high concentration ratio was reinforced by the fact that some of the same oil firms controlled significant segments of the oil industry in the United States and the Caribbean. Another aspect of the structure of the oil industry was the special role played by the American government in enabling the U.S. oil industry to regulate oil output and therefore crude oil prices in the U.S. market.

The development of Middle East oil and the setting of its prices were done in a manner that preserved the stability of the price structure and prevented an outbreak of ruinous price and supply wars among oil-producing companies. The stability of the prices of Middle East oil in the decade prior and after the creation of OPEC may be seen in the price data in Table 1.2. The price quotations in the table illustrate that with minor changes, mostly downward, Middle East oil prices remained stable for more than two decades before being raised as a result of the 1971 Tehran Price Agreement.

The stability of Middle East oil prices was reinforced by the collusive action of the sellers which took the form of price leadership and was exercised by different sellers at different times. The rotation of leadership was possible because each of the major sellers controlled a considerable share of the market. Moreover, the prices during this period were being reduced in order to allow

Table 1.2
Evolution of Crude Oil Prices: OPEC Reference Basket, 1950–2000 (price per barrel)

Year	Price
1950	1.75
1960	1.73
1970	1.67
1974	10.77
1980	28.67
1982	32.38
1984	28.20
1986	13.53
1988	14.24
1990	22.26
1992	18.44
1994	15.53
1996	20.29
1998	12.28
2000	27.60

Sources: OPEC, *Annual Statistical Bulletin*, several issues (Vienna: OPEC); *Middle East Economic Survey* (Nicosia, Cyprus: Middle East Economic Survey).

Note: 1950 price refers to the posted price of Arabian Light at Ras Tanura.

Middle East oil to expand its share of the energy market. Another force was also operating to encourage price reductions. This was the challenge posed by new entrants in international oil—the independents, or the newcomers.

THE INDEPENDENTS: ENTRY AND IMPACT

Any attempt to explain the behavior of the price of crude oil during the period under consideration would be incomplete without a discussion of the role of independents. In considering oil output and prices, both in the OPEC region and worldwide, it should be remembered that during the first half of the twentieth century the bulk of oil output outside the United States and the Soviet Union was produced by the seven largest vertically integrated multinational oil companies which, as late as 1963, were responsible for 86 percent of the oil produced in the OPEC region, but by 1970 their share had declined to 77 percent of the total output. The difference between OPEC's total output and that of the seven majors was produced by a number of oil enterprises that came to be known as the independent oil companies, or the newcomers.

Several factors made it either feasible or imperative for the newcomers to venture into the international oil industry. One such factor was the need to secure sources of crude oil to meet refinery requirements in consumption centers. Such backward integration was necessary if the refinery operations in the home countries were to be free from the supply decisions of the major international oil companies. Another consideration was the change from coal to oil as the major energy source in many European countries. This shift from indigenous to foreign energy sources gave oil a national security dimension and, in turn, encouraged national oil companies to enter into the international oil industry to secure oil for national markets. In other words, it was felt that national economies should not be totally dependent on the fortunes and behavior of the seven major oil companies. A third consideration was the desire of the oil-producing countries to grant concessions to oil companies other than the majors and if the independents were forthcoming with better terms, then so much the better. In order to secure concession agreements from oil-producing countries, the independents did in fact offer better terms to the host governments. Still another factor encouraging the entrance of new companies was the emergence of national oil companies in the oil-producing countries themselves. These companies were organized to produce oil in the areas that companies had had to relinquish or, as in the case of Iraq, areas that were taken over from the original concession holders. Last but not least was the rapid increase in the world demand for oil which further spurred the newcomers.

In addition to the oil offered by the independents, there was Soviet oil that was reintroduced to world markets outside Eastern Europe in 1953. In its drive to recapture its pre–World War II share of the world market, the Soviet Union resorted to trade agreements and other inducements, especially in its trade with developing countries. The Soviet Union found receptive buyers in Western Europe, as well as in other parts of the world. This was not surprising since the Soviet Union did not require payment in U.S. dollars, the currency of transaction in international oil, and since oil-importing countries were interested in conserving their foreign-exchange earnings, expanding their own exports, and increasing their bargaining position vis-à-vis their traditional suppliers, the major oil companies.

The combined effect of U.S. oil policy, which restricted oil imports, and of the Soviet Union's policy which promoted oil exports, exerted a downward pressure on crude-oil prices. This pressure manifested itself in the granting of discounts off the posted prices to nonaffiliated refiners. But as the pressure continued, the marketing affiliates of the majors found themselves at a competitive disadvantage in relation to third-party buyers. In order to preserve their own positions in consuming centers, the majors started to lower the prices charged to their own affiliates. Since the oil companies, both majors and nonmajors, were paying taxes to host governments on the basis of posted prices, the posted prices became also tax-reference prices.

The extent of the reduction of the prices of crude oil due to the increase in the supply of oil can be appreciated from the following price data compiled by Neil Jacoby. According to Jacoby, prices of crude oil delivered to Western Europe rose by 22 percent between 1953 and 1957, from $3.08 to $3.75 per barrel. But with changing market conditions in the late 1950s, the average price had dropped by 40 percent between 1957 and 1965, from $3.75 to $2.27 per barrel. Even as late as 1972 the price was $2.95 per barrel, or lower than it had been two decades earlier, despite the general inflation and the price rise of the early 1970s. The decline in the delivered prices of oil sold to Japan was even more dramatic than that in Western Europe. The average delivered price to the Japanese market peaked at $3.48 per barrel in 1957. By 1970 the price of oil had declined by 48 percent, to $1.80 per barrel—and that decline occurred in the face of a rapidly growing Japanese demand (Jacoby 1974: 226–230).

To summarize, Middle East oil prices prior to the formation of OPEC were determined by the interaction of several influences, all of which tended to strengthen the monopoly elements of the industry. In the first place, oil resources were developed by a few large multinational, vertically integrated firms. These firms were engaged in joint-ownership contractual arrangements that enabled them to regulate Middle East oil output to meet primarily the needs of their own operations in consumer markets throughout the world. The small number of these firms, their interdependence, and the standardized nature of the product provided the necessary conditions for oligopolistic pricing and monopoly profits. This was enforced by three factors. First, the phenomenal rise in the demand for oil in the postwar period provided expanded markets for the increased output of the oil companies without their having to resort to price competition. Second, the fact that marginal cost was so low relative to the price enabled the companies to engage in price reductions without having to be concerned about the profitability of their investment at this phase of the industry. The third factor was the role of government both in the United States and in the oil-producing countries. The U.S. government, by providing the necessary output-regulating mechanisms in the United States, enabled the industry to charge monopolistic prices without having to be concerned about the consequences of entry in the industry. And by relating Middle East prices to the American prices, the oil industry was in a position to set what amounted to price ceilings for Middle East oil prices. While the American prices provided a ceiling, the floor was set by the governments of oil-producing countries. This was a direct consequence of profit-sharing agreements adopted in the early 1950s that continued in effect until the early 1970s. The respective governments' interests in seeing the companies avoid price reduction is clear, since any such reduction would result in a reduction in these governments' per-barrel revenue.

In spite of the institutional rigidities in the system and the monopolistic aspects of the industry, the control of the majors was being eroded in the 1950s, owing to the emergence of new forces in the international oil markets, including the entry of new oil firms in the international oil market, the reentry of Soviet oil in the world market, the American oil import-quota system, and the rising importance of national oil companies in both oil-importing and oil-exporting countries. These agents of change resulted in larger quantities of oil being offered on the world market outside and beyond the control of the major oil companies. This rise in supply and in the number of buyers and sellers had the effect of reducing the price-setting powers of the established oligopolists, which in turn led to a series of reductions in the price of crude oil. Initially, the companies absorbed these cuts when they chose not to reduce posted prices, but eventually, in 1959 and 1960, the companies reduced the posted prices.

PRICE ADMINISTRATION, 1960–1971

From 1960 (when OPEC was formed) to 1971, (when the Tehran Price Agreement was concluded), the basic determinants of crude-oil prices remained the same. In other words, OPEC during this period failed to alter the structure of relations responsible for establishing these prices. As might have been anticipated, the first resolution of the newly created OPEC declared that crude-oil prices should be restored to the pre–August 1960 levels, and a request to this effect was issued to the companies involved. OPEC, however, failed to articulate why the prices should be restored to their pre-August level or to any level, for that matter. OPEC also neglected to consider a plan of action should the companies fail to respond to its demand. Thus, in the absence of either a price-change rationale or a potential threat of sanctions, the oil companies found no compelling reason to change their position. And so the first plea of OPEC's founding members was ignored.

In 1968 OPEC adopted a statement which articulated certain principles of petroleum policy for member countries. These principles included direct exploitation of oil resources by the government, participation in the ownership of the operating companies, relinquishment of areas not developed by the companies, and conservation. It furthermore affirmed that posted prices should be determined by the governments and that these prices should be linked to the prices of imported goods in order to prevent erosion in oil-revenue purchasing power.

The principle on prices contained three elements: (1) posted prices should be determined by the government; (2) these prices should move in such a manner as to prevent any deterioration in their relationship to the prices of manufactured goods traded internationally; and (3) these prices should be consistent with each other among various member countries, subject to location and quality differentials (OPEC 1969: 17–22).

PRICING OF IRAQ CRUDE OIL IN THE ERA OF OPEC

Although the pricing issue was the immediate force behind the creation of OPEC and despite the adoption of several resolutions calling for the restoration of prices to their pre–August 1960 level, OPEC achievement in this area was dismal and by 1963 OPEC was forced to abandon its pursuit of price restoration. OPEC had to wait until 1971, when the Tehran Price Agreement finally recognized OPEC as a price power. The Tehran Price Agreement, and the other agreements it generated, represent a landmark in OPEC's history and in the evolution of its pricing behavior.

An initial attempt at gaining some control over the determination of output and prices was made in 1970 when the Libyan government ordered a series of output cutbacks for conservation purposes. This was followed by a negotiated price agreement that raised prices and tax rates. These two measures were the first successful attempt by a government of an oil-producing country to assert its sovereignty over this vital economic resource since the Iranian nationalization twenty years earlier.

The Libyan success seemed to have triggered a number of irreversible developments that hastened the transfer of economic control from the companies to the governments. First, in order to avoid a repetition of the Libyan experience, the companies decided on their own initiative to raise prices and tax rates for other countries without having to resort to negotiations. Second, the Libyan experience proved that, in the presence of certain market conditions and the appropriate combination of economic variables, negotiations with oil companies could be conducted according to a well-defined timetable, rather than have them be protracted over several years, as was the habit of the oil companies. Third, like any oligopoly, the Libyan government found it easier to target for negotiations the smaller oligopolist (oil company) and the one that was most dependent on Libyan oil. Once their ranks were broken, the larger oligopolists had no choice but to follow suit and agree to the same terms. Fourth, and most important, OPEC member countries found it possible to reach an agreement among themselves on a group of demands to be negotiated collectively with the oil companies.

The success of Libya set the stage for the celebrated Tehran negotiations. These negotiations, which were OPEC's first major experiment in collective bargaining, also marked the first time that the oil companies agreed to negotiate with OPEC as an intergovernmental organization in an effort to modify concession agreements and raise prices. The joint strategy that was adopted by the companies was encouraged in the United States by the State Department and facilitated by the Department of Justice's issuance of a business review letter that provided the companies with antitrust clearance. The negotiations between OPEC and the oil companies culminated in the Tehran Price Agreement of February 1971, but not before a special OPEC conference had threatened to legislate the terms of the proposed agreement and to impose an embargo on companies that refused to comply with the legislation.

The financial terms of the five-year agreement provided for the following: (1) a stabilization of the income tax rate at 55 percent; (2) a uniform increase of $0.33 per barrel in the posted prices of crude oils exported from Gulf terminals; (3) another uniform increase of $0.02 per barrel for freight disparity; (4) further uniform increases of $0.05 per barrel effective June 1, 1971, and on January 1, 1973, 1974, and 1975; (5) an increase of 2.5 percent in posted prices effective June 1, 1971, and on January 1, 1973, 1974, and 1975; (6) elimination of existing OPEC allowances; and (7) adoption of a new system for the adjustment of gravity differentials. In terms of government revenue, these terms amounted to a gain of $0.30 per barrel in 1971, rising by another $0.20 per barrel in 1975 (Alnasrawi 1985: 23–26).

It should be noted that the Tehran Price Agreement covered oil exports from Gulf terminals only. Exports from Mediterranean terminals in the case of Iraq, Saudi Arabia, and Libya were subject to another round of negotiations that were concluded in April in the case of Libya and in June in the case of Saudi Arabia and Iraq. Algeria and Venezuela chose to legislate their own price changes, while Indonesia followed its own path outside the framework of the Tehran Price Agreement. But as soon as the Tehran and other price agreements were concluded, negotiators had to deal with oil prices again in light of the international monetary crisis that culminated in the collapse of the international monetary system and the end of the convertibility of the dollar into gold.

The de facto devaluation of the dollar prompted OPEC to ask for an upward adjustment in crude-oil prices to compensate for loss in the dollar's purchasing power vis-à-vis other major currencies. An agreement, Geneva I, was reached, according to which these prices were raised by 8.5 percent to reflect the official devaluation of the dollar in terms of gold. The devaluation of the dollar, in turn, was undertaken within the context of realignment of a number of currencies under the provisions of the Smithsonian Agreement of December 1971.

The force of the provisions of the Smithsonian Agreement proved short-lived, however. In February 1973 the United States devalued the dollar once again by 10 percent in terms of gold (the official gold price was raised from $38.00 per ounce to $42.22 per ounce). Once again another set of negotiations was launched, resulting in another agreement, Geneva II, which adjusted OPEC crude-oil prices upward to reflect the dollar's second devaluation (Alnasrawi 1985: 23–26).

The Tehran Price Agreement was not a long-lasting accord because its provisions could not withstand the ensuing changes in the international oil industry and the world economy. These changes, which had been gathering force for some time, anticipated the 1973 oil-price revolution.

IRAQ AND THE PRICE REVOLUTION OF 1973

The average annual growth rate of energy consumption had, up to 1973, been higher than that of the consuming countries' gross national products, 5.1 percent versus 4.7 percent for the period 1965–1973. And the growth rate of oil was much higher than that of other energy sources, 7.7 percent versus 3.2 percent for the same period. It is clear from these growth rates that oil was used not only to satisfy the expanding world energy demand but to displace other forms of energy—mainly coal—as nonenergy input. It is important to note that between 1957 and 1970 government per-barrel revenue in the Middle East stood at $0.86. During the same period, however, prices of overall exports of industrialized countries increased by 22 percent. Thus, while these countries' oil-import prices declined in real terms, OPEC member prices of imported goods from these countries rose substantially (Exxon 1977: 1–5).

In conjunction with the forces that led to an increase not only in demand for OPEC oil but in OPEC's share in oil trade and in consumption there was a new awareness on the part of producing countries that certain measures should be adopted to limit output for the purpose of conservation. Libya in 1970 and Kuwait in 1972 decided that in the long-term interest of their economies, oil output should be stabilized or even reduced. Oil supply conditions were not helped when Iraq nationalized the Iraq Petroleum Company in 1972.

The supply and demand picture that was emerging, in which a buyer's market was becoming a seller's market, seemed at the time to be permanent rather than transitory. In addition to these market forces, OPEC member countries were closely observing the spiraling worldwide inflation that had the effect of eroding the real per-barrel income from oil.

As these forces of change were unfolding, a number of oil-producing countries began to question in rapid succession the wisdom of having locked crude-oil prices into a five-year agreement with the oil companies. It was not long before the belief prevailed among member countries that crude-oil prices should be raised.

The question before member countries in 1973 was whether prices should be set unilaterally by OPEC—a practice that had been in effect in Venezuela, Indonesia, and Algeria—or whether a negotiated revision of the Tehran Price

Agreement should be undertaken. The members decided to negotiate and to try to gain acceptance for a rise in posted prices of $2.00 per barrel as of October 1, 1973. The suspension of negotiations, on October 11, 1973, prompted the OPEC government on October 16 to unilaterally raise posted prices by $2.00 per barrel (see Table 1.2). The next day, Arab oil producers, with the exception of Iraq, decided to reduce output and impose an embargo on oil exports to the United States and The Netherlands, in retaliation for their support of Israel during the October war. The cutback measures reduced the November output of Arab countries by some 20 percent from the September output and created a shortage that caused market prices to skyrocket. As a result, the Nigerian government was able to sell its royalty oil at $20.00 a barrel and the National Iranian Oil Company sold its oil in the open market at $17.00 a barrel when the same oil was being sold to oil companies at the posted price of $5.00 a barrel. This change in supply conditions encouraged the Iranian government to lead a drive at OPEC's December 1973 meeting to raise the posted price to $11.65 as of January 1, 1974.

In the aftermath of the 1973–1974 oil price increases Saudi Arabia began to exert its considerable oil power to stabilize prices. The assumption of price leadership role by Saudi Arabia in OPEC was helped by several factors. First, the government of Saudi Arabia could, if it wished, expand output to maintain price stability. Second, the Saudi government believed that OPEC's fortunes were tied to economic conditions in the industrialized countries. OPEC, therefore, should follow a policy of price stability and price predictability. As the data in Table 1.2 show, prices remained relatively stable for most of the 1970s until 1979 when the Iranian Revolution administered a new shock to the price system.

When the Iranian Revolution was pending, an early market effect was the reduction in oil output as a result of strikes by Iranian oil workers. Although output was restored, its level was not allowed to match the average output for the first three quarters of 1978. The shock of the Iranian Revolution of 1979 was compounded by the shock of the Iraq–Iran War that broke out in September 1980. The combined effect of the revolution and the war forced these two countries' oil exports to decline by more than 5 MBD or 25 percent of OPEC exports. This shortage and the panic-buying associated with it pushed the price of oil from $14.00 per barrel in January 1979 to the unprecedented level of $34.00 per barrel in November 1980.

THE 1980s AND THE END OF THE PRICE REVOLUTION

The oil supply shortages associated with the Iranian revolution and the Iraq–Iran War proved to be transitory as Saudi Arabia sharply increased its production to make up for the shortfall. The Saudis, however, persisted in maintaining high levels of production even after the panic-buying had receded and market prices were falling. Moreover, the sluggishness in the performance of the economies of the industrial countries, the continued efficient use of energy, and the rising importance of non-OPEC oil exports caused a decline in the demand for OPEC oil and led to lower crude oil prices.

However, the underlying market conditions that led to price decline forced OPEC to accept a smaller share of the world market as it continued to defend its official price of $28.00 per barrel. Non-OPEC exporters were free, of course, to lower prices and expand their market share. This untenable situation finally forced Saudi Arabia and other OPEC members toward the end of 1985 to abandon the role of price administrator and residual supplier and adopt a strategy to maximize market share. Toward this end OPEC discarded the policy of setting official prices for crude oil and a new formula was adopted. According to the new formula an oil exporter price is determined by the price a refiner in a consuming country receives for petroleum products. This new method of pricing, combined with a maximum market share strategy, led in 1986 to a collapse of crude oil prices, falling at one point to as low as $7.00 per barrel. This price collapse resulted in the drastic decline in oil revenue for OPEC member countries from $130 billion on exports of 13.3 MBD in 1985 to $77 billion on exports of 15.5 MBD in 1986. Iraq's oil revenue in this period plummeted from $10 billion to $7 billion.

The 1986 price and revenue collapse forced Saudi Arabia and other OPEC countries to return to a system of production quotas and to an agreed upon official or reference price of $18.00 per barrel, a price that was deemed necessary for these countries' social and economic development. Between 1987, when the new price went into effect, and 1999 the price ranged between $12.28 per barrel (in 1998) and $22.26 per barrel (in 1990).

SPECIAL VULNERABILITIES OF IRAQ'S OIL INDUSTRY

The Iraqi oil industry suffers from particular vulnerabilities which the other oil sectors in the Middle East are not exposed to; certainly not to the extent to which Iraq's oil sector is exposed.

One of the most serious problems for the Iraqi oil industry, and by extension for the entire economy of Iraq, has been the instability which has characterized the political system since the inception of the modern state of Iraq in 1921. From the early days of the new state Britain used its position of power to extract an oil concession from a government that was under the control of the British government itself. In the absence of a strong and knowledgeable central government the evolution of the industry was left to the oil companies. These companies had to balance their own individual corporate interests vis-à-vis the interests of their partners and competitors on the one hand and the competing interests of the various producing countries in which they were operating on the other. Since the concession regime gave the companies the power to determine the level of output in Iraq this meant that Iraq's bargaining power vis-à-vis the companies was compromised. This is so because while the companies operating in Iraq were in a position to meet their oil requirements from other producing countries in the Middle East, Iraq, on the other hand, had no alternative sources of revenue. In other words, Iraq's staying power in any confrontation or negotiation with the companies was limited by the government's need for revenue.

Iraq's particular geographic location dictated that most of its exported oil had to be transported through pipelines traversing other countries which exposed the exported oil to developments and conditions beyond Iraq's control. Thus the Arab–Israeli conflicts of 1948, 1956, and 1967 forced the suspension of oil pumping for different periods of time.

At other times, as happened in 1966–1967, Iraq's oil exports were suspended due a dispute between the country where Iraq's pipelines go through, Syria, and the oil exporting company, IPC. The dispute, to which Iraq was not a party, was over the oil transit fees and local oil prices. The failure of the negotiations that had started in 1966 led the Syrian government to shut down the pipeline for nearly three months and impound IPC assets in Syria. While the owners of IPC could make up for Iraq's oil from other producing countries in the region, Iraq lost a considerable amount of revenue since the pipeline transported two-thirds of Iraq's oil export. The loss to Iraq of two-thirds of its oil revenue spelled out difficulties for the economy and instability for the state.

The same pipeline was closed again in 1982 by the Syrian government in support of the Iranian effort during the Iraq–Iran War. The Syrian decision to close the pipeline left Iraq with only one pipeline with capacity of 0.750 MBD, across Turkey, for its oil export. It is worth pointing out that this last figure represented less than one-fourth of Iraq's oil exports in 1979. To compensate for the loss of the Syrian outlet Iraq was able to build a pipeline through Saudi Arabia. This pipeline, together with the pipeline across Turkey, increased Iraq's export capacity to 2.4 MBD by 1989. The invasion of Kuwait and the ensued U.N. economic sanctions halted oil export. Although exports through the pipeline across Turkish territory were resumed in December 1996, the Saudi–Iraqi pipeline remains inoperable.

NOTE

1. Some parts in this chapter and the next two chapters draw on Abbas Alnasrawi, *The Economy of Iraq: Oil, Wars, Destruction of Development and Prospects, 1950–2010* (Westport, CT: Greenwood Press, 1994).

REFERENCES

Alnasrawi, A. (1975). "The Petrodollar Energy Crisis: An Overview and Interpretation." *Syracuse Journal of International Law and Commerce* 3 (2): 369–412.
———. (1985). *OPEC in a Changing World Economy.* Baltimore: Johns Hopkins University Press.

Al-Pachachi, N. (1968). "The Development of Concession Arrangements and Taxation in the Middle East." *Middle East Economic Survey* (supplement), March 29, pp. 1–11.

Blair, J. H. (1976). *The Control of Oil.* New York: Pantheon Books.

Exxon Corporation. (1977). *World Energy Outlook.* New York: Exxon.

Federal Trade Commission. (1952). *International Petroleum Cartel.* Staff Report submitted to U.S. Senate Subcommittee on Monopoly of the Select Committee on Small Business, 82d Congress, 2d Session. Washington, D.C.

Jacoby, N. H. (1974). *Multinational Oil.* New York: Macmillan.

OPEC. (1969). *Annual Review and Record, 1968.* Vienna: OPEC.

Smithies, A. (1949). "Economic Consequences of the Basing Point Decisions." *Harvard Law Review* 62 (2): 308–318.

Stocking, G. W. (1970). *Middle East Oil: A Study in Political and Economic Controversy.* Nashville: Vanderbilt University Press.

CHAPTER 2

The Rise and Decline of a National Oil Industry

One of the most serious developments in the history of the Arab region following the defeat of the Ottoman Empire in World War I was the entry of foreign multinational capital to develop the region's oil resources. Such development was designed to export oil worldwide, thus forging new links between oil producing countries and the international economic system.

The Iraq Petroleum Company, which was owned by five multinational oil companies (British Petroleum, Exxon, Mobil, Shell, and Compagnie Francaise des Petroles), was awarded in 1925 a concession for the exploration and production of oil in Iraq. The concession covered most of the territory of Iraq. And those areas of Iraq that were not covered by the IPC concession were given under similar concessions to two subsidiaries of IPC: Basrah Petroleum Company (BPC) and Mosul Petroleum Company (MPC).

In Saudi Arabia the concession went to Exxon, Mobil, Texaco, and Standard Oil of California. In Kuwait the concession was awarded to BP and Gulf Oil, while in Qatar and the United Arab Emirates the concessions went to the same five companies that obtained the Iraqi concessions. And in Iran BP was, until 1951, the sole holder of that country's concession.

OIL IN THE CONCESSION ERA

The concession system had certain unique characteristics, which solidified the control of these multinational oil firms over the oil sectors of producing countries. The most pronounced features, as was discussed in the previous chapter, were the duration of the concession and the area it covered; and the companies' power to determine output, price, and export levels.

This position of collusive control by few multinational oil companies gave them the power to regulate output in every country where they were operating. Such regulating was not only intended to meet corporate commercial interests throughout the world, but it gave them the power to influence economic and political developments in oil-producing countries and ensure compliance with corporate plans. The ability of companies to ensure country compliance may be explained by at least three considerations.

First, as time went by during the postwar period, governments of oil-producing countries became increasingly dependent on the oil sector as the primary source of budget revenue to finance ordinary expenditure such as defense, health, education, and housing as well as development spending. Dependence on oil revenue increased sharply starting in the early 1950s when the method of calculating government revenue was changed from a flat rate of $0.22–$0.25 per barrel to 50 percent of the difference between production cost and posted price. The change in the method of calculation resulted in the quadrupling of government per barrel revenue. This increase in per-unit payment together with the rise in oil output and export in the decade of the 1950s had the effect of sharply raising government revenue. Thus, in 1949 total receipts by the government of Iraq amounted to $19 million. By 1959 these receipts had increased to $243 million. But the other side of this rise in government income was the rise in dependency on changes in world demand for oil and the policies of the companies regarding output and price over which the government had no influence. The position of control that the oil companies had over the oil sector was made clear in the aftermath of the 1951 Iranian nationalization of the oil sector which plunged Iran's oil output from 700,000 barrels a day in 1950 to a mere 28,000 barrels per day after the nationalization. The primary explanation for this drop was Iran's inability to sell its oil in the face of an oil company boycott of the nationalized oil. Iran's ensuing economic difficulties set the stage for the 1953 CIA-backed coup that overthrew the elected government of Mohammad Mossadegh and prepared the way for the entry of multinational oil companies to share with British Petroleum in the exploitation of Iran's oil resources.

The second explanation for company power was the nature of corporate joint ownership of operating companies in different countries. Exxon, for example, had access to oil resources in all the Arab countries, except Kuwait and Iran. BP, by the same token, had oil interests in Iran and all the Arab countries except Saudi Arabia. This joint ownership gave oil companies the flexibility to increase output in one country at the expense of another without harming their worldwide interests. This flexibility was demonstrated after the Iranian nationalization when the companies were able to make up the loss of the Iranian oil by increasing output in Kuwait, Saudi Arabia, and Iraq. This flexibility was demonstrated again after 1954 when Iran's oil had to be reintroduced into the world market, which meant that the rate of production growth in the other countries had to be lowered.

The third explanation for the power of the companies may be found in the pattern of relationships between these companies and their home governments, which used their positions of power in the world to enable these oil firms to obtain concessions, to penetrate markets, and to back them in their dealings with the host governments. A few examples will illustrate this point.

As was stated earlier, the British government, as the mandatory power, played a crucial role in securing Iraq's oil for BP and other majors. Similarly the French and American governments made certain that their own corporate citizens had access to that oil.

Again, when the monarchy in Iraq was overthrown in July 1958, the U.S. government considered military intervention in Iraq to undo the newly established republican regime. But a decision was reached that military action could not be justified as long as the new government respected Western oil interests, which it did. The near military invasion of Iraq led Robert Engler to observe that this "gunboat diplomacy was clearly in line with the State Department's commitment to pipelines and profits" (Engler 1961: 264).

In assessing the triangular relationship between the oil companies, governments of oil-producing countries, and the U.S. government, the Senate Committee on Foreign Relations stated that the system of allocation of output between various oil-producing countries was administered by the multinational oil firms with the help of the U.S. government. The committee went on to say that the system was premised on two basic assumptions: (1) that the companies were instruments of U.S. foreign policy, and (2) that the interests of the companies were basically identical with those of the United States. Furthermore, the committee identified U.S. foreign policy objectives as follows: (1) that the United States provide a steady supply of oil to Europe and Japan at reasonable prices for post–World War II recovery and to sustain economic growth, (2) that stable governments be maintained in pro-Western oil-producing countries, and (3) that American-based firms be a dominant force in world oil trade (U.S. Senate Committee on Foreign Relations 1975: 2).

While the companies were solidifying their position in oil-producing countries, forces of nationalism were moving in the other direction. The nationalization of the Iranian oil sector, the nationalization of the Suez Canal in 1956, and the overthrow of the Iraqi monarchy in 1958 were serious challenges to the prevailing political and economic order, especially the oil concession system.

As was indicated earlier in this chapter, the concession system emerged at a time when governments had neither the political power nor the knowledge to determine terms more favorable to them than the ones they had to accept. In short, the very nature of the concession system contained within it inevitable points of conflict that centered, among other things, on the duration of the concession, the relinquishment of areas undeveloped by the companies, settlement of disputes, the disposal of associated natural gas, managerial functions, employment of nationals, production cost elements, and price-setting power.

But the state was in no position to protect its interests vis-à-vis oil company decisions or with respect to changes in the international economy. This is illustrated by the fact that revenue per unit of oil output remained constant and in some instances declined in the period of 1950–1970 due to the series of price cuts that oil companies introduced in order to expand their markets. Thus the per barrel revenue for Iraq's oil which was $0.86 in 1955, declined to $0.77 in 1961, but increased to $0.91 in 1969 (*Middle East Economic Survey* 1970: Table 3). By contrast the prices of goods imported by oil-producing countries continued to rise during the same period. This is reflected in the upward movement of the prices of goods exported from industrial countries, which increased by 22 percent in the United States, 14 percent in Canada, 17 percent in the United Kingdom, 14 percent in France, 21 percent in Germany, and 4 percent in Japan—the main trading partners of oil-producing countries (*Petroleum Intelligence Weekly* 1972: 5–6). The third element relates to changes in the delivered prices that oil-consuming countries actually pay for their imported oil. According to an index of three cost components—price of crude oil, tanker freights, and currency valuations—between 1957 and 1970 the cost of imported oil in Germany had declined by 40 percent; in The Netherlands by 35 percent; in Japan by 31 percent; and in Italy by 30 percent (*Petroleum Intelligence Weekly* 1972: 5–6). It is very clear from the data that the working of the international economic system was such that the terms of trade had moved in favor of industrial countries and resulted in the transfer of resources from oil-producing to major oil-consuming countries.

MANAGEMENT OF IRAQ'S OIL OUTPUT

It can be said that the determination of Iraq's oil output had gone through three distinct phases. First, there was the era of the concession system that lasted from 1925, when the IPC oil concession was granted, and 1961, when the government passed Law No. 80. Second, there was the period from 1961–1990, when the government took the initiative to build a national oil industry (see Table 2.1). This era was inaugurated by the adoption of Law No. 80 of 1961 which confined the operations of IPC. This was also the era that witnessed the rise of OPEC's interest in regulating member country levels of output. Third, there is the current period, which might be described as the U.N. Security Council era, that started in 1990 when economic sanctions were imposed on Iraq.

Table 2.1
Crude Oil Production, 1961–2000 (million barrels per day)

Year	Iraq	OPEC	World
1961	1.0	9.4	22.3
1965	1.3	14.3	30.2
1970	1.5	23.4	45.7
1975	2.3	27.2	53.4
1980	2.6	26.9	59.7
1985	1.4	14.9	57.7
1990	2.1	20.5	65.4
1992	0.5	23.9	65.8
1994	0.7	24.6	67.0
1996	0.7	24.8	70.0
1998	2.2	27.8	73.4
2000	2.5	28.1	71.9

Source: BP, *Statistical Review of World Energy 2001* (London: BP, 2001); OPEC, *Annual Statistical Bulletin* (Vienna: OPEC, 1990).

In the first phase oil output was determined solely by IPC, which delivered the oil it produced to its owners. A key feature of the international oil industry in the Middle East was the creation of production companies. Companies such as Kuwait Oil Company (KOC), Iraq Petroleum Company, and the Arabian American Oil Company (Aramco) were owned jointly by a number of the major oil companies. While these operating companies were independent legal entities, their investment and output patterns were determined, as mentioned earlier, by the parent companies in response to the regional and worldwide interests of the latter. The sole objective of these companies was to produce oil and deliver it to their owners, the majors.

Thus IPC, for instance, was owned by five companies, all of whom owned interest in Iran's oil concession; two held interests in Aramco; one held interest in KOC; and all five owned the operating companies in Qatar and the United Arab Emirates.

It is clear from this pattern of ownership that even without formal collusion, the companies' common knowledge of each partner's oil requirements had the effect of enabling any parent company to regulate output from its worldwide sources. Not only did common knowledge of the requirements of various partners aid in planning a company's oil lifting requirements, but the instrument of joint ownership had other important implications for determining the pattern of investment and the level of future output.

The manner in which output and investment decisions were made for IPC is a good illustration of these implications. By agreement, the owners of IPC were entitled to receive oil at cost in proportion to their ownership shares in IPC. Those partners in need of more oil were required to buy it from other partners at a price halfway between the cost of production and the posted price. Moreover, investment plans for IPC were made for five-year intervals to start five years prior to the beginning of the investment period. (Thus, investment for the period 1957–1961, for example, had to be planned in 1952.) In addition to these built-in rigidities, there was also the so-called five-sevenths rule, according to which the total amount of oil to be produced was computed by adding up the amounts nominated by various partners and then reducing it if the highest single nomination exceeded five-sevenths of the sum of the two lowest nominations (Penrose 1971: 205–206, 213). Obviously, such rules made it extremely difficult for the government of Iraq to hope for an increase in output, considering the fact that the producing company was locked into a ten-year operating procedure that deprived it of flexibility. Yet the companies that owned IPC had alternative sources of oil in other oil producing countries, a fact which helped them to regulate their total supply with relative ease.

Another feature that contributed to the regulation of output was the long-term contracts for the sale and purchase of oil concluded between some of the major oil companies. These contracts were negotiated to last for long periods of time and to cover substantial quantities of oil priced on a cost-plus basis. The contracts were also restrictive with respect to markets where buyers could dispose of their purchased oil. It is relevant to mention here that since the oil so contracted was priced on a cost-plus basis, these contracts served as a useful means of disclosure in terms of production-cost elements. Some of these contracts (such as between BP and Exxon or BP and Mobil) were so similar in detail that the competitors were made privy to the production plans and the cost of production of their rivals. Moreover, by giving BP the choice of delivering the contracted oil from either Kuwait or Iran, Exxon and Mobil were given access to the production data of another competitor, Gulf, which (with BP) owned the Kuwaiti concession. And since Gulf had its own long-term contract to sell oil to Shell, the other companies involved—BP, Exxon, and Mobil—found themselves having access to Shell's production and market plans.

The significance of the disclosure clauses in these contracts can be seen in at least two areas. First, any seller contemplating a move to alter the current price was in a better position to predict his rivals' reaction than if he had no such information. Second, this disclosure, plus the joint ownership of the producing companies, provided the sellers with the motive to adopt a uniform or similar production-cost accounting system which, in turn, enabled similar assessment of output programs.

To recapitulate, the international oil industry in oil-producing countries had near absolute control over the determination of output volumes from the producing fields in these countries' national territories. The nature of the concession system, the creation of jointly owned operating companies, and the long-term contracts concluded by the major oil companies that owned the operating companies tended to strengthen the position of the majors in regulating output from their widely scattered sources of supply in the Middle East, North Africa, the Far East, and Venezuela. Yet, the position of the multinational oil companies could not remain unchallenged. The strength of the oil companies derives, in the last analysis, from the stability of the forces underlying the international economic system.

THE RISE OF IRAQ NATIONAL OIL COMPANY

The second phase could be said to have started in 1961 when Law No. 80 was adopted. As was stated earlier, throughout the 1950s, Iraq had long-standing points of conflict with the oil companies. The change in the political system that was brought about by the 1958 revolution accelerated the pace of the dispute between the two parties, with Iraq attempting to change some of the practices of the companies with respect to the level of oil output and the elements of production cost. The failure to reach a settlement on the issues of the dispute led the government of Iraq to enact in 1961 the celebrated Law No. 80 (entitled Defining the Exploitation Areas for the Oil Companies), which confined the companies to only one-half of 1 percent of the concession area. In other words, the government of Iraq appropriated to itself all the acreage that had not been exploited by the operating oil companies: IPC, BPC, and MPC.

The dispute with the oil companies continued throughout the 1960s, with Iraq's oil output failing to increase at the same rate as that of other countries in the region. Thus, between 1960 and 1970, the annual rate of growth of Iraq's oil output was 4.7 percent, compared with an annual growth rate of 13 percent for the region as a whole. The dispute between Iraq and the companies helped the companies introduce the Libyan oil to the world market, as well as boost oil output in Iran, Saudi Arabia, and Kuwait at rates that were higher than would otherwise have been the case.

The most important accomplishment of this phase was the building of a national oil industry in Iraq. In order to realize this broad national policy objective, the Iraq National Oil Company (INOC) was created in 1964. But the newly created entity was not given the necessary legal and financial resources to develop the reacquired resources. It took another three years and two laws before INOC was given the exclusive rights to exploit the country's oil resources in 1967.

In cooperation with the former Soviet Union, Iraq was able in 1972 to produce oil from areas covered by Law No. 80. Moreover, agreements were concluded between INOC and the Soviet Union, East Germany, and Hungary that provided for loans, technical assistance, training, and equipment to help INOC build a national oil industry. A novel feature of these agreements was that repayment of the loans would be made in the form of oil which these agreements were to help produce (Iraq National Oil Company 1973b: 15–17).

In 1975 Iraq completed the nationalization of IPC, BPC, and MPC and turned over their operations to INOC. Between 1972, when IPC was nationalized, and 1979, just prior to the outbreak of the Iraq–Iran War in 1980, Iraq's oil output increased from 1.5 MBD to 3.5 MBD. In addition to producing oil, Iraq succeeded also in developing other facets of a well-developed national oil industry, including the training of specialized labor force, building of pipelines, refineries, export facilities, and loading terminals, acquisition of oil tankers, and creation of marketing networks at home and abroad. The decision to develop a national oil sector was intended to use the country's oil wealth as the mainstay of the economy: Iraq National Oil Company became responsible for the execution of that part of the national oil policy that aimed at creating and developing a large, solid, and integrated oil industry that would become the mainstay of accelerated economic development (Iraq National Oil Company 1973a: 5).

The inherent weakness and danger in such policy is its equation of national ownership of the oil sector with freedom of action. It is true of course that by nationalizing its oil sector Iraq could appropriate to itself the entire amount of the rent (that is, the difference between the cost of production and the price) instead of receiving only a fraction of that rent as was the case under the concession system. It is also true that by taking over the operations of the oil sector Iraq was able to free itself from the uncertainty associated with decisions made by multinational firms over which it had no control. Yet the mere transfer of ownership to a national authority did not by itself free Iraq from the uncertainty of the constantly changing forces of supply and demand of the wider world economy. To put it differently, while Iraq succeeded in increasing its oil income per unit of output and in mapping the size and direction of its oil sector, its dependency on the world economy nevertheless remained unchanged.

Another observation with respect to the new emphasis on the oil sector is in order. The success of the nationalization measures and the rise in oil prices and the stress on developing the oil sector as the "mainstay of accelerated economic development" in Iraq bound rather dangerously Iraq's prospects of economic development to only one sector, the performance of which is ultimately beyond the control of the government. Thus changes in the demand, supply, and prices of oil and other forms of energy are bound to have direct impact on Iraq's oil industry and by extension the entire economy. Similarly, any damage to or disruption of Iraq's oil facilities are bound to affect the economy. The bombing of Iraqi oil facilities in the course of the Iraq–Iran War of 1980–1988 forced Iraq in the early phase of the war to slash its oil exports by 72 percent, from 3.3 MBD to 0.9 MBD.

One of the historical ironies of the 1970s was the success of the Iranian revolution in overthrowing the militarily powerful Shah's regime in Iran in 1979. The newly established Islamic Republic's policy to lower oil output and export created an opportunity for Iraq to expand its oil export, making it the largest OPEC oil exporter after Saudi Arabia. The changes in Iraq's oil fortunes in the early 1970s and the rise in oil prices that accompanied the Iranian revolution pushed Iraq's oil revenue from $1 billion in 1972, to $6.5 billion in 1974, to $10.9 billion in 1978, and to $26.1 billion in 1980. In other words, Iraq's oil revenue increased by twenty-six times in less than a decade.

The war with Iran and the changing demand conditions in the 1980s resulted in sharp decline in Iraq's oil revenue from $26.1 billion in 1980, to $10.4 billion in 1981, and $6.9 billion in 1986.

The impact of what happened in the oil sector on the rest of the economy was immediate and widespread. The government was forced to curtail imports, suspend development projects, introduce austerity measures, and become a major foreign debtor. Although oil production, exports, and revenue increased after the end of the war with Iran in 1988 the 1990 invasion of Kuwait and the consequent embargo on all transactions with Iraq changed everything.

OIL OUTPUT UNDER SANCTIONS

The impact of the economic sanctions on Iraq's oil output was immediate, falling from 3.3 MBD in July 1990, to 0.95 MBD in August, and to 0.48 MBD in September. For the year 1991 Iraq's output averaged 0.28 MBD compared with 2.1 MBD in 1990. Between 1992 and 1996 Iraq's output ranged between 0.3 and 0.4 MBD. Starting in December 1996 Iraq was allowed to produce enough oil to generate $4 billion per year in accordance with the provisions of the U.N. Security Council (UNSC) resolution 986. In 1997 Iraq's output recovered to reach 1.4 MBD to rise to 2.2 MBD and 2.5 MBD in 1998 and 1999 respectively. In December 1999 the UNSC decided to lift the cap on Iraq's oil exports.

The embargo conditions under which the oil industry had to operate led a U.N. mission to Iraq in 1998 to conclude that the Iraqi oil industry was in a lamentable state and recommended to the UNSC that imports of spare parts and equipment by Iraq be authorized. Two years later another group of oil experts was sent to Iraq and reached a similar conclusion: The lamentable state of the Iraqi oil industry had not improved (United Nations 2000: 3).

OPEC, IRAQ, AND THE INVASION OF KUWAIT

Iraq, like other OPEC member countries, declares periodically, that it would set its oil output and prices in accordance with OPEC member country oil ministers' collective decisions. Such decisions are much easier to adhere to when, generally speaking, there is a seller market or when member countries are producing at capacity. Adversely, when there is excess capacity, member countries attempt to expand their sales through hidden discounts, countertrade arrangements, or outright price cuts. Since there is a high degree of interdependence among the sellers any increase in the sale of one oil-producing country is bound to affect other countries' sales and revenue. This high degree of interdependence among the few sellers is similar to the oligopolistic behavior of the oil companies that was discussed earlier.

The similarity in price behavior between oil-producing countries and the major oil companies should not be carried too far for the simple reason that while the oil companies are guided by the principle of profit maximization governments of oil-producing countries are guided by political considerations as well. Essentially, the political survival of a government in an oil-producing country is affected by the manner in which its income from oil is distributed throughout the economy. Furthermore, as oil became the single most important source of revenue it conferred upon the state unprecedented power over the economy; over regional and personal distribution of income; over urban–rural income differentials; over the level of employment and its sectoral distribution; over the structure of the economy; and ultimately over the very nature of the state and the future of the country itself.

The availability and level of oil revenue give governments of oil-producing countries certain leverages in their regional and international contexts to influence events and developments beyond their borders. It can be said, therefore, that the interest of the state in changes in oil output, price, and revenue goes beyond the mere commercial interest as these changes impinge not only on the domestic economic and political agenda but also on the state's regional and international agenda, linkages, and obligations.

Since OPEC member countries took over from oil companies in the 1970s the power to set prices and output, their decisions have been guided by their understanding of the workings of the world oil market and by their own perception of what constituted their own national interest. The principle of the sovereignty of the state was, in the final analysis, the guiding principle of each state. In this context national interest took precedent over the collective interest of the group. Because member countries varied considerably in their endowments of oil reserves, in the size of their populations, in the stage of their economic development, and in the network of their international commitments outside OPEC it was natural that they would have different assessments of the value of their oil reserves and consequently the amount of oil to be produced and the price at which oil will be sold.

These differences gave rise within OPEC to two distinct views of how much oil should be produced and the price at which such oil was to be sold. One group of countries led by Saudi Arabia and supported by other Arab Gulf states—Kuwait, United Arab Emirates, and Qatar—viewed stable or even relatively low price to be important for all member countries' long-term interest. And in order to keep prices from rising these states were prepared to increase oil output. Their ability to pump more oil to sell at a lower price and still maintain their revenue was bolstered by the fact that they had a small population, had accumulated considerable financial investment, and had large oil reserves. These states argued that it was in the interest of oil-producing countries to maintain prices at levels acceptable to the main consuming countries— the industrialized countries of the West—in order not to compel the West to find alternative sources of oil, alternative sources of energy, or to adopt excessive conservation measures.

If Saudi Arabia and its allies within OPEC can be described as "output maximizers" there was another of group of countries which may be described as "price maximizers." The latter group of countries were endowed with smaller oil reserves and/or larger populations and therefore tend to have lower per capita income than members of the other group. Moreover, these countries tend to run a balance-of-payments deficit and therefore incur foreign debt obligations. Their position on the price of oil is greatly influenced by their relatively small oil reserves, hence they would like to get as much income as possible. Their position is also influenced by their ambitious development plans which call for a large component of foreign exchange. And since all oil-exporting countries are paid in U.S. dollars for their oil these countries would like to see upward price adjustments to offset any erosion in the value of the dollar due to inflation or foreign exchange fluctuations. Countries in this group include Algeria, Indonesia, Iran, Iraq, Libya, Nigeria, and Venezuela.

One of the notable features of Saudi oil policy and OPEC since the 1973 oil price explosion was the ability of the Saudi government to impose its policy of relative price freeze on other members of OPEC. The Saudi tactic was very simple but effective. Whenever member countries advocated a price increase that was not in line with Saudi thinking the Saudi government threatened an increase in its output that would result in lower prices and smaller market share to the price-raising country. This Saudi oil policy in turn helped serve the U.S. government's long-standing objectives of access to adequate supplies of Middle East oil at "reasonable prices." The policy coordination between the governments of Saudi Arabia and the United States was described in these terms:

To achieve the U.S. objective of access to adequate supplies at "reasonable prices," the United States uses its bilateral relationships with friendly producers in attempts to influence their pricing and production decision. This is especially apparent with Saudi Arabia with which . . . the United States has a "very active" bilateral policy. Frequent visits by cabinet-level officials including the Secretaries of State, Treasury, Defense, and Energy, during the past several years illustrate this bilateralism. (General Accounting Office 1982: 49–50)

The erosion of OPEC's market share and revenue after 1982, once the panic demand conditions induced by the Iranian revolution and the Iraq–Iran War were satisfied, was transformed into a disastrous price collapse in 1986 as OPEC abandoned all restraints on output in order to regain its market share. But this unrestrained behavior forced the price down from $29.00 per barrel in 1983 to less than $10.00 per barrel (at one point $7.00 per barrel) in 1986 and caused the combined oil revenue of OPEC to plummet from $130 billion in 1985 to $77 billion in 1986 or by 41 percent while its combined oil exports increased by 18 percent, from 12.9 MBD to 15.2 MBD during the same period.

The 1986 price collapse forced OPEC in October of that year to return to its system of quotas and to an agreed upon official or reference price of $18.00 per barrel, a price that was deemed by all member countries to be necessary for their social and economic development. The significance of this accord was the linkage which member countries established between their economic and social development and a certain level of output to be sold on the world market at a certain price. Therefore, any attempt by a member country to produce above its quota meant that it would have to sell its oil at a lower price than the $18.00 per barrel reference price agreed upon by OPEC. This in turn meant that the noncomplying country will expand its share of the market at the expense of fellow producers, causing a decline in their oil revenue with unwanted implications for their economic and social development.

A number of countries nevertheless chose not to abide by their own agreement and allowed their output to rise and exert downward pressure on the price which fell well below the $18.00 per barrel benchmark; averaging $16.92 per barrel in 1987; $13.22 in 1988; and $15.69 in 1989. While Kuwait and the UAE were among the countries that produced above their respective quotas, Iraq was not in a position to do so since its export outlets were severely limited as a result of the Iraq–Iran War. The government of Iraq felt doubly frustrated as the country's economic crisis continued to deepen in the postwar period. The oil price movements prior to the invasion of Kuwait in August 1990 illustrate the chaos in the oil market which the following brief review will illustrate.

In October 1988 the selling price of oil had sunk to $12.00 per barrel but by the end of 1988 it had recovered to reach $14.00 per barrel. The upward movement in the price continued throughout 1989 and in January 1990 the price reached $19.98 per barrel. But this price was not allowed to continue as Kuwait and other producers increased their output causing the price to fall sharply to $14.02 in June of that year—a decline of 30 percent which wiped out a major portion of the anticipated oil income of Iraq and other countries.

Kuwait's position as a leading output maximizer within OPEC, was articulated in February 1990 by its oil minister when he stated that his country was producing above its quota and he thought that his government's obligation to stay within the quota applied when the price of the OPEC basket was below $18.00 per barrel and if the price was above $18.00 per barrel he thought everyone should be, and even encouraged to be, producing above quota. The Kuwaiti oil minister went on to say that the OPEC current price of $18.00 per barrel would remain at that level and not be adjusted for inflation and dollar depreciation for at least three or four years. As to the OPEC quotas he said he would like to see them scrapped as soon as possible since from a practical standpoint they were already irrelevant, so all that was needed was a recognition of that fact (*Middle East Economic Survey* 1990b: A1–A5).

By contrast Iraq could not increase its exports; it wanted to adhere to the OPEC quota system; it had no investment in retail outlets; and it had no portfolio to draw income from. Instead, Iraq had become more dependent than ever on its oil revenue (Salman 1990a: D1–D6).

Aside from the particular situation of Iraq the problem with Kuwait's policy position was the central fact that Kuwait was not acting in a vacuum since there was a high degree of interdependence among oil-producing countries and that one country's gain could not be attained except at the expense of other countries. Moreover, Kuwait could not announce the demise of the quota system and still remain a member of OPEC. In short Kuwait or any other member of OPEC could not have it both ways. The immediate effect of the Kuwaiti oil policy was to force a downward slide in the price of oil which declined by one-third in the first six months of 1990, as was mentioned earlier.

On May 30, 1990, Iraqi President Saddam Hussein made a statement at the Arab Emergency Summit Conference in Baghdad in which he spoke of the economic damage inflicted upon Iraq as a result of the oil price decline. Given Iraq's export capacity at the time he asserted that a drop in the price of $1.00 per barrel meant a loss of $1 billion of oil revenue per year. Moreover, he expressed the Iraqi government's belief that the price could be raised to $25.00 per barrel within two years without harming export levels. This in turn meant that the longer the price remained low the larger the economic loss that Iraq would have to endure. From Saddam Hussein's perspective the punishing effects on the Iraqi economy of Kuwait's oil policy of overproduction were similar to the economic damage inflicted by conventional wars. The desperate state of the Iraqi economy was made clear by Saddam Hussein when he said that a few billion dollars could solve much that has been at a standstill or postponed in the life of the Iraqis. In the middle of July Iraq stepped up its campaign against Kuwait and the United Arab Emirates and widened its scope against Kuwait. In a memorandum to the League of Arab States Iraq accused the government of the UAE of participating with the Kuwaiti government in what was described as "a planned operation to flood the oil market with excess production." The Iraqi memorandum characterized Kuwait's actions as tantamount to military aggression and accused its government of being determined to cause a collapse of Iraq's economy (*Middle East Economic Survey* 1990b: D1–D9).

In addition to the issues of oil production and the long-standing border dispute there were two other issues that Iraq added to the list of its grievances against Kuwait. The first related to the dispute over the Rumaila oil field in which Iraq accused Kuwait of using diagonal drilling to pump oil from that part of the field which is located in Iraq's territory. The second related to the financial assistance that Kuwait had extended to Iraq during the war with Iran. While Kuwait maintained that those funds were loans, Iraq's position was that they were grants. From Iraq's perspective such assistance or loans or debts should have been written off for several reasons. First, the war with Iran was waged not only to defend Iraq's own sovereignty but also to defend the eastern flank of the Arab homeland, especially the Gulf region, a view that has been confirmed, according to the Iraqi government, by the leaders of the Gulf themselves. Second, Kuwait benefited financially from the war by selling more oil at higher prices. Third, the length of the war and therefore its cost was not foreseen.

On July 27, 1990, in the shadow of Iraqi troop movement along the Iraqi–Kuwaiti border, OPEC agreed to set a higher reference price of $21.00 per barrel and adopt new quotas without allowing any member country to exceed its allocated share for any reason whatsoever (*OPEC Bulletin* 1990: 7).

But on August 2 Saddam Hussein decided to invade and occupy Kuwait. And on August 6 the United Nations Security Council decided to impose a comprehensive economic embargo on Iraq. The imposition of blockade against any exports from Iraq and an occupied Kuwait gave rise to demands that OPEC member countries be allowed to increase output beyond their quotas. On August 29 OPEC decided to suspend quota allocations so that member countries might expand their output without restrictions. This latest decision was described as having been adopted by OPEC under considerable pressure by the United States, a pressure that amounted to a direct order (Ibrahim 1990).

THE IRAQI OIL INDUSTRY UNDER
THE CONTROL OF THE UNITED NATIONS

The imposition of sanctions by the U.N. Security Council led to the deterioration of Iraq's oil industry in all its phases and sectors by depriving it of essential imports of spare parts and equipment. Ironically, the oil-for-food program did not, prior to 1998, provide for imports for the oil sector.

As it became evident that Iraq could not produce sufficient oil to meet its allowable revenue targets some relaxation of the rule became inevitable. This relaxation became necessary in order to generate the required revenue for the continuation of the oil-for-food program and also to provide revenue for the U.N. Compensation Commission and funding for the U.N. activities in Iraq.

In February 1998 the UNSC decided under resolution 1153 to raise Iraq's allowable export of oil from $2 billion to $5.2 billion for each six-month phase of the program. It also decided in the same resolution that a group of oil experts be sent to Iraq to ascertain the oil industry's capacity to generate the new level of allowable target. Given the low price of Iraqi oil at the time, $10.50 per barrel in 1998 as compared with a price of $18.00 in 1996 when the program was launched, and given the deteriorating conditions of the Iraqi oil industry, Iraq informed the United Nations that it was not possible to achieve the required increase in production to generate the $5.2 billion. The government instead projected a level of revenue between $3.5 and $4 billion. This projection, however, was considered rather optimistic by the group of oil experts that the secretary-general had sent to Iraq in March 1998. Instead, the experts reported that Iraq could generate $3 billion in a 180-day period at a price of $10.50 per barrel, and $3.9 billion should the price rise to $12.50 per barrel, provided that an infusion of spare parts and equipment was achieved. The delivery of such capital goods was necessary in the experts' views due to the fact that the oil industry of Iraq was in a lamentable state and that the developed oil fields had their productivity reduced, some irreparably, during the last two decades. Given these conditions the oil experts stressed that a sharp increase in production without concurrent expenditure on spare parts and equipment would severely damage oil-containing rocks and pipeline systems, and would be against accepted principles of good oil field husbandry (*Middle East Economic Survey* 1998: D1–D6).

The report of the experts served as a basis for resolution 1175 which the UNSC adopted in June 1998, allowing Iraq over a period of six months to import $300 million of oil industry spare parts and equipment to stem the deteriorating conditions of the industry. Yet Iraq could not benefit from this allocation fully since the UNSC Sanctions Committee either denied or delayed approval of some of the equipment. These holds which the Sanctions Committee placed on contracts caused the whole program to be ineffective.

The failure of this import program was brought to light by another group of experts that the secretary-general sent to Iraq in January 2000. The first conclusion of the second group was that the lamentable state of the Iraqi oil industry had not improved as could be seen from the continued decline in the conditions of all sectors of the industry leading to decline in oil output and export. The oil experts predicted that this trend would continue, and the ability of the Iraqi oil industry to sustain the current reduced production levels would be seriously compromised until action is taken to reverse the situation. The experts indicated that the government of Iraq raised oil output adopting high-risk techniques in expectation of the arrival of spare parts and equipment. Obviously the failure of such equipment to arrive endangered oil fields on the one hand and forced production to decline until such time when the holds placed on the import of such equipment are lifted (United Nations 2000: 3).

The deteriorating conditions of the oil industry were also revealed by comparing per barrel investment in Iraq with that in the Middle East. According to the experts between December 1996, when the oil-for-food program was launched, and January 2000, Iraq exported 2 billion barrels of oil and invested $1.2 billion in the oil sector in operating expenditure, or $0.30 per barrel per year, which amounted to 20 percent of the comparable operating expenditure in the oil industry in the Middle East, which was calculated to be $1.50 per barrel per year. The report also pointed out the deteriorating conditions in the other sectors of the industry such as refining and transportation and concluded that the reasons for the ineffectiveness of the spare parts and equipment program were many and the situation can be summed as "too little, too late," and recommended that the system of holds be revamped and the allocation for the oil sector import program be doubled to $600 million (United Nations 2000: 7).

Although the UNSC passed resolution 1302 in June 2000, allowing Iraq to raise its oil sector imports to $1.2 billion per year, the benefits of the new resolution were not much better than those of the 1998 resolution as evidenced by the Sanctions Committee's continued resort to placing holds on oil sector import contracts. In a statement before the UNSC the Executive Director of the U.N. Iraq Programme expressed his fear that without the supply of spare parts the current volume of production and export levels are not sustainable, unless the necessary spare parts and equipment are delivered. He went on to point to a contradiction in the policy of UNSC on this issue. While the UNSC doubled the allocation for oil spare parts and equipment, something that was essential for the lifeline of the humanitarian program, its Sanctions Committee continued to delay the approval of oil sector imports to the point that the number of holds has become unacceptably high. He went on to say that while everyone was calling on OPEC to increase the export of oil Iraq's minimum requirements of spare parts and equipment have been facing serious obstacles at the UNSC Sanctions Committee (Sevan 2000: 2–4).

The effect of the holds on oil production and export was echoed by Iraq's oil minister when he stated that oil production was increased dramatically in late 1998 and early 1999 on the assumption that spare parts would arrive on schedule and that the damage to the oil fields would be short-term in nature. But when the ministry of oil realized in early 1999 that the holds on oil equipment were becoming large and there was less and less processing of contracts it began to scale down production to contain damage to the oil fields (*Middle East Economic Survey* 2000: A1–A4).

REFERENCES

Engler, R. (1961). *The Politics of Oil: A Study of the Private Power and Democratic Directions*. Chicago: University of Chicago Press.

General Accounting Office. (1982). *The Changing Structure of the International Oil Market*. Washington, D.C.: U.S. Government Printing Office.

Ibrahim, Y. M. (1990). "OPEC Members Close to Raising Output Ceiling." *The New York Times*, August 20, p. A1.

Iraq National Oil Company. (1973a). *Iraq National Oil Company and Direct Exploitation of Oil in Iraq*. Baghdad: National Oil Company.

Iraq National Oil Company. (1973b). *Oil in Iraq: From Concessions to Direct National Investment, 1912–1972* (in Arabic). Baghdad: National Oil Company.

Middle East Economic Survey. (1990a). February 12.

———. (1990b). April 20.

———. (1990c). July 23.

———. (1990d). August 20.

———. (1990e). September 17.

———. (1998). April 20.

———. (2000). September 25.

OPEC. (1990). *OPEC Bulletin*. Vienna: OPEC.

Penrose, E. (1971). *The Growth of Firms, Middle East Oil and Other Essays*. London: Frank Cass & Co.

Petroleum Intelligence Weekly. (1972). March 27, pp. 5–6.

Salman, R. (1990). "Iraq's Oil Policy." *Middle East Economic Survey*, March 12, pp. D1–D6.

Sevan, B. V. (2000). Introductory Statement by Benon V. Sevan, *Report of the Secretary-General Pursuant to Paragraph 5 of Security Council Resolution 1302 (2000) of 8 June 2000*. New York: United Nations.

United Nations. (2000). *Report of the Group of United Nations Experts Established Pursuant to Paragraph 30 of the Security Council Resolution 1284 (1999)*. New York: United Nations.

U.S. Congress. Senate. (1975). Committee on Foreign Relations. Subcommittee on Multinational Corporations, 93d Congress, 2d Session. *Multinational Corporations and U.S. Foreign Policy*. Washington, D.C.

CHAPTER 3

Oil and Development in Iraq

The idea that oil is an exhaustible national resource, the revenues from which should be used for investment purposes, goes back to 1927 when the government received its first royalties from oil. It was decided at the time to view such royalties as a budgetary surplus to be used for infrastructure projects such as roads, bridges, irrigation, and buildings. The dual budgeting system, ordinary and capital, continued to be in effect until 1950. The era of oil-financed development which begun in earnest in 1950 may be divided into three distinct periods: (1) oil-financed development under the monarchy, 1950–1958; (2) oil-financed development from 1958 to 1968; and (3) oil-financed development since 1968 when the present regime under the rule of the Baath Party and Saddam Hussein seized power in that year.

THE DEVELOPMENT BOARD AND ITS PROGRAMS
FROM 1950 TO 1958

The rise in Iraq's oil production in the postwar period from 0.1 million barrels per day (MBD) in 1949 to 0.7 MBD in 1955 and the resulting increase in oil revenue, which went up from $87 million to $207 million during the same period, prompted the government to embark upon a policy of channeling oil revenue for development purposes through a new agency called the Development Board created in 1950.

The law that created the board stipulated that all revenues from oil be credited to the board, which was entrusted with the task of drawing up and implementing a general economic and financial plan for the development of the resources of Iraq and the raising of the standard of living of its people through the implementation of projects in the fields of water storage, flood control, irrigation, drainage, industry, mining, and communications. These projects were to be handed over to the specialized government ministries for administration and maintenance (Government of Iraq 1950).

The first general program for the Development Board's projects covered the period of 1951–1956 and envisaged a total expenditure of $185 million on agriculture, flood control, irrigation, land reclamation, transport, communications, buildings, and housing. However, soon after this program was adopted, the 1952 agreement with oil companies which increased Iraq's per barrel revenue considerably was concluded. The projected increase in oil revenue prompted the board to adopt the second general program for the period 1951–1957 with total expenditures of $423 million. The continued increase in oil revenue prompted another revision in the plan and was replaced by a new five-year plan for the period 1955–1960. The new plan envisaged a total expenditure of $851 million (Government of Iraq 1955).

While this program was being implemented optimistic projection of oil revenues led to the adoption of yet a new, the fourth, program for the period of 1955–1961 with estimated total expenditures of $1.4 billion. Thus in the span of few years, because of the continued rise in oil revenue projected development spending increased from $185 million to $1.4 billion or by 757 percent. This frequent upward revision of both revenue and projected development spending was driven by the continued rise in oil income which had to be passed on to the development board and was unrelated to the board's technical ability to implement its projects. Therefore, it is not surprising to notice that one of the striking features of development spending is that actual expenditure lagged considerably behind planned expenditures. This is evident in every sector, although the performance in some sectors was much worse than others. By contrast actual revenue tended to be very close to planned revenue. Thus while the board had planned to spend $874 million during this period (1951–1958) actual expenditure was only $498 million, or 57 percent of the total (see Table 3.1). Oil revenue, it should be noted, provided 96 percent of development actual spending in this period. Sectoral distribution of spending shows that 35 percent of actual spending went to the agricultural sector, 22 percent to transportation and communication, 14 percent to building and housing, 11 percent to industry, with the remaining 20 percent to all other projects (Alnasrawi 1994: 18–21).

One of the serious features of this period's spending was the relative neglect of the agricultural sector where only 52 percent of that sector's planned spending was actually invested. The neglect of the industrial sector was even more serious where only 37 percent of planned spending was actually in-

Table 3.1
Planned and Actual Development Expenditures and Revenues, 1951–1958
(millions of dollars)

		Planned $	Actual $	Actual:Planned %
I.	Expenditure			
	Agriculture	330	172	52
	Industry	143	53	37
	Transportation and			
	Communications	186	108	58
	Building and housing	107	67	63
	Other	108	99	91
	Total	874	499	57
II.	Revenue			
	Oil	754	689	91
	Total	772	718	93
III.	Actual Expenditure: Actual Revenue			70

Source: Calculated from Government of Iraq, *Law No. 6 of 1952*, schedules A and B; Government of Iraq, *Law No. 54 of 1956*; Central Bank of Iraq, *Quarterly Bulletin*, selected issues; Iraq Ministry of Development, *Annual Report on the Accounts of the Development Board and the Ministry of Development for the Fiscal Year 1954* (Baghdad: The Ministry, 1957); Government of Iraq, *Annual Abstract of Statistics* (Baghdad, Government of Iraq, various years).

Note: The fiscal year in Iraq ran from April 1 to March 31. As of January 1, 1976, the fiscal year was changed to coincide with the calendar year. Details may not add up to totals because of rounding.

vested. In a country heavily dependent on consumer goods imports and where more than three-fourths of its labor force was dependent on agriculture the neglect of the two most important goods-producing sectors cast serious doubts on the nature and direction of the policies of the board.

Basically, the essence of planning for economic development is to mobilize national savings into productive investment in order to generate a rate of increase in national output that is higher than the rate of increase in population. The difference between the two growth rates would help increase the standard of living. This task also requires that investment spending be made in such a way as to yield the highest possible rate of growth of output with the least possible waste. But this does not answer the question as to who would be making the necessary decisions to attain these objectives. While in the industrialized countries the question has long been settled in favor of the private sector and market forces this was not so in the case of developing economies.

There is general agreement that the numerous imperfections of the market will impede the necessary process that would transform a basically underdeveloped economy like Iraq's into a growing economy. Given this reality, planning becomes a necessary tool to accelerate economic development. In Iraq, the government found it necessary to expand its role in the economy when it decided to utilize oil revenues to finance investment projects, and to adopt policies to stimulate the non-oil sectors of the economy.

A comprehensive development program must, therefore, consist of objectives and aggregate targets in terms of the following: (1) national income and employment; (2) a public investment program for the economy's different sectors; (3) projection of private investment among various major sectors; (4) a combination of fiscal, monetary, and trade policies to stimulate and influence private investment; (5) definition of the role of the private sector; and (6) policies designed to effect basic institutional changes.

Should it prove to be beyond the ability of a country like Iraq to meet these requirements, then the next best thing would be to try to provide for broad targets in terms of income and employment. In other words, the plan must provide a sense of direction for the economy and national income accounts should help planners determine growth targets. If these aggregates were not used as a basis for development planning, then the plan will be no more than a list of investment projects with no context. This was the case in Iraq during the first decade of its development experiment as will be seen later in this chapter.

The first program, as a matter of fact, did not even mention such concepts as national income, employment targets, and fiscal and monetary policies. The lack of basic understanding of economic planning and its goals is reflected in the meager allocation for agriculture. In a country like Iraq, where agriculture was the most important sector, the first plan allocated only $4 million for agricultural development proper with the bulk of the $84 million within the agricultural sector allocations earmarked for irrigation projects. This neglect of agriculture was matched by a comparable neglect of the industrial sector. The second program followed the path of the first in emphasizing the importance of irrigation, roads, and buildings.

The third program, adopted in 1955, had total planned expenditure of $852 million and revenue of $604 million. Funds for agricultural and industrial development did not increase in the new plan. Agriculture development's share was reduced from $32 million or 7 percent of the total in the previous plan to only $18 million or 2 percent of the total in this plan. Industry, on the other hand, received $122 million or 14 percent of the total as compared with 20 percent previously. As oil revenue continued to rise and to deal with mounting criticism of the development policies the board sought foreign advice to guide its action. In 1956 the fourth development plan with projected total spending of $1.4 billion and revenue of $1.1 billion was adopted. The advice that the board received from its foreign consultants seems to have indicated that the stress should continue to be on infrastructure and away from industry and agriculture (Alnasrawi 1994: 23).

The neglect of these two sectors by the board under the monarchy paved the way for Iraq's rising dependency on food and other consumer goods imports and on the oil sector as the primary provider of foreign exchange.

THE NEGLECT OF THE AGRICULTURAL SECTOR

When the development programs were launched in the early 1950s Iraq was an agricultural country with about four-fifths of its labor force employed in agriculture. This sector's contribution to Iraq's non-oil GDP during the period under consideration ranged between 22 percent and 36 percent. Like other developing countries Iraq's agricultural sector suffered from chronic underemployment and seasonal unemployment reaching as high as 75 to 80 percent (Food and Agriculture Organization 1959: 12). It is imperative, therefore, that agriculture be the primary interest of development policy in order to increase employment and raise the rate of economic growth. The development of the agricultural sector is vital to the process of economic development because (1) it releases agricultural labor for nonfarm employment, (2) it helps increase exports and reduce imports, (3) it is expected to meet the inevitable rise in demand for food associated with growing population and higher income, and (4) it generates more savings to finance investment in the agricultural sector and other sectors of the economy.

Any development policy, therefore, should have as its priority the reduction of the high rate of unemployment by investing in the goods-producing sectors. Investment in the industrial sector was also necessary in order to provide employment opportunities for the absorption of the surplus farm labor and for the natural growth in the labor force. To channel the unemployed to the newly created industries requires a rise in the productivity of agriculture in order to meet the rising urban demand for agricultural products. It also requires an increase in the purchasing power of the rural population, thereby increasing the demand for industrial products. It is safe to say that without the simultaneous increase of investment and output in both sectors, the twin goals of a higher standard of living and higher rate of employment would not be attained.

One of the most outstanding and influential features of agriculture in Iraq during this period was the immense concentration of landownership among a tiny fraction of landholders. No less important than the structure of landowner-ship was the pattern of the then prevailing practices of distribution of agricul-tural output between landowners and cultivators. Depending on the region of the country, extent of investment by owners, and methods of irrigation the share of the landlord ranged between one-half and five-sevenths of the crop. But the relationships between the landlord and his cultivators went beyond the mere distribution of benefits as the practice of cultivating only one-half of the land and the low productivity of cultivated land forced the peasants to end up not only with meager returns for their labor but they were never able to pay back the debt that they perpetually owed to landlords. The historical evolution of these relationships that outlined peasant obligations to landlords and which were codified by a series of laws turned cultivators into virtual serfs with monumental human, social, and economic costs for the entire country.

Such a system of land tenure gave rise to two interrelated problems of in-come distribution. Within the rural sector a minority of landlords received most of the output while the majority of rural population ended up living in conditions of grinding poverty. And since the majority of the population was made up of rural peasantry, with agriculture contributing about one-fourth of the national product, the distribution of national income tended to have another bias in favor of the urban population. This resulted in a pattern of income distribu-tion in which the per capita income of the rural villager was less than one-half of that of the town or city dweller. Such an impoverished rural majority could not be expected to provide the necessary market for expanding local industry, not to mention the ability to generate savings for investment.

With these structural problems, one would have expected the development programs to include an agricultural development policy that would lead to a better distribution of landownership, better methods of cultivation, and a dif-ferent pattern of rural income distribution. To attain such outcomes would have required agrarian reform in Iraq. But the introduction of agrarian reform to solve the land problem was not possible since the very nature of the power structure of the political system was such that the landed class and their political supporters dominated the legislative apparatus and other decision-making bodies. The change in the land tenure system had to await the July 1958 revolution which overthrew the monarchy and with it the land tenure system.

The failure of the board's agricultural development policy, which set Iraq on the path of dependency on food imports, was matched by its failure to invest in the industrial sector as will be seen in the following paragraphs.

THE NEGLECT OF THE INDUSTRIAL SECTOR

In Iraq, industrialization is important not only as a means of raising em-ployment and income and achieving economic diversification but also be-cause of its contribution to the development of agriculture: An expanding industrial sector is essential to solving the problem of agricultural unemployment and poverty.

With the ever-rising flow of oil revenue, the question of industrial development should have assumed priority but this was not the case, especially in the early years of development planning in Iraq. The first program did not allocate any funds for this sector. The second program allocated 20 percent of its total budget to this sector while the third and fourth programs allocated 14 percent and 13 percent of their budgets respectively to industry.

It should be pointed out that the board, in its lack of emphasis on investment in the industrial sector, was influenced by the advice of foreign consultants as well as the World Bank. The gist of the advice was that Iraq should concentrate on agriculture and should avoid giving incentives to domestic industry or provide protection for it. But the board followed these experts' advice on industry and did not follow it in the case of agriculture which resulted in lack of development in both sectors. In fact, with abundant supply of capital, Iraq could afford to follow a policy of rapid economic development achieved in part through rapid industrialization without restricting consumption. What makes this approach more appealing is the knowledge at the time that the flow of oil revenue and consequently the availability of capital, was assured.

OIL AND DEVELOPMENT PLANNING, 1958–1968

When the 1958 revolution occurred, the fourth general program for the Development Board's projects, from 1955 to 1961 was in its fourth year. The new republican leaders pledged to alter the economic priorities of the previous regime and reorganize the structure of the development-planning administration to correct some of the shortcomings of the previous regime. According to these leaders the failure of planning under the monarchy was unavoidable because of the dependency of the economy, especially the sectors of oil, finance, banking, and foreign trade on foreign imperialism. This dependence was made worse by the development policy which perpetuated Iraq's status as a market for foreign capital and consumer goods and as an exporter of raw materials and fuel at low prices. This explains why agriculture, with its feudal base, was the predominant sector and why industry was insignificant and why output, productivity, income, and employment were low. These conditions led in turn to serious inequality in the distribution of income, inflation, internal migration to the capital city and other major cities, and immigration (Food and Agriculture Organization 1959: 36–37).

Although revenues from oil could (and should) have been used in a manner that would have created an independent economy, the policies of the Development Board failed to do so. In a nutshell, the board's development policies led to strengthening the dependency of the economy on oil, thus wasting Iraq's most important resource while consolidating and strengthening the feudal base of the economy.

The new regime decided to abolish the Development Board and the Ministry of Development and replace them with the Economic Planning Council and the Ministry of Planning. A Provisional Economic Plan was adopted to provide continuity in implementing projects started under the Development Board. The provisional plan was followed by a five-year Detailed Economic Plan for the period from 1961 to 1966.

The Detailed Economic Plan (DEP) which became effective in January 1962, was an improvement over the previous plans in its sophistication. It established a target rate of growth and calculated the capital–output ratio, and concluded that investment should be about 35 percent of the national income.

The DEP designed an expenditure budget of $1.6 billion distributed among the four major sectors as follows: agriculture, 20 percent; industry, 29 percent; transport and communications, 24 percent; and building and housing, 25 percent. In assessing the performance of the plans under Abdel Karim Qasim, the leader of the revolution that toppled the monarchy in July 1958, it can be said that (1) there was a noticeable shift in emphasis from irrigation to industry. This can be explained by the fact that some irrigation projects had been completed while other projects were not urgently needed. Yet agriculture seemed to have been pushed to the background as it received the lowest share of the total funds; (2) the DEP gave the impression of emphasizing housing by allocating 25 percent of the funds to this sector. However, an inspection of the details revealed that out of a total of $392 million only $39 million was spent on low-income housing with the bulk of the funds spent on the ministry of defense projects and army officers' housing; (3) the DEP did not pay much attention to how to integrate the private sector in the plan; and (4) the rate of performance in terms of actual spending for the period of 1958–1963 was 46.2 percent of planned spending compared with a rate of 57 percent during the period of 1951–1957.

The most important change to take place during the Qasim era, however, was the enactment in 1958 of the Agrarian Reform Law. The new law increased the size of agricultural land holdings from 1,000 to 2,000 donums, depending on the method of irrigation. Land in excess of these limits was to be taken over by the government. The landowners were to receive compensation in the form of treasury bonds. Peasants were to receive small holdings, thirty to sixty donums, and to join cooperative societies supervised by civil servants. The law set five years for the completion of the process of land distribution (Government of Iraq 1958).

This revolutionary change in the land tenure system was not accompanied, however, by corresponding increases in investment in the agricultural sector. On the contrary, and as was stated earlier agriculture was not made a top priority by the new regime.

The extent of the failure of Iraq's agricultural development policy is reflected in the significant decline of the contribution of the agricultural sector in both absolute and relative terms. Thus the value of agricultural output which stood at $240 million in 1953 rose by an average rate of 1.1 percent to $242 million during the five-year period from 1959–1963. It is important to note that the Food and Agriculture Organization (FAO) projected that the contribution of the agricultural sector to the national income in 1965 would be $784 million, in 1956 prices. But such contribution was $225 million in 1963 and $336 million in 1965 (Iraq Ministry of Planning 1969) (see Table 3.2).

The failure of agricultural development policy is also reflected in the decline in agricultural productivity. Thus while the cultivated area of wheat, barley, and rice increased from 2.8 million in 1957 to 3 million hectare in 1963, the total output of these three main field crops declined from 2.5 million tons to 1.4 million tons respectively. In short, the failure of agricultural development policy had the effect of turning Iraq from a food-exporting to a food-importing country, and also failed to achieve any measurable redistribution of income.

Table 3.2
Planned and Actual Development Expenditures, 1958–1963 (millions of dollars)

Expenditures	Planned	Actual	Actual:Planned
	$	$	%
Agriculture	332	139	42
Industry	213	112	52
Transportation & Communication	447	163	37
Building & Housing	502	167	53
Other	121	67	55
Total Expenditure	1615	749	46
Total Actual Revenue		811	
Actual Expenditure: Actual Revenue			92

Source: Calculated from Government of Iraq, *Law No. 6 of 1952*, schedules A and B; Government of Iraq, *Law No. 54 of 1956*; Central Bank of Iraq, *Quarterly Bulletin*, selected issues; Iraq Ministry of Development, *Annual Report on the Accounts of the Development Board and the Ministry of Development for the Fiscal Year 1954* (Baghdad: The Ministry, 1957); Government of Iraq, *Annual Abstract of Statistics* (Baghdad, Government of Iraq, various years).

The regime of Abdel Karim Qasim was overthrown in February 1963 in a coup led by the Baath Party in alliance with elements of the armed forces. The new leaders, both civilian and military, had no program for the country, the government, or development planning. This observation is supported by no other than the leading civilian personality of the regime who asserted that the leaders of the new regime were lost in the government and that their coup had the characteristic of a leap into the unknown.

In November 1963 the military wing succeeded in purging the government from its civilian counterpart. The new regime remained in power until July 1968 when it was ousted by yet another Baath Party–led coup. This regime remains in power at the present time.

The new regime decided to continue the implementation of the Qasim government's Detailed Economic Plan until it could formulate its own plan— the Five-Year Economic Plan (FYP) for the years 1965–1969.

The economic objectives of FYP included raising the standard of living, lessening the dependence on the oil sector, more investment in both agriculture and industry, expansion of employment, wider geographic distribution of planned investment, and the gradual reduction in the concentration of income and wealth.

The FYP had a budget of $1.6 billion with agriculture and industry given 53 percent of the total budget. The oil sector was called upon to supply 70 percent of the plan's budget. Actual spending declined under the plan and amounted to 55 percent of the budget while actual spending in agriculture and industry amounted to 43 percent of what was budgeted to these two sectors. Once again planners failed to spend all the oil income earmarked for them.

In projecting the growth of the economy for the years 1965–1969 the FYP provides illuminating data regarding the performance and the changing structure of the Iraqi economy during the 1953–1963 period. Some of the changes are the following: (1) gross domestic product grew at an annual rate of 6.4 percent; such a relatively high rate of growth, it should be noted, was influenced by the growth of the oil sector, (2) the non-oil GDP grew at an annual rate of 5.5 percent, (3) the growth rate of agriculture was found to be zero, (4) nonagricultural sectoral annual growth rates were industry at 11.5 percent; electric power, 16.7 percent; banking and insurance, 11.3 percent; transportation, 6 percent; public administration and defense, 10.5 percent; wholesale and retail trade, 5.7 percent; services, 8.3 percent; and construction and building, 2.4 percent, (5) during this period imports increased by 67 percent, and (6) Iraq's non-oil exports financed only 19 percent of its imports in 1963 compared to 35 percent in 1953 (Iraq Ministry of Planning 1969: 1–5).

A glaring built-in failure of the plan was its admission that it could not provide employment to all the new entrants in the labor force. Although the planners projected an increase of 664,000 workers in the size of the labor force the plan itself projected that only 322,000 workers would find employment. This meant that the unemployment rate which was said to be 3.1 percent in 1964 would rise to 13.5 percent in 1970, with the number of unemployed rising from 76,000 to 418,000 during the same period.

In assessing the performance of FYP the ministry of planning arrived at these conclusions: (1) oil continued to be a dominant sector in the economy and the dominant commodity in Iraq's export; (2) FYP was given credit for laying a strong foundation for the economy and for achieving a "big push"; and (3) FYP was also given credit for introducing modern technologies in several sectors of the economy (Iraq Ministry of Planning 1971: 42–43).

The FYP was in its fifth year when the Baath Party seized power in 1968 (see Table 3.3). The new regime allowed the FYP to complete its course while a new five-year plan was being prepared.

Table 3.3
Allocated and Actual Expenditures and Revenue: Five-Year Plan, 1965–1970 (millions of dollars)

	Allocated ($)	Actual ($)	Actual to Allocated %
Expenditures			
Agriculture	486	158	32
Industry	524	279	53
Transport and Communication	308	186	60
Building and Housing	377	199	53
Others[1]	175	202	116
Total	1871	1023	55
Revenue			
Oil	1092		
Other[2]	479		
Total	1571	1099	70

Source: Ministry of Planning, *Detailed Framework of the Five-Year Economic Plan, 1965–1969* (Baghdad: The Ministry, 1969), 45–47; Ministry of Planning, *Evaluation of the Five-Year Economic Plan 1965–1969* (Baghdad: The Ministry, 1971), 26 (in Arabic).

1. Includes international obligations and Ministry of Defense projects.

2. Foreign and domestic loans constitute almost three fourths of this item.

THE ERA OF NATIONAL DEVELOPMENT PLANS

The Baath Party's new five-year National Development Plan (NDP) took two years to prepare. This particular plan had the distinction of having been adopted at a time when major changes in the oil industry were pending. It was during this plan's period, 1970–1974, that the Tehran Price Agreement and the two Geneva agreements which adjusted oil prices upward were concluded. More important, it was during this plan's life that the government nationalized the oil industry in 1972 and OPEC embarked on its historic oil price revolution of 1973–1974.

Although the plan spoke of lessening dependence on the oil sector, actual policy actually led in the opposite direction and resulted in of more dependence on the oil sector rather than less. This can be seen from the hasty revision of the NDP itself in response to the unanticipated rise in oil revenue. Thus in reaction to oil-revenue increases the plan revised development spending upward from $1.6 billion to $5.8 billion. In the meantime the role of oil revenue in development finance was raised from $1.3 billion to $4.7 billion, or from 80 to 90 percent of the projected planned spending.

The $5.8 billion of planned spending was allocated as follows: agriculture, 19 percent; industry, 20.2 percent; transport and communication, 11.4 percent; buildings and services, 14.6 percent; and other, 34.8 percent. The last category was to provide funding to a number of unrelated projects such as state-owned enterprises, international obligations, general reserve, and other investment expenses. It is worth noting that over one-half of the allocation to state-owned enterprises was earmarked to oil sector projects. The performance of NDP shows that it managed to spend 61.6 percent of its appropriations. Comparing actual to target growth rates we find that the targets were surpassed in economic indicators such as GDP, private consumption, public consumption, exports, and imports. On the other hand, actual rates of growth failed to reach their targets in agriculture, industry, construction, communication, power generation, and employment. In other words, NDP failed to reach its targets in all goods-producing sectors except the oil sector (Alnasrawi 1994: 64–72).

The 1970–1974 NDP had the dubious distinction of being the last published multiyear development plan in Iraq (see Table 3.4). Instead, the political leadership decided to resort to segmented, annually approved investment programs. This was done for the years 1975–1977 and then the government announced, but did not publish, the adoption of a 1976–1980 NDP.

Beginning in 1978 the government chose not to publish sources of development finance. Instead, the revenue equivalent of spending was simply decreed. Thus the 1978 law which decreed that $9.5 billion was allocated to meet the expenditures of the investment program in that year also decreed that the revenues of the program for that year shall be estimated at $9.5 billion (Alnasrawi 1994: 147).

Table 3.4
NDP: Sectoral Allocations and Revenue, 1970–1974 (billions of dollars)

	Original	Revised
	$	$
Sectoral Allocations		
Agriculture	.55	1.10
Industry	.40	1.17
Transport & Communications	.18	.66 .
Buildings & Services	.20	.85
Other	.28	2.02
Total	1.60	5.80
Revenue		
Oil	1.28	4.66
Other[1]	.34	.52
Total	1.61	5.18

Source: Ministry of Planning, *Law of National Development Plan 1970–1974* (in Arabic) (Baghdad: The Ministry, 1971).

1. Includes foreign and domestic loans and loan repayments.

Following the start of the war with Iran in 1980 development spending was initially accelerated but had to be subordinated to the goals of the war. In 1982, however, development spending was drastically curtailed as Iraq lost much of its oil export and revenue and as the government was forced to introduce austerity measures throughout the economy. With this turn of events development spending in Iraq ceased to be a priority of the state. The disinterest of the Baath in development planning was further underscored by the Baath regime when it decided in 1987 to abolish the Planning Board and replace it by a unit called the Planning Body within the Ministry of Planning.

Iraq emerged from the war worrying more about inflation, the consequences of the war, and about how to deal with its new status as a country overwhelmed with foreign debt than with how to restore its development structures and mechanisms. Less than two years after the end of the war with Iran the government plunged the country in another catastrophe when it decided to invade Kuwait.

In short, Iraq's experience with development planning after 1980 was first halted under the impact of the Iraq–Iran War, then negated following the invasion of Kuwait and the imposition of sanctions by the U.N. Security Council.

IRAQ'S ECONOMIC DEVELOPMENT BETWEEN OIL AND POLITICAL INSTABILITY

Iraq's experiment in planned economic development in the sense of utilizing oil revenue to diversify the economy and lessen its dependence on oil began under the monarchy in 1950 with the creation of the Development Board. Prior to the overthrow of the monarchy in 1958 several plans were adopted and revised, each one of which had higher levels of spending than the previous one. And each one of them was more dependent on the revenue from oil than the previous one. And although the majority of the people lived in rural Iraq these plans failed to invest in the agricultural sector with the result that the country became increasingly more dependent on food imports.

The configuration of political forces under the monarchy was such that an alliance was formed between political opposition parties and certain elements in the army that succeeded in 1958 in overthrowing the monarchy. In the less than five years of its life, the new republican regime was faced with a number of severe problems and challenges. These included an open split among the new regime military leaders, an open rebellion by a segment of the armed forces, an assassination attempt on the life of the regime's strong man, Abdel Karim Qasim, an open political feud with President Nasser of Egypt and his followers in Iraq, a rebellion by the Kurds in the northern part of the country, a fallout with the regime's political supporters, the drift toward erratic and authoritarian rule, and a general drift toward stagnation. By 1963 the political power base of the regime was so weakened that its overthrow was not an insurmountable task. The task was accomplished in February 1963 and Qasim was immediately executed by the new rulers.

The military–Baath alliance that succeeded the Qasim regime of 1958–1963 and ruthlessly suppressed Qasim's political supporters fell into a quagmire of chaos, arbitrariness, and disintegration prompting the military wing of the alliance to oust its civilian counterpart in November 1963. The head of the regime, Abdel Salam Aref, who perished in a helicopter accident in 1966, was succeeded to the presidency by his brother, whose regime was toppled in July 1968 by another coup organized by another military–Baath alliance. This time it was the civilians who in time succeeded in bringing the military under their firm control.

Between 1968 when the Baath seized power and 1979 when Saddam Hussein became president, the Baath succeeded in consolidating its power through a mixture of rewards, coercion, and unprecedented use of internal security methods. The ruling group managed to stave off all attempts to unseat it and stamp out any political opposition from within or without the party. Rebellions were ruthlessly suppressed and whole communities were deported or reloacted in different parts of the country. Another factor that enabled the Baath to remain in power was the phenomenal rise in oil revenue in the decade of the 1970s.

But beginning in 1979 the ruling group under Saddam Hussein became preoccupied with its own survival. First, there was the ruthless purge of a major segment of the political leadership by Saddam Hussein only weeks after he assumed the presidency. A year later he took the country into the destructive eight years of war with Iran which ended in 1988. Two years later, he gambled with the fortunes of the country when he took it into the adventurous invasion of Kuwait in August 1990. This invasion provoked the imposition of economic sanctions against Iraq and was followed by the Gulf War of 1991 which inflicted enormous destruction on the people and the economy while the sanctions are still in effect today.

From this brief review it can be said that the country's political history was an endless series of coups and countercoups, conspiracies, purges and counterpurges, violent seizure of power and ruthless suppression of dissent, and last but not least, wars, adventures, and sanctions. In all this history the people had no voice as there has been a virtual absence of democratic institutions and peaceful transfer of power.

Moreover, changes in political leadership and personalities entailed changes in economic priorities, direction, and policies. While well thought out or planned changes are necessary and beneficial for development, the changes in Iraq were so frequent, sudden, and violent as to negate the benefits of planning. Frequent changes in leaders and cabinets led inevitably to prolonged delays in plan formulation, adoption, and execution.

While internal political instability was a serious force it was not the only force to impinge on the course of economic development in Iraq. The instability of Iraq's regional context tended to accentuate and add to the negative consequences of domestic political instability. The presence of Britain in Iraq was a powerful force in shaping economic and political developments during the period 1921–1958. The partition of Palestine and the creation of the state of Israel in 1948 which gave rise to the Arab–Israeli conflict entailed the diversion of considerable resources from civilian to military uses. The French–British–Israeli invasion of Egypt in 1956, the Israeli invasion of Lebanon in 1982, the border disputes with Iran and Kuwait, and the disputes with Turkey and Syria over the division of the Tigris and the Euphrates rivers were all forces that affected the pace of development within Iraq.

Beyond the regional context, Iraq's development policies were undoubtedly affected by the evolving international context in the Middle East. Between the time when the state was created in 1921 and the 1958 revolution, Iraq's economic policies were influenced by England. The mandatory position that Britain had over Iraq, the treaty obligations which tied Iraq to England, the identification of the political class with British interest, Iraq's membership in the sterling area, Iraq's pattern of foreign trade, and the role of oil in its economy were among the forces that cast Iraq into a dependency relationship with Britain.

Following the 1958 revolution there occurred a series of major changes in Iraq's foreign and economic policies. It is important to stress that the 1958 revolution was a middle-class led nationalist movement that had the support of all opposition political parties. Thus, soon after the new republican regime was installed it decided as an assertion of its independence to withdraw from the sterling area, leave the Western-dominated military alliance Baghdad Pact, open up diplomatic and economic relations with the Soviet Union and the East European countries, enact agrarian reform, expand social services, nationalize over 99 percent of all the oil concession areas, prepare the groundwork for a national oil industry, and expand the role of the public sector in the economy. These changes which were initiated by the Qasim regime continued to provide the policy framework for all the regimes that followed.

It should be clear by now that the 1958 revolution constituted a rupture or a break in the ideological underpinning of Iraq's economic policies. Prior to 1958 there was some form of tripartite alliance between the landowning classes as represented by the tribal chiefs, the Crown, and the political class. Behind this domestic alliance there was the imperial presence of England in the form of military bases, treaty alliance, oil interests, and civil and military advisers. The economic orientation of the era of monarchy was, broadly speaking, laissez faire. In the early part of the period most of the national output was generated in the agricultural sector. By the same token most of the population worked and lived in rural Iraq. Most of the manufacturing industry in this period was of the cottage industry variety. As time went on, especially during the Great Depression and the war years of the 1930s and the 1940s, the local and modest industrial output found a receptive domestic market.

Although the decade of the 1950s witnessed the activities of the newly established Development Board as well as a substantial growth in Iraq's oil export and revenue, there is no evidence to indicate that the political system was interested in changing the characteristics or the structure of the economy. Development policy tended to strengthen the economic status quo as its benefits tended to flow to landowners instead of peasants and urban workers.

The political and economic orientation of 1921–1958 was rejected by the 1958 republican regime. This rejection was based on the assertion that the

Iraqi economy prior to 1958 was distorted in favor of imperial and feudal interests since the economy was allowed to grow with the most important sector, oil, being at the mercy of foreign oil firms. Moreover, the enclave-type nature which the foreign-dominated oil sector enjoyed became a mere financier of feudalism and reactionary classes which in turn served and perpetuated foreign interests in Iraq at the expense of the majority of the people. The dualism of the economy as reflected in a modern oil sector and backward agricultural sector and weak industry is responsible for the low level of national income, its maldistribution, and for the impoverishment of the masses. Although conditions of poverty could have been ameliorated, the policies of the Development Board had the effect of serving the interests of large landowners. Moreover, development spending should have encouraged the emergence of market conditions conducive to the rise of a national bourgeoisie. Such evolution failed to occur because a pliant Iraqi government preferred to increase imports rather than domestic output thus recycling oil revenue to the benefit of foreign exporters and contractors. In short, the new regime concluded that in order to ease the state of tension between the ruling elite and the people it was decided to increase Iraq's oil revenue on the one hand and waste such increase in revenue on the other. In order to accomplish this task the Development Board was created to spend the oil revenue on nonproductive projects and for the benefit of the few (Government of Iraq 1959: 69–101).

To reorient the direction of the economy and change the number and the composition of development beneficiaries the new regime took it upon itself to change the objectives and policies of development. These changes tended to favor public sector industrial investment, provide more protection to local industry, cause agrarian reform, and increase welfare programs and social services. It is worth noting that in spite of the revolutionary rhetoric of the new regime its policies tended to encourage the private sector either through land distribution in the case of the agricultural sector or by extending incentives and protection to industry.

While Qasim's regime represented a major break with past economic and development policies and had clear and definite views about steering the country and the economy in a different direction the leaders of the February 1963 coup that overthrew Qasim's had the distinction of not having any program or policy.

Naked repression and struggle for power and personal rivalries led to the November 1963 coup when the military wing of the government decided to oust their civilian partners. The new leaders who remained in power until July 1968 and who were in sympathy with the policies of President Nasser of Egypt decided to implement some of his economic measures in Iraq. The most significant of these measures was the 1964 sudden nationalization of a major segment of the private sector which transferred to government ownership thirty industrial and trading enterprises and all commercial banks and insurance companies.

According to the government the justifications for the enactment of the nationalization measures included social justice, the drawing of clear lines of demarcation between the private and public sectors, private sector exorbitant profits at the expense of consumers, emergence of a social class with controlling power over banking, insurance, trade, and industry accompanied by rising economic, social, and political influence (Ali 1991: 137–141). This expansion of the public sector role in the economy was continued and enhanced by the Baath regime that came to power in 1968.

When the Baath came to power it proclaimed that its ultimate goal was to establish a socialist economy. In the meantime the Baath Party announced that in the transition it would implement the following measures: expansion of the public sector role in agriculture at the expense of the private sector; total control over foreign trade; central government control over domestic trade; strengthening the role of public sector in industry; and managing social services according to the requirements of transition to socialism.

During the 1970s the government was successful in translating its ideological pronouncements into economic policies, especially after the nationalization of the oil industry. But in the 1980s the government, under the impact of the Iraq–Iran War, formally reversed its position on the private sector and decided to expand its role through its enactment of privatization measures.

ASSESSMENT OF IRAQ'S DEVELOPMENT
FROM 1950 TO 1990

One of the most outstanding features of the more than three decades from 1958, when the republican regime was established, until 1990 is that the general outline of development—its rhetoric, framework, objectives, sectoral allocations, total and sectoral performance, problems, and its utter dependence on oil—remained more or less the same. Although several plans and several regimes and many cabinets and changes characterized the period the variations did not amount to what successive governments claimed to be revolutionary changes. To be sure there were different emphases at different times reflecting regime political and economic priorities but by and large it was the Qasim's regime that set the tone and the objectives of development for the period under analysis. Even in those instances when this or that regime seemed to have deviated from Qasim's centrist position with respect to the relative importance of the public and the private sectors vis-à-vis each other, such as the nationalization measures of 1964 or the attempt to force collective farming or allowing the public sector to overwhelm the private sector, there were always forces at work which ultimately led to a pull toward the center. By the same token, when the deviation from the centrist position was found to have gone too far in favor of the private sector the political authorities found it advisable to steer toward the center again.

DEVELOPMENT ALLOCATION
AND ACTUAL SPENDING, 1958–1980

One of the common and striking features of Iraq's economic development over the thirty-year period of 1950–1980 is the failure of planners and implementers to spend the funds allocated in development plans and programs (see Table 3.5). This is true whether one speaks of the promarket-oriented regime under the monarchy, the centrist regime of the Qasim period, or the Baath regime which strongly advocated a public-sector dominated economy. This observation applies also to all sectors of the plan. It is true of course that there were variations in performance or in expenditure efficiency or the ratio of actual spending to allocation from year to year or from sector to sector but at no time did one plan or one program complete its term without a surplus.

In the first twenty-five years (1951–1975) of its development history Iraq planned to spend $14.2 billion but actually spent $9.2 billion or 64 percent of what was appropriated (see Table 3.6). In the 1976–1980 period the government planned to spend $53.2 billion but it actually spent $34 billion. Taking the entire period from 1951–1980 we find that Iraq appropriated $67.4 billion but it actually spent $43.2 billion. Relating actual development spending to oil revenue, which amounted to $100.6 billion for the period of 1951–1980, we find that the planners managed to spend no more than 43 percent of oil revenue (see Table 3.7). There are several reasons for the failure of the various planning mechanisms and administration to spend their allocations. One of the most serious flaws of Iraq's development planning since the inception of the development board was the fact that it was driven by the level of oil revenue. Regardless of the nature of the political regime its orientation, its proclaimed philosophy and/or rhetoric development was in reality a function of oil revenue. The picture that emerges is one that called for accelerated growth in the oil sector and the utilization of the oil income to develop the non-oil sectors of the economy. While the first goal was to a considerable extent accomplished, thanks to a combination of a number of factors including a series of economic and political policy decisions, foreign assistance (especially from the Soviet Union), OPEC, and the changing nature of the international oil market, the second goal was far from being attained.

But since development policies are conceived and implemented in a given historical context, Iraq's development experience had to be shaped by its own internal political instability as well by Iraq's regional and international contexts. Iraq's own political instability took the form of sudden and violent changes in government and political leadership. As these changes deprived economic development plans from the necessary stability and continuity they resulted in the failure of the plans to attain their goals under all regimes during the last five decades.

This instability was aggravated at times by regional developments such as the Arab–Israeli conflict or border disputes. Moreover, the mere fact that Iraq

Table 3.5
NDP: Revised Allocations, Actual Expenditure, and Revenue, 1970–1974
(billions of dollars)

	Revised Allocation $	Actual Expenditure $	Actual to Allocation %
Expenditures			
Agriculture	1.10	.63	57
Industry	1.17	.99	84
Transport and Communications	.66	.53	54
Building and Services	.85	.51	61
Other	2.02	.88	44
Total	5.80	3.54	62

Revenue	Estimated	Actual	Actual to Allocation %
Oil	4.66	4.17	89
Non Oil	.52	.45	71
Total	5.18	4.62	89

Source: Calculated from Government of Iraq, *Law No. 6 of 1952*, schedules A and B; Government of Iraq, *Law No. 54 of 1956*; Central Bank of Iraq, *Quarterly Bulletin*, selected issues; Iraq Ministry of Development, *Annual Report on the Accounts of the Development Board and the Ministry of Development for the Fiscal Year 1954* (Baghdad: The Ministry, 1957); Government of Iraq, *Annual Abstract of Statistics* (Baghdad, Government of Iraq, various years).

was a major oil-exporting country placed it directly in the sphere of the security and/or national interests of the major powers of the day, be it Britain, France, or the United States.

Throughout the period of the second half of the twentieth century, all of Iraq's development plans were drawn up with oil revenue as the major if not the sole source of development finance. As time went on planning in Iraq was

Table 3.6
NDP: Target and Actual Values of Certain Economic Indicators, 1974
(billions of dollars)

Economic Indicator	Target	Actual	Actual to Target %
Gross domestic product	3.49	10.04	288
Oil extraction	1.23	6.07	495
Total exports	1.40	5.83	418
Total imports	.79	2.72	344
Agriculture	.95	.70	73
Manufacturing	1.20	.53	44
Construction	.52	.21	40
Transportation and Communication	.56	.37	67
Electricity and Water	.11	.04	40
Private Consumption	2.05	3.14	153
Public Consumption	.96	1.43	149
Employment (Thousands)	9.50	8.40	88

Source: Ministry of Planning, *Law of National DSevelopment Plan 1970–1974* (in Arabic) (Baghdad: The Ministry, 1971); Arab Monetary Fund, *National Accounts of Arab States 1971–1982* (Abu Dhabi: The Fund, 1983); United Nations, *Monthly Bulletin of Statistics*, various issues.

distorted by the expectation of how much oil revenue would be forthcoming. In other words, successive governments, regardless of their ideological bent, allowed development spending to rise with the ever-rising level of oil revenue regardless of the economy's absorptive capacity or the availability of technical and specialized requirements.

The biggest failure, however, relates to the very nature of the outcome of fifty years of development which entailed the spending of tens of billions of

Table 3.7
Planned and Actual Development Expenditures, 1951–1980 (billions of dollars)

	Planned Expenditure $	Actual Expenditure $	Actual Planned Expenditure %
Agriculture			
1951-1975	3.06	1.46	48
1976-1980	7.29	3.50	48
Subtotal	10.35	4.96	48
Industry			
1951-1975	3.70	2.42	66
1976-1980	15.18	10.01	66
Subtotal	18.88	12.43	66
Transport and Communication			
1951-1975	2.33	1.58	68
1976-1980	7.83	5.33	68
Subtotal	10.16	6.91	68
Buildings and Service			
1951-1975	2.73	1.70	62
1976-1980	8.30	5.15	62
Subtotal	11.03	6.85	62

dollars. It will be recalled that the linkage of oil to development was to use oil revenue to raise the rate of economic growth, diversify the economy, and lessen dependence on the oil sector. Yet fifty years of oil and development

Table 3.7 (*continued*)

	Planned Expenditure $	Actual Expenditure $	Actual Planned Expenditure %
Other			
1951-1975	2.41	2.00	83
1976-1980	14.57	12.10	83
Subtotal	16.98	14.10	83
Total			
1951-1975	14.22	9.16	64
1976-1980	53.19	34.04	64
Grand Total			
1951-1980	67.41	43.20	64

Source: Assembled from Tables 3.1–3.6; Government of Iraq, *Annual Abstract of Statistics* (Baghdad, Government of Iraq, various years).

seem to have left Iraq with economic stagnation, absence of economic diversification, and heavier dependence on the oil sector.

REFERENCES

Ali, A.M.S. (1991). "Evaluation of the Role of the State in Arab Countries." In *The Role of the State in the Arab Countries*, ed. Ali Nassar (in Arabic). Kuwait: Arab Planning Institute.

Alnasrawi, A. (1994). *The Economy of Iraq: Oil, Wars, Destruction of Development and Prospects, 1950–2010*. Westport, Conn.: Greenwood Press.

Batatu, H. (1982). *The Old Social Classes and the Revolutionary Movements of Iraq: A Study of Iraq's Old Landed and Commercial Classes and of Its Communists, Ba'thists, and Free Officers*. Princeton, N.J.: Princeton University Press.

Food and Agriculture Organization. (1959). *Iraq, Country Report*. Rome: Food and Agriculture Organization.

Government of Iraq. (1950). *Law No. 23* (in Arabic). Baghdad: Government of Iraq.

———. (1955). *Law No. 43* (in Arabic). Baghdad: Government of Iraq.

———. (1958). *Law No. 30* (in Arabic). Baghdad: Government of Iraq.

———. (1959). *The July 14 Revolution in Its First Year* (in Arabic). Baghdad: Government of Iraq.

Iraq Ministry of Planning. (1969). *The Detailed Framework of the Five-Year Economic Plan, 1965–1969* (in Arabic). Baghdad: Iraq Ministry of Planning.

Iraq Ministry of Planning. (1971). *Evaluation of the Five-Year Economic Plan, 1965–1969* (in Arabic). Baghdad: Iraq Ministry of Planning.

CHAPTER 4

Invasion, Sanctions, and Bombing

A comprehensive system of economic sanctions was imposed by the U.N. Security Council on Iraq four days after it had invaded Kuwait on August 2, 1990. Although the original objectives of the sanctions were achieved by March 1991 Iraq is still laboring under UNSC sanctions.

In the following pages the evolution of the sanctions as well as their impact on Iraq will be undertaken. The analysis will be confined in this chapter to the period up to April 1991 when an entirely different system of sanctions was imposed.

Prior to the analysis of sanctions it is important to say few words about the role that the Iraq–Iran War and changes in the fortunes of OPEC played in setting the stage for the invasion of Kuwait.

IMPACT OF THE IRAQ–IRAN WAR

When the government of Iraq decided to launch the war against Iran in September 1980 the Iraqi economy was on the threshold of another decade of economic growth. The immense increase in oil revenue from less than $1 billion in 1970 to $26 billion in 1980 had made it possible for the government to increase spending simultaneously on infrastructure, the bureaucracy, goods-producing sectors, social services, imports, and the military. The destruction of oil facilities caused by the war led oil output to decline sharply from 3.4 MBD in August 1980 to 0.9 MBD in 1981. This in turn resulted in the collapse of Iraq's oil revenue from $26 billion in 1980 to $10 billion in 1981, or by 60 percent.

For a country that has grown dependent on a single export these external shocks forced the economy to cope with a number of serious problems, some of which had become structural. Among such problems are the following:

1. Iraq's major oil exporting capacity was either destroyed, blocked, or closed.
2. Iraq's heavy industries were destroyed or in need of major repair.
3. The infrastructure was extensively damaged.
4. A major segment of the labor force (one-fifth) was in the armed forces.
5. Agricultural and industrial growth was either stagnant or negative.
6. Rural workers had either been drafted into the army or drifted to the city.
7. The large number of foreign workers imported during the war had become a burden on the economy.
8. Dependence on food imports increased.
9. Inflation had become a structural problem.
10. Privatization was not succeeding according to expectations.
11. Iraq had become a major debtor country.
12. Levels of imports had declined.
13. Development planning and spending had virtually ceased.
14. The higher living standards which were promised during the war could not be delivered in the postwar period.

In short, the government's big gamble of winning a quick victory over Iran led the economy to a dead end with no prospect for recovery. What staved off total economic collapse was the pumping of funds and credit by the Gulf states, OECD, and the former Soviet Union (Alnasrawi 1994: 83–100).

MILITARIZATION OF THE ECONOMY

One of the most significant changes to take place in the Iraqi economy in the decades of the 1970s and the 1980s was the massive shift of labor from the civilian economy to the military and the sharp increase in military spending and military imports.

In 1975 Iraq had 3 percent of its labor force in the armed forces. By 1980 the armed forces absorbed more than 13 percent of the labor force. And by the time the war with Iran ended in 1988 the government was employing more than 21 percent of the labor force or one million persons in the armed forces.

The other side of this expansion in the armed forces was the sharp rise of the military's claims on Iraq's fiscal resources. Thus in 1970 the government spent less than $1 billion on the military, or 19 percent of the GDP—a high ratio by world standards. By 1975, the government increased military spending by more than fourfold to $3.1 billion. By 1980, the government raised military spending more than sixfold over the 1975 level to $19.8 billion, or nearly 39 percent of the GDP. The share of military spending of the GDP continued to rise to absorb between one-half and two-thirds of the GDP in the 1980s.

Another way of looking at the burden of military spending is to relate it to Iraq's oil revenue. Thus during the eight-year period 1981–1988, military spending amounted to $120 billion or 256 percent of the same period's oil revenue of $46.7 billion. The eight-year deficit of $73.3 billion was financed by drawing from Iraq's international reserves, foreign debt, suppliers' credit, grants from Gulf states, abandonment of development plans, and reduction of imports and social services (Alnasrawi 1994: 83–100).

THE INVASION OF KUWAIT AND THE IMPOSITION OF SANCTIONS

Iraq entered the postwar period with a smaller and disorganized economy that was overburdened with unemployment, inflation, and foreign debt. To cope with the economic crisis, and to also fund an ambitious program of military industrialization Iraq had to rely on a shrinking source of oil revenue which in 1988 generated only $11 billion compared to $26 billion in 1980.

The exhausted state of the economy was made worse by the 9 percent decline in GDP in 1989 over 1988—a decline that constituted a severe blow to the government and forced it to adopt an austerity program of spending. But to reduce government spending in a period of severe economic crisis had the effect of worsening the crisis. What the economy needed at that particular juncture was an increase in the supply of goods to dampen inflation and restore some of the living standards that were severely eroded during the war. In order to achieve these objectives Iraq had only one option—to raise oil revenue. And it was in this particular arena that the stage was set for Iraq's conflict with Kuwait.

During the decade of the 1980s Iraq witnessed not only the devastation of its economy due to the eight-year war with Iran but it and other OPEC member countries suffered from a drastic decline in their oil revenue. The primary explanation for this decline was the oil price collapse of 1986. In order to stabilize their revenue OPEC member countries agreed in October of that year to return to their system of quotas, which they had abandoned earlier in that year, and to set the price at $18.00 per barrel, a price that was deemed by all member countries to be necessary for their social and economic development. The significance of the October 1986 accord was in the linkage it created between economic and social development on the one hand and certain levels of output to be sold on the world market at a given price on the other. This linkage meant also that a country that chooses to expand its output above its quota would do so at the expense of fellow producers causing a decline in their oil revenue and unwanted implications for their development.

Yet several countries, especially Kuwait and the United Arab Emirates, chose not to comply with their quotas, thus forcing the price to decline to $12.00 per barrel by October 1988. Although market conditions improved, causing the price to reach $20.00 per barrel in January 1990, Kuwait and other noncomplying OPEC countries, however, decided to raise their output to such a level that the price declined by one-third by June of that year—a decline that wiped out a major portion of the oil income of Iraq and other OPEC countries. It is important to note that given Iraq's oil export capacity at the time a drop in price of $1.00 per barrel meant a loss of $1 billion in oil revenue per year. It is worth noting that Iraqi President Saddam Hussein articulated an ominous position at the May 1990 meeting of the Arab Emergency Summit Conference when he characterized oil policies leading to above-quota production and lower prices as causing damage to the Iraqi economy that was similar to the economic damage inflicted by conventional wars (Alnasrawi 1994: 105–118).

In addition to the issue of production and prices Iraq accused Kuwait of using diagonal drilling to pump oil from that part of the Rumaila oil field that was located inside Iraqi territory.

On July 17, 1990 the Iraqi president accused rulers of the Gulf states of being tools in an international campaign waged by imperialists and Zionists to halt Iraq's scientific and technological progress and to impoverish its people. Ten days later, and in the shadow of the Iraqi troops movement along the Iraqi–Kuwait border, OPEC decided to raise the reference price for its oil from $18.00 to $21.00 per barrel and adopt new quotas. But on August 2 the government of Iraq decided to invade and occupy Kuwait.

The invasion of Kuwait was looked at by Iraq as a short-cut solution to its economic crisis and to the regime's failure to improve living standards. This policy decision was articulated by the deputy prime minister for the economy when he stated that Iraq will be able to pay its debt in less than five years; that the "new Iraq" would have a much higher oil production quota; that its income from oil would rise to $38 billion; and that it would be able to vastly increase spending on development projects and imports (Alnasrawi 1994: 105–118).

Iraq's invasion of Kuwait prompted the U.N. Security Council under the leadership of the United States to vote on August 6 to adopt resolution 661 which imposed a sweeping and comprehensive system of sanctions that are still in effect.

THE EARLY PHASE OF SANCTIONS

On August 2, 1990 Iraq's armed forces invaded and occupied Kuwait. A few hours following the invasion the UNSC adopted resolution 660 which condemned the invasion and called for the immediate and unconditional withdrawal of Iraq's forces from Kuwait. It also called upon the two countries to begin negotiations for the resolution of their differences. On that day President George Bush signed an executive order freezing Iraq's financial assets.

On August 6 the UNSC adopted resolution 661 which imposed sanctions on Iraq in order to achieve two objectives: to secure the withdrawal of Iraqi forces from Kuwait and to restore the authority of the Kuwaiti government. To attain these two objectives the resolution decreed (1) the banning of all imports from Iraq and Kuwait; (2) the banning of all exports except supplies intended strictly for medical purposes, and, in humanitarian circumstances, foodstuffs; (3) the freezing of all Iraqi government funds and other assets held abroad and banning all financial transactions with it; and (4) the creation of a sanctions committee composed of all fifteen Security Council members to oversee the implementation of the resolution.

On August 25 the UNSC adopted resolution 665 which transformed the sanctions into a blockade when it authorized member states to have their maritime forces use such measures as may be necessary under the authority of the Security Council to halt all inward and outward shipping, to inspect and verify their cargoes and destinations, and to ensure strict implementation of the provisions related to such shipping laid down in resolution 661. The passage of resolution 665 may be looked at as constituting a turning point in the dispute between Iraq and the UNSC since this particular resolution authorized for the first time the use of force against Iraq. It is interesting to note that while the UNSC was tightening its sanctions and blockade around Iraq it was also aware of the looming conditions of humanitarian emergency. This was made clear in resolution 666 which the UNSC adopted on September 13 and which recognized that circumstances may arise in which it will be necessary for foodstuffs to be supplied to the civilian population in order to relieve human suffering.

Yet on September 25 the maritime blockade was reinforced by an air blockade when the UNSC adopted resolution 670. This resolution stated that the sanctions on Iraq apply to all means of transport, including aircraft. The resolution instructed all states to deny permission to any aircraft to take off from their territory if the aircraft would carry any cargo to or from Iraq or Kuwait. The resolution also required member states to deny permission to any aircraft destined to land in Iraq or Kuwait to overfly their territory.

While the UNSC was tightening the blockade evidence of food shortages and deteriorating living conditions was mounting. Thus as early as August 12 the Iraqi president admitted for the first time in public that the sanctions were imposing hardship on the economy when he appealed to the people to do two things: (1) halve their usual food consumption and change their diets, and (2) forgo the purchase of clothes for at least one year (*Middle East Economic Survey* 1990: B2).

Three weeks after the call for frugality on the part of the people the government decided to institute a system of food rationing effective September 1,

1990. The ration under this system provided 1,270 calories per day per person, or a fraction of precrisis levels. A daily diet of less than 2,000 calories per person meant that Iraq was transformed overnight from a middle-income, relatively prosperous country to one of the poorest countries in the world (Simons 1998: 47).

While the economy of Iraq was continuing its decline the UNSC was setting the stage to establish Iraq's liability to pay compensation for any loss, damage, or injury arising from the occupation of Kuwait. Toward this end the UNSC adopted on October 29 resolution 674 which reminded Iraq of its liability and invited states to collect relevant information regarding their claims, and those of their nationals and corporations, for restitution or financial compensation by Iraq. This resolution, it should be pointed out, provided the basis for the creation of the U.N. Compensation Fund in the post–Gulf War period.

Four weeks after the adoption of the compensation resolution the UNSC passed on November 29 resolution 678 which set the stage for the Gulf War. In this resolution the UNSC authorized member states to use force, or as the resolution spelled it out, "to use all necessary means" to expel Iraqi forces from Kuwait unless Iraq terminated its occupation before January 15, 1991.

Since Iraq did not terminate its occupation of Kuwait by the appointed date the coalition forces under the leadership of the United States inaugurated the Gulf War on January 16, 1991 with a massive bombing campaign of Iraq.

THE AIR WAR AND THE IRAQI ECONOMY

On January 16 the coalition forces led by the United States inaugurated the six-week operation Desert Storm with an intensive bombing campaign of Iraq that culminated in the expulsion of Iraqi forces from Kuwait by the end of February.

Prior to the bombing phase of the Gulf War one group of military planners were of the opinion that the bombing should concentrate on the basic elements of Iraqi military power while another group of planners within the U.S. Air Force (USAF) sought a much wider scope for their bombing. To these planners there was no question that USAF should exercise air supremacy over Iraq, and in order to do so Iraq's air defenses would be the first targets of the bombing. The question was what to bomb next. The answer to this question was that bombing must be extended to Iraq's center of gravity. Since the planners could not come up with what constituted Iraq's center or centers of gravity they reached outside the military establishment to interview academics, journalists, ex-military types, and Iraqi defectors to determine what would make an impact psychologically on the population and the regime. And the conclusion was that the cutting edge would be Baghdad itself. This approach meant targeting the economic and political structure of Iraq, starting with Saddam Hussein, his command and control structure, infrastructure including electricity plants and oil refineries, and weapons of mass destruction (Freedman and Karsh 1993: 316–317).

True to the approach that stressed the targeting of centers of gravity the bombing of Iraq was aimed not only at military targets but also at such assets as civilian infrastructure, power stations, transport and telecommunications networks, fertilizer plants, oil refineries and other petrochemical plants, roads, railroads, iron and steel plants, bridges, schools, hospitals, government buildings, storage facilities, industrial plants, and civilian buildings. And the assets that were not bombed were rendered dysfunctional due to the destruction of power-generating facilities. One of the most severely damaged sectors of the infrastructure was power generation. The postwar assessment of recovery times gave the oil industry up to two years; electric power five to nine years; telecommunication, anything from three to twelve years; and transportation, three to six years (Freedman and Karsh 1993: 322).

The impact of the intensity and the scale of the bombing was assessed by a special U.N. mission to Iraq immediately after the war as follows:

It should, however, be said at once that nothing that we had seen or read had quite prepared us for the particular form of devastation which has now befallen the country. The recent conflict had wrought near-apocalyptic results upon what had been, until January 1991, a rather highly urbanized and mechanized society. Now, most means of modern life support have been destroyed or rendered tenuous. Iraq has, for some time to come, been relegated to a pre-industrial age, but with all the disabilities of post-industrial dependency on an intensive use of energy and technology. (United Nations 1996: 186–188)

This vast scale of destruction should not be surprising in light of the fact that the initial plan of bombing had focused on 84 targets but had grown to 174 targets by September 13, 1990. By the time the air campaign began on January 16, 1991 the plan had grown to include 386 targets which was expanded in the course of the war to include 723 targets (U.S. House Armed Services Committee 1992: 86).

In a postwar study of the air campaign it was acknowledged that the strategy went beyond bombing armed forces and military targets such as air defenses, airfields and warplanes, missiles, and chemical, nuclear, and munition plants. In addition to purely military targets the bombing revealed that: (1) some targets were attacked to destroy or damage valuable facilities that Iraq could not replace or repair without foreign assistance; (2) many of the targets chosen were selected to amplify the economic and psychological impact of sanctions on Iraqi society; and (3) targets were selected to do great harm to Iraq's ability to support itself as an industrial society. Thus the damage to Iraq's electrical facilities reduced the country's output of power to 4 percent of its prewar level. And nearly four months after the war the national power generation was only 20–25 percent of its prewar total or about the level it was at in 1920 (Hiro 1992: 354; Gellman 1991).

ESTIMATES OF WAR-RELATED HUMAN LOSSES

Neither the U.S. government nor the Iraqi government has seen fit to release data on the extent of the war-caused human and material losses. Data on such losses are in the realm of estimates hence the wide variation.

The Gulf War related human losses fall in three categories: (1) military and civilian losses during the war itself from January 16 to February 28, 1991; (2) civilian and military human losses during the unsuccessful popular March 1991 uprising against the Baath regime and its institutions; and (3) civilian losses which can be attributed to the effects of the destruction of infrastructure and other facilities and the continued embargo. The last category will be dealt with in a later section.

As to Iraq's losses of military personnel, estimates of such losses vary considerably. Thus in March 1991 Secretary of Defense Richard Cheney said, "If anybody is curious about what we think happened, we think there were a lot of Iraqis killed. Our military effort was aimed specifically at the destruction of these forces that took Kuwait, the destruction of [Saddam Hussein's] offensive capability, the destruction of divisions he used over the years to terrorize his neighbors, and we did that" (Clark 1994: 44).

Also in March 1991 Operation Desert Storm Commander in Chief General H. Norman Schwarzkopf said, "We must have killed 100,000" (Clark 1994: 43). But in May 1991 the Defense Intelligence Agency issued its estimate that 100,000 Iraqi troops were killed with an "error factor" of 50 percent meaning that 50,000 to 150,000 might have been killed (Hiro 1992: 396).

In 1992 the Pentagon estimated that 9,000 Iraqi troops were killed in the air war plus 120,000 Iraqi troops escaped or were killed during the ground war. The last figure was arrived at by estimating that out of 183,000 Iraqi troops present at the start of the ground war 63,000 were captured with the balance assumed to have escaped or been killed (U.S. House Armed Services Committee 1992: 33). Dilip Hiro, using different sources, concluded that 82,000 Iraqi soldiers lost their lives in the six-week Gulf War (Hiro 1992: 396).

Similarly, estimates of civilian deaths during the war show very widespread losses ranging from 11,000 to 24,500 (Kainker 1991: 345). Ramsey Clark, however, maintains that experience, reason, Commission of Inquiry research, and actual counts completed show that by early 1992 more than 150,000 civilians died, including 100,000 postwar deaths (Clark 1994: 83, 209). Moreover in the month-long uprising against the government that followed the war it was estimated that between 20,000 and 100,000 civilians lost their lives. In addition it was estimated that 15,000 to 30,000 Kurds and other displaced persons died in refugee camps and on the road and that another 4,000–16,000 Iraqis died of starvation and disease (Murphy 1991).

In addition to the loss of human lives the war and its aftermath inflicted other forms of losses on the civilian population, some of which are difficult to quantify. No information, for instance, has been released regarding the injured, the maimed, and the traumatized whose numbers and the extent of their plight are not known. It is similarly difficult to estimate the losses endured by the large numbers of refugees and displaced persons whose plight was caused by the manner in which the government crushed the March 1991 uprising. Suffice it to say that in the aftermath of the uprising nearly two million people left their homes, fleeing to Iran and Turkey (Graham-Brown 1999: 23).

THE CEASE-FIRE RESOLUTIONS

On February 28, 1991 President George Bush made a speech in which he announced that he would offer the government of Iraq a cease-fire provided that it comply with certain conditions which he laid down. One such condition was to require Iraq's full compliance with all relevant UNSC resolutions, including abrogation of Iraq's decision to annex Kuwait and accepting the principle of responsibility for paying compensation for damage and injury (Hiro 1992: 392). Iraq agreed immediately to the announcement and the cease-fire went into effect on February 28, 1991.

Following Iraq's acceptance of the cease-fire conditions the UNSC moved on March 2 to formalize it by adopting resolution 686. This was a provisional arrangement pending the adoption of a permanent cease-fire resolution. This was accomplished on April 3, 1991 when the UNSC adopted resolution 687. This resolution and its implications for the Iraqi economy and the future of Iraq will be addressed in the next chapter. In the following paragraphs an analysis of the impact of the sanctions in their earlier phase is undertaken.

ECONOMIC CONSEQUENCES OF THE SANCTIONS

Iraq was in a weak position when it invaded Kuwait. Its economy was still recovering from the impact of the Iraq–Iran War, its oil industry had suffered major setbacks in the previous decade, its foreign reserves had been exhausted, its foreign debt had mounted, its currency was depreciating, its dependency on food imports was rising, its stocks of wheat and rice were enough for three months, and its GDP had been declining over the previous two years. Moreover, the freezing of Kuwait's assets beyond the reach of Iraq turned the occupation of Kuwait into a giant economic liability. It was in these vulnerable economic conditions that the government of Iraq found itself when the sanctions were imposed. Under these conditions the impact of the sanctions proved to be immediate and effective.

As was stated earlier the sanctions were imposed on Iraq on August 6, 1990 and were tightened by the naval and air blockades instituted in the following month.

The first economic casualty of the sanctions was oil. Iraq's oil output in July 1990 was 3.3 MBD. In subsequent months the output plummeted to 0.45 MBD or 14 percent of preinvasion output—enough to meet local consumption. Since Iraq's oil was being exported through Turkey, Saudi Arabia, and the Gulf, it was rather easy to shut off the pipelines and use maritime force to block all oil exports. And since the price of oil had been raised by OPEC to $21.00 per barrel, Iraq's oil revenue would have been much higher than in 1989.

Ironically, while the annexation of Kuwait doubled the size of oil reserves endowment under the control of Iraq and increased the combined output capacity of the two countries to 4.6 MBD, Iraq found itself, because of the embargo, unable to benefit from this wealth. Interestingly, Iraq even failed in its attempt to give its oil away to Third World countries when the Iraqi government declared its readiness to supply needy Third World countries with Iraqi oil free of charge provided that the takers must arrange for the transport of oil (*Middle East Economic Survey* 1990: A5).

The effectiveness of the embargo was such that in a testimony before the U.S. Senate Foreign Relations Committee it was reported that the embargo had effectively shut off 90 percent of Iraq's imports and 97 percent of its exports and produced serious disruptions to the economy and hardships to the people.

The embargo-induced economic loss in the six months prior to the January bombing of Iraq was estimated by the Iraqi government to be 24 percent of GDP or $18.1 billion—$10 billion in lost oil exports, $5.1 billion in lost production, and $3 billion in other losses (*Middle East Economic Digest* 1991: 22). But these losses and the hardships associated with them were minor in comparison to the destruction inflicted upon Iraq by the Gulf War.

It will be recalled that the Iraqi government's decision to invade Kuwait was driven primarily by the desire of the regime to find a solution to the economy's deepening crisis. The economic crisis was a direct result of the bankrupting effects of the Iran–Iraq War. The economic destruction of the Gulf War that followed the August 1990 invasion of Kuwait was superimposed on an economy that was reeling from the multiple shocks of a war that was ended less than two years earlier.

The economic destruction of 1991 took many forms. First, there was the destruction of nonmilitary and military assets. The extent of the massive destruction of or damage to the infrastructure and other sectors of the economy as assessed by the United Nations was referred to earlier. The scope of the damage was widened as the list of targets was constantly expanded in the course of the war. It was also suggested that a number of targets were destroyed to increase Iraq's dependency on the West, particularly the United States, after the war (Gellman 1991).

As to the cost of all the assets destroyed during the war, such cost was estimated to be $232 billion, or several times the level of Iraq's GDP in 1989 (Arab Monetary Fund 1992: 18).

In addition to the replacement cost of the destroyed assets one must add, of course, the value of lost output, replacement cost of equipment and related supplies, inflation-related losses, depreciation of the Iraqi dinar, and lost imports. Furthermore, one must add also the loss of export earnings; that is, lost oil revenue.

The most obvious and most readily measurable loss is that of lost oil revenue which would have exceed $20 billion in 1990 and increased in 1991. Since Iraq's GDP in 1989 was $55.3 billion this means that Iraq lost between 35–40 percent of its GDP from this sector alone due to the sanctions. A reduction in oil revenue of this magnitude is bound to have a devastating impact on private consumption, public consumption, development spending, and private sector investment.

The impact of the embargo on imports on the economy was severe since in an open economy like Iraq's such embargo affects the availability not only of consumer goods but also the availability of inputs and capital goods essential for the functioning of all sectors of the economy. These shortages induce decline in output on the one hand and inflation on the other.

Since the Iraqi economy is totally dependent on its foreign sector and since it is in no position to pull itself up by its own boot straps it is only logical to conclude that it will continue to suffer from stagnation and decline so long as the sanctions continue. And the longer the sanctions remain in place the greater their potential impact due to the multiplier process.

IMPACT ON PERSONAL INCOME, CONSUMPTION, AND COST OF LIVING

It has been suggested that when people get to the point where they start selling their property and their jewelry, we know, statistically, that they are approaching the famine stage. This should not be surprising in a country where a comprehensive embargo has been in effect with inflation reaching a record figure of 2,000 percent and wages not rising for more than three years. The factors are hitting the poorest—about 85 percent of the population—the hardest, with their situation getting worse every day. The government rationing system provides only 55 percent of calorie requirements. Yet the embargo has barely affected the regime's top cadres who, far from feeling the pinch, benefit hugely in one way or another from hefty profits in the private sector (Chipaux 1991: 13).

A measure of the collapse of the Iraqi economy may be seen in the change in Iraq's per capita GDP, measured in 1980 prices, which rose from $1,745 in 1970 to $4,083 in 1980. By 1988, however, it had declined to $1,756 and to $627 in 1991. Indeed one has to go back to the decade of the 1940s to find comparable per capita GDP. The depth of the deteriorating living conditions of most Iraqis was captured by the findings of the International Study Team. After having analyzed the behavior of prices, incomes, and employment for the year ending in August 1991 the study made these observations:

1. While there has been a shift in the distribution of employment from the formal to the informal sectors of the economy monthly earnings remained stagnant.

2. Consumer prices during the same period increased considerably, especially the food price index, which increased by 1,500 to 2,000 percent in that year.

3. Real monthly earnings or the food purchasing power of private income has declined by a factor of fifteen or twenty or to 5–7 percent of its August 1990 level.

4. Real monthly earnings are lower than the benchmark used by the government of Iraq before August 1990 to identify "destitute households" eligible for government support.

5. These earnings are lower than the monthly earnings of unskilled agricultural workers in India—one of the poorest countries in the world (Dreze and Gazdar 1992: 933–935).

The bombing of infrastructure, collapse of the economy, ravaging inflation, bombing of hospitals and power generating plans, lack of food, medicine, and purified water resulted in drastic declines in health conditions which led to a decline in life expectancy and a phenomenal rise in death rates, especially among children. In a UNICEF study published in 1996 it was reported that as many as 4,500 child deaths per month can be attributed to the sanctions (Simons 1998: 215). Another U.N. agency, the World Health Organization (WHO) observed that, due to the sanctions, the vast majority of the population was forced to survive on a semistarvation diet giving rise to serious implications for the health status of generations to come (WHO 1996: 16). The sanctions-induced rise in mortality rates led Richard Garfield to conclude that this is the only instance of a sustained, large increase in mortality in a stable population of more than two million in the last two hundred years (Garfield 2000: 36–47).

In a joint report by the Food and Agriculture Organization (FAO) and the World Food Programme (WFP) it was observed that under normal circumstances, Iraq would be neither a food-insecure country nor would it qualify to receive international humanitarian assistance due to its abundant natural resources and its fiscal capacity to import all its food needs. But since its economy has been devastated by the Gulf War and the sanctions Iraq has found itself forced to cope with persistent deprivation, chronic hunger, endemic undernutrition, and widespread human suffering. The report also noted the existence of prefamine indicators such as exorbitant prices, a sharp fall in the value of the Iraqi dinar, collapse of real incomes, soaring unemployment, drastically reduced food intakes, high morbidity levels, escalating crime rates, and rapidly increasing numbers of destitute people. The situation would have been much worse had it not been for the food rationing system that was put in place in September 1990. But the food distributed under the rationing system which is carbohydrate-based and provided only a fraction of the necessary caloric intake resulted in the deterioration of the nutritional status of the population at an alarming rate since these food intakes were lower than those of the populations in the disaster-stricken African countries (FAO and WFP 1993).

THE RESPONSE OF THE U.N. SECURITY COUNCIL

As was stated earlier resolution 661, which the UNSC adopted four days after the invasion of Kuwait, imposed a total ban on all imports by Iraq except for supplies intended strictly for medical purposes, and, in humanitarian circumstances, foodstuffs. The definition of what constitutes "humanitarian circumstances" was to be determined by the UNSC or its Sanctions Committee. Even when the Sanctions Committee eventually recognized the existence of urgent humanitarian needs in Iraq in March 1991, nothing was done to alter the situation. This meant that the bulk of the enormous food needs of the Iraqi people—more than 10,000 tons per day of food grain alone—were unmet. The case of medical supplies was not much better (Dreze and Gazdar 1992: 924).

This was not an oversight on the part of the UNSC. There was no escaping the fact that the policy was intended to inflict suffering on the population in the hope that the government of Iraq would change its policy. As was noted at the time, "We want to hurt Iraq but cannot be seen to use famine to bring the country down" (Freedman and Karsh 1993: 191).

The humanitarian emergency conditions in Iraq and the pending human catastrophe were highlighted in the March 20, 1991 report by a mission led by U.N. Undersecretary-General Martti Ahtisaari. The bleak picture that the report presented regarding living, health, and economic conditions in Iraq was described as follows:

I, together with all my colleagues, am convinced that there needs to be a major mobilization and movement of resources to deal with aspects of this deep crisis in the field of agriculture and food, water, sanitation and health. . . . It is unmistakable that the Iraqi people may soon face a further imminent catastrophe, which could include epidemic and famine, if massive life-supporting needs are not rapidly met. . . . Time is short. (United Nations 1996: 186–188)

Only two days after the release of this report the Sanctions Committee made the following determination: "In the light of the new information available to it, the Committee has decided to make, with immediate effect, a general determination that humanitarian circumstances apply with respect to the entire civilian population of Iraq in all parts of Iraq's national territory" (United Nations 1996: 189). But since Iraq's foreign-held assets were frozen and its oil exports were embargoed the Sanctions Committee's determination proved to be of no benefit to Iraq.

IMPACT OF THE SANCTIONS: THE FIRST YEAR

The sanctions were imposed on Iraq in August 1990. The Gulf War which caused the destruction of the country's infrastructure lasted from the middle of January to the end of February 1991. The cease-fire was immediately followed by a general uprising throughout the country against the regime of Saddam Hussein and the institutions of the Baath Party. It is obvious that whatever human and physical damage was inflicted upon Iraq cannot be attributed to the sanctions alone. It is true, of course, that for the period preceding the bombing campaign most of the decline in the economy can be attributed to the sanctions but the same cannot be said for developments after the war. This is particularly true when we realize that the destruction of the infrastructure had the effect of reinforcing the impact of the sanctions and vice versa.

The Ahtissari report cited left no doubt as to the breadth and depth of the catastrophes that engulfed Iraq immediately after the war. Thus in May 1991, the Harvard Study Team Report projected that some 85,000 children under the age of five would die over the next year from the effects of the new conditions (Harvard Study Team 1991: 1). Another effect of the war and sanctions was their impact on life expectancy due to the vastly deteriorated living and health conditions. Another report concluded that about 170,000 people have died as a direct and indirect result of the embargo (Harvard Study Team 1991: 1). It was also estimated that lack of food and medicine increased the under-five mortality rate from 29.5 per 1,000 live births in 1988 to 92.7 per 1,000 live births in 1992 (Harvard Study Team 1991: 1).

One of the major problems with vast consequences for the people and the economy has been the destruction of electricity-generating capacity which reduced power output to a small fraction of its prewar level. The Ahtissari report observed that without normal supply of electricity food that is imported cannot be preserved and distributed, water cannot be purified, sewage cannot be pumped away, crops cannot be irrigated, and medicines cannot be shipped to where they are needed (United Nations 1996: 188).

This breakdown combined with the fact that industrial employment was reduced by 90 percent and the phenomenal rise in prices led to the impoverishment of the majority of Iraqi society.

As Dreze and Gazdar observed, in Iraq, as in all modern societies, household access to food and other basic commodities is determined by their private and public goods. Private income depends primarily on employment which in turn depends on demand for labor, wages, and prices. Public goods depend on the state's ability and willingness to provide health services, education, safe water, public health, and food subsidies (Dreze and Gazdar 1992: 922).

Of particular importance in the Iraqi context was the combination of sanctions-induced commodity shortages, sanctions-caused loss of foreign exchange, loss of private sector output and employment, serious decline in the market exchange rate (value) of Iraqi dinar, loss of the government's primary source of income, and the sharp rise in prices which afflicted all sectors of the economy. By August 1991 all these factors led to the collapse in private-income purchasing power over food by a factor of fifteen to twenty or 5–7 percent of their level since August 1990 (Dreze and Gazdar 1992: 926). Food-price increases in Iraq for the period August 1990 to August 1991 are shown in Table 4.1.

Table 4.1
Food Price Increases in Iraq, August 1990–August 1991

Food Item	Price per Unit (ID)		Percentage increase
	Aug. 90	Aug. 91	
Wheat flour	0.05	2.42	4,431
Powdered milk	0.75	27.33	3,561
Sugar	0.20	4.42	2,108
Cooking oil	0.48	10.33	2,038
Rice	0.23	4.08	1,701
Tea	1.70	23.67	1,292
Cost (at current prices) of the average 1990 food basket for a family of six	66.00	1,010.00	1,446

Source: J. Dreze and H. Gazdar, "Hunger and Poverty in Iraq," *World Development* 20 (7) (1992): 927.

What compounded the effects of the sanctions upon household purchasing power was the inability of the government to continue to fund its presanctions provision of public services. The sharp decline in oil revenue prompted the government to do two things, both of which tended to depress living standards and contribute to the impoverishment of the people. First, the government reduced the scope of its supply of social services. Second, in order to finance its expenditure the government resorted to the printing of money, thus deepening inflationary pressures in the economy.

What mitigated against further decline in living conditions was the food-rationing system that the government introduced in September 1990 which provides food rations at nominal cost to households.

Sanctions, deteriorating economic conditions, inflation, and rising unemployment depressed real earnings to unprecedented levels. Thus it has been found that real monthly earnings for unskilled labor as well as in most other occupations are less than 7 percent of what they were in August 1990 and lower than the benchmark used by the government of Iraq before August 1990 to identify "destitute households" eligible for government social security payment. What is striking about this new condition is that, in terms of current income, the majority of the Iraqi population is below the Indian poverty line (Dreze and Gazdar 1992: 934–935).

The response of the UNSC to Iraq's predicament after the war was far from satisfactory as will be seen in the next chapter.

REFERENCES

Alnasrawi, A. (1994). *The Economy of Iraq: Oil, Wars, Destruction of Development and Prospects, 1950–2010.* Westport, Conn.: Greenwood Press.

Arab Monetary Fund, League of Arab States, Arab Fund for Economic and Social Development, and Organization of Arab Oil Exporting Countries. (1992). *Unified Arab Economic Report* (annual, in Arabic). Abu Dhabi: United Arab Emirates.

Chipaux, F. (1991). "Saddam Sits Pretty as Iraqi People Suffer." *Manchester Guardian Weekly*, August 11.

Clark, R. (1994). *The Fire This Time: U.S. War Crimes in the Gulf.* New York: Thunder's Mouth Press.

Dreze, J., and Gazdar, H. (1992). "Hunger and Poverty in Iraq." *World Development* 20 (7): 921–945.

Food and Agriculture Organization, and World Food Program. (1993). *FAO/WFP Crop and Food Supply Assessment Mission to Iraq.* Rome: Food and Agriculture Organization.

Freedman, L., and Karsh, F. (1993). *The Gulf Conflict, 1990–1991.* Princeton, N.J.: Princeton University Press.

Garfield, R. (2000). "Changes in Health and Well-Being in Iraq during the 1990s: What Do We Know and How Do We Know It." In Campaign Against Sanctions on Iraq, *Sanctions on Iraq: Background, Consequences and Strategies.* Cambridge: The Campaign.

Gellman, B. (1991). "Allied Air War Struck Broadly in Iraq: Officials Acknowledge Strategy Went Beyond Purely Military Targets." *The Washington Post*, June 23, p. A1.

Graham-Brown, S. (1999). *Sanctioning Saddam: The Politics of Intervention in Iraq.* London: I. B. Tauris.

Harvard Study Team. (1991). *Public Health in Iraq after the Gulf War.* Washington, D.C.: Wagner Communications.

Hiro, D. (1992). *Desert Shield to Desert Storm: The Second Gulf War.* New York: Routledge.

Kainker, L. (1991). "Desert Sin: A Post-War Journey Through Iraq." In *Beyond the Storm: A Gulf Crisis Reader*, ed. P. Bennis and M. Moushabeck. New York: Olive Branch Press.

Middle East Economic Digest. (1991). August 30.

Middle East Economic Survey. (1990). August 20.

Murphy, C. (1991). "Iraqi Death Toll Remains Clouded." *The Washington Post*, June 23, p. A1.

Simons, G. (1998). *The Scourging of Iraq: Sanctions, Law and Natural Justice*, 2d ed. New York: St. Martin's Press.

United Nations. (1996). *The United Nations and the Iraq–Kuwait Conflict*. New York: United Nations.

U.S. House Armed Services Committee. (1992). *A Defense for a New Era: Lessons of the Persian Gulf War*. Washington, D.C.: U.S. Government Printing Office.

World Health Organization. (1996). *The Health Conditions of the People in Iraq Since the Gulf Crisis*. Geneve: World Health Organization.

CHAPTER 5

Sanctions after the Gulf War

Following the expulsion of Iraqi forces from Kuwait the UNSC adopted on March 2, 1991 resolution 686 which dealt with matters that arose directly from the invasion and annexation of Kuwait and the subsequent Gulf War. These matters included demands by the UNSC that Iraq rescind the annexation of Kuwait, accept liability for loss, damage, and injury that resulted from the invasion and occupation, release prisoners of war, and return seized assets.

THE NEW ORDER OF RESOLUTION 687

Four weeks after the adoption of resolution 686, the UNSC adopted on April 3, 1991 resolution 687 which established Iraq's obligations in the postwar period. In the words of the U.N. secretary-general,

Security Council resolution 687 (1991) represents one of the most complex and far-reaching sets of decisions ever taken by the Council. The longest text ever adopted by the Council. . . . Implementation of resolution 687 (1991) sent the United Nations into uncharted territory in many areas, among them the Organization's work in demarcating the boundaries between Kuwait and Iraq, its collaboration with the IAEA in the nuclear area, its administration of a compensation fund and the use by the Security Council of subsidiary bodies such as the Special Commission (UNSCOM) and the Sanctions Committee. (United Nations 1996: 29)

In order to have a permanent cease-fire and to have the sanctions lifted Iraq had to agree to a number of conditions regarding the following: (1) boundary settlement; (2) the deployment of a U.N. observer unit to monitor the border; (3) the elimination of Iraq's chemical and biological stockpiles and its ballistic missiles, the creation of a U.N. Special Commission to carry out immediate on-site inspections in order to take possession of these weapons and supervise their destruction and the development of a plan for the future ongoing monitoring and verification of Iraq's compliance with the ban on these weapons; (4) the unconditional undertaking by Iraq not to acquire or develop nuclear weapons or nuclear-weapons usable materials to be verified by on-site inspection. A special plan is to be developed for the future ongoing monitoring and verification of Iraq's compliance with the nuclear ban; (5) acceptance by Iraq of its liability for any direct loss, damage (including environmental damage and the depletion of natural resources) or injury to foreign governments, corporations, and individuals as a result of the invasion. The resolution decided to also create a compensation fund to pay out claims. The fund was to be financed from a portion of Iraq's oil revenue. The determination of this portion will take into account the humanitarian needs of the Iraqi people; (6) the UNSC demanded that Iraq adhere to its foreign debt obligations; and (7) Iraq was called upon to cooperate in the effort to facilitate the repatriation of other countries' prisoners and detainees. The resolution decided to lift the sanctions on Iraq's imports of food and other materials and supplies for essential civilian needs. As to the eventual lifting of the sanctions the resolution stated that the ban on Iraq's exports will be lifted when the UNSC approved the program for the compensation fund and agreed that Iraq had complied with the weapons provision of the resolutions (United Nations 1996: 30–33).

Although the resolution lifted the ban on Iraq's imports of foodstuffs, materials, and supplies for essential civilian needs this was of no consequence since Iraq lacked the financial resources, as oil exports remained under embargo, to benefit from this window of opportunity. It is relevant to note that the UNSC was aware of the humanitarian crisis engulfing Iraq at the time of the resolution since it empowered the Sanctions Committee to approve adequate financial resources to enable Iraq to import commodities to meet humanitarian needs. Iraq's several requests to the Sanctions Committee that it be allowed the financial exception stipulated in the resolution were turned down. And the financial exception was later cancelled by the UNSC when it adopted resolution 778 in October 1992 (al-Anbari 1996).

It is important to note that when the initial sanctions regime was imposed on Iraq in August 1990 its purpose was to bring the invasion and occupation of Kuwait by Iraq to an end and to restore the sovereignty, independence, and territorial integrity of Kuwait. Although these objectives were attained in the early part of March 1991 the UNSC saw fit to introduce a whole new regime of sanctions with an entirely different set of conditions as outlined previously.

THE SECRETARY GENERAL'S MISSIONS TO IRAQ

In March 1991, prior to the adoption of resolution 687, the U.N. secretary-general dispatched a mission to Iraq to report to him on conditions in the country in the aftermath of the Gulf War. The mission was led by the U.N. Undersecretary General Matti Ahtissari and included representatives of several U.N. agencies such as United Nations Children's Fund (UNICEF), United Nations Development Programme (UNDP), Office of the United Nations Disaster Relief Coordinator (UNDOR), the Office of the United Nations High Commisioner for Refugees (UNHCR), the Food and Agriculture Organization, and the World Health Organization.

The mission reported on the "dimensions of the calamity" and stressed the need for "a major mobilization and movement of resources to deal with aspects of this deep crisis in the fields of agriculture and food, water, sanitation and health. . . . It stated that it was unmistakable that the Iraqi people may soon face a further imminent catastrophe, which could include epidemic and famine, if massive life-supporting needs are not rapidly met" (United Nations 1996: 186–188). Only two days after the submission of this report the Sanctions Committee made a general determination that humanitarian circumstances apply with respect to the entire civilian population of Iraq in all parts of Iraq national territory. The Sanctions Committee went on to state that the civilian and humanitarian imports identified in the Ahtissari mission report are to be considered integrally related to the supply of foodstuffs and medicines and as such they are exempt from sanctions (United Nations 1996: 189). But as was noted earlier neither the UNSC nor the Sanctions Committee provided the legal and the financial means to respond to the humanitarian needs identified in the Ahtissari report.

As the plight of the ordinary people of Iraq continued to worsen the U.N. secretary-general decided to send another mission that visited Iraq in July 1991 under the leadership of his executive delegate Sadruddin Aga Khan. In addition to representatives from other U.N. agencies such as UNICEF, WHO, UNDP, and FAO this mission included "consultants, specialists and eminent personalities from outside the United Nations system" (United Nations 1996: 277).

The mission stated that the tragic consequences of the conflict were compounded by massive displacements of ill-prepared populations, by ecological disasters, and by the collapse of the structures that sustain life in today's human societies. The mission asserted that in Iraq the effects of the upheaval are leading to the gradual but inexorable collapse of essential services, leading to the risk of a humanitarian crisis whose eventual dimensions would dwarf today's difficulties. The mission went on to record its observations regarding the conditions of the sectors of concern to it.

In the water sector the mission noted that the damage to water treatment plants and the inability to import needed spare parts have cut off an estimated 2.5 million persons from the system. As to the 14.5 million people who continue to receive their water through the system, they are provided with one-quarter of the prewar amount per day and much of it is of doubtful quality. The national sewage system suffered major damage, causing outbreaks of diseases caused by contaminated water and sewage problems. Similarly the health of the population is challenged by insufficient access to quality medical care and inadequate nutrition. Public health programs and hospitals were forced to reduce their services for lack of supplies, electricity, medicines, equipment, and spare parts.

The mission observed that the food supply position was deteriorating rapidly in all parts of the country. Current retail prices of wheat and rice have skyrocketed forty-five and twenty-two times their respective levels of the previous year. Average incomes, on the other hand, have shown only moderate gains. On the basis of several studies the mission warned of a pending widespread and acute food-supply crisis which, if not averted through timely intervention, will cause massive starvation throughout the country.

As to power generation capacity it was observed that by July 1991 Iraq was able to produce 25 percent of its prewar capacity. In the absence of major imports of new parts power output should be expected to decline.

Again, the oil sector and the telecommunication sectors require considerable imports of equipment to restore production and services. The mission made the important observation that in many cases problems with importing had more to do with financing such imports than actual prohibitions. In other words, Iraq should be permitted to sell oil to pay for its imports.

As the mission concluded that the scale of damage and decline in Iraq in the past year had indeed been dramatic, it focused its attention on the necessity to rehabilitate five sectors: water, health, food supply, power generation, and oil. These sectors are not only important in and of themselves but their continued deterioration or rehabilitation would have serious implications for the future of the people and the economy. Suffice it to say that the restoration of power generation is so essential for the functioning of the entire economy and all human services that its rehabilitation had to be given priority. Although Iraq managed to restore about 40 percent of the 1990 electricity production level this restoration was accomplished through such methods as cannibalizing parts from damaged units. This means that without major imports of new parts power output can be expected to decline (United Nations 1996: 274–276).

As to the costs of returning these systems to their prewar condition the mission had these estimates: $12 billion for the power-generating capacity; $6 billion for the oil sector; $2.64 billion for food imports; $0.450 billion for the water and sanitation systems; $0.5 billion for imports for the agricultural sector; and $0.5 billion for health sector imports. Anticipating that such sums, totaled at $22.1 billion, were not likely to be approved by the UNSC, the mission provided cost estimates for greatly reduced level of services which came to $6.8 billion including $1.62 billion for general food imports and $0.5 billion for health services. It is important to point out that the mission's calculations were made for providing reduced levels of services except for the health sector. Thus the mission cost estimates were designed to provide two-fifths of the prewar per capita levels of clean drinking water and putting a corresponding proportion of the damaged sewage-treatment capacity back in operation. Similarly food imports were based on the ration level that the World Food Programme provides to sustain disaster-stricken populations. Power-generation estimates were based on restoring one-half of the prewar capacity in the country.

The mission provided another cost estimate of $2.63 billion for an initial four-month period and stressed that the massive financial requirements to establish even this reduced level of service are of a scale far beyond what is likely to be available under any U.N.–sponsored program. Furthermore, any appeals for aid to Iraq will have to compete with a number of emergency situations around the world with very compelling needs.

Given Iraq's wealth the mission recommended that funds be generated either by the unfreezing of its foreign assets held abroad or through the sale of oil (United Nations 1996: 277–279).

THE RESPONSE OF THE UNSC TO THE CRISIS

On August 15, 1991 the UNSC adopted resolution 706 which authorized Iraq to sell $1.6 billion of oil over a period of six months. This figure was confirmed in resolution 712 adopted on September 13, 1991. Although the report of the executive delegate was used by the UNSC to justify its decision it failed, however, to accept the mission's estimates of the financial resources necessary to help Iraq care for its people. This can be seen in the huge difference between what the mission had recommended and what the UNSC voted on. Thus while the mission estimated that Iraq would need $6.8 billion over one year or $2.63 billion over four months the UNSC voted to authorize the sale of $1.6 billion for six months. Not only did the authorized $1.6 billion fall short of the mission's estimates but the gap between the two figures becomes much wider once we realize that of the UNSC's recommended figure several deductions totaling $666 million were made in accordance with the resolution and reduced what was available to Iraq to $934 million for the so-called humanitarian imports. These deductions included 30 percent or $480 million for the Compensation Fund with the balance going to fund the U.N.'s other operations such as Iraq–Kuwait boundary demarcation, expenditures of the International Atomic Energy Agency, United Nations Special Commission, monitoring contracts of oil sales and inspection, costs of monitoring and distribution of humanitarian assistance by the United Nations in Iraq, and direct procurement of food and medicines by the United Nations (*Middle East Economic Survey* 1991: D6).

There are several issues that this program gives rise to but were left unanswered. In the first place the UNSC failed to provide any rationale for the $1.6 billion oil sales, actually $934 million after the deductions stated. Given the fact that Iraq needed, before the Gulf crisis, $3 billion per year just to cover its imports of food and medicine, the appropriation of $934 million is rather small by comparison. Leaving historical standards aside, the UNSC also failed to explain why this authorization fell short of what the U.N. secretary-general's executive delegate had recommended. Moreover, the secretary-general himself had attempted but failed in his request that the allocation be increased by $800 million to $2.4 billion before the deductions to bring the funding for the humanitarian program to $1.7 billion. In other words, the UNSC went ahead and authorized the sale of oil to fund a much smaller program of $934 million or 54 percent of what the secretary-general and his executive delegate have recommended (United Nations 1996: 299–300).

The second issue relates to the decision by the UNSC to deduct 30 percent of the oil sales and earmark it for the Compensation Fund. The question here is similar to the earlier one: What was the rationale for selecting this particular ratio of 30 percent? It turned out that the selection of this particular ratio was arrived at by the secretary-general in the following manner. The starting point in the computation was Iraq's oil production in July 1990 of 3.14 MBD from which was deducted 0.3 MBD for local consumption, leaving 2.85 MBD available for export. It was also assumed that this level of export would be reached in 1993. As to the price of oil, it was assumed that the price of OPEC oil would be $21.00 per barrel in 1993. Allowing for quality and locational differentials Iraq's oil price would be $20.04 per barrel. Under these assumption Iraq was assumed to generate $21 billion in oil revenue in 1993. These calculations also assumed that the demand for oil would rise by 2 percent per year and that OPEC member countries would return to the production quotas that they agreed upon in July 1990, thus allowing Iraq to reach this level of oil exports without causing a price collapse. Having arrived at an estimate of Iraq's oil revenue the next step was to compute foreign exchange requirements for strictly civilian imports and foreign debt service. By taking account of historical relationships of consumption and investment to GDP and their import intensity, it was estimated that about $8 billion may be required to sustain a level of civilian imports in 1991 consistent with the need of the Iraqi economy. These imports were projected to reach $10 billion or 48 percent of the $21 billion of oil revenue in 1993. As to debt service, the secretary-general assumed that Iraq will be able to reschedule its debt of $42.1 billion at standard Paris Club terms and that debt service would absorb another 22 percent of the 1993 oil revenue, leaving 30 percent of the oil revenue to be earmarked for the Compensation Fund (United Nations 1996: 258–259).

There are, of course, several problems with this scenario. One such problem is Iraq's ability to produce and export the projected levels of oil. Actual experience shows that actual output was far below the projected level. OPEC member countries chose not to go back to their July 1990 production quotas and the price of OPEC oil did actually collapse to $16.33 per barrel in 1993 and to $12.28 per barrel in 1998. Indeed, for the period 1991–1999 the price never reached $21.00 per barrel. This had to wait until the year 2000. But what is most revealing about the calculations is their estimates of the civilian Iraqi economy's needs for foreign exchange of $8 billion and $10 billion in 1991 and 1993 respectively, yet the decision of the UNSC was to limit such civilian imports to $934 million for six months or $1.87 billion per year.

The other problem with the program is the complexity of its execution. In order for Iraq to sell oil its State Oil Marketing Organization (SOMO) must negotiate oil sales and sign sales contracts for potential purchases that must be approved by the Sanctions Committee. These contracts are to be reviewed by U.N. agents at SOMO to ensure compliance with U.N. regulations and report their findings to the oil overseers at the United Nations in New York. The contracts are further reviewed by the overseers to verify compliance with U.N. regulations, including the standard that pricing is consistent with world prices and market trends. Once the contract and supporting documents are found to be in order the overseer will notify his approval to the purchaser, SOMO, the U.N. inspector in the port of Ceyhan, Turkey who is responsible for authorizing the loading of oil. Full proceeds from the sale of oil are to be deposited by the purchaser into the escrow account established by the United Nations and administered by the secretary-general (United Nations 1996: 298–301).

The procedure for Iraq's imports is more complicated and more time consuming. The starting point in the process is the government's submission to the office of the humanitarian coordinator in Baghdad of a list of what it intends to import. This list, which may be revised by the humanitarian coordinator, is then sent to the Sanctions Committee for action. After taking action on the list the Sanctions Committee forwards the list to the secretary-general who will make the list known to member states and to the humanitarian coordinator who would inform Iraq of the clearance by the committee. At this point Iraq may enter into contracts with potential exporters. These contracts are then forwarded to the committee by the potential exporter's mission to the United Nations. If the committee found the contracts for foodstuffs and medicines to be in order the committee would so inform the secretary-general and the exporter's mission to the United Nations; that is, the exporter can expect payment from the escrow account. If the committee, in the case of materials and supplies for essential civilian needs, cannot approve the shipment whether the contract is found in order, the goods are not allowed to be shipped. Final payment would be effected by the secretary-general following authorization by the committee. Such authorization is issued by the committee after its acceptance of delivery reports by U.N. agents stationed at unloading ports and points (United Nations 1996: 340–342).

Given the network of restrictions on its freedom of action with respect to the sale of oil, commodity imports, and the distribution of such imports within the country the government of Iraq chose not to accept the program provided under resolutions 706 and 712. Basically, the government felt that it would be a violation of its sovereignty to have a parallel authority in the country that could wield considerable power. Instead, the government resorted to negotiations with the United Nations to see whether the system could be modified to the point of acceptability. Several rounds of negotiation did take place but the effort failed to bridge the gap between the two sides and the attempt was suspended in July 1993.

According to Walid Khadduri there were two groups of professionals who favored a resumption of Iraqi oil exports under the restrictive conditions of resolutions 706 and 712. These two groups were the bureaucrats of the United Nations and the Iraqi oil technocrats. The U.N. staff was concerned about the mounting expenditure incurred by the United Nations on its humanitarian and monitoring operations in Iraq. In addition there was the U.N. Compensation Fund which was in urgent need of funds to finance its administrative and technical operations, not to mention the need for a massive flow of funds to make payment for war reparations.

Iraqi technocrats, who favored the resumption of oil exports despite the harsh nature of resolutions 706 and 712, were of the opinion that there was no way out of the country's mounting difficulties unless oil exports were resumed. They argued that even though the initial oil sales would be limited and subject to cumbersome restrictions, the volume would eventually increase and the procedures would be relaxed. Furthermore, proceeds from oil sales would give a much needed boost to the faltering economy and the collapsing dinar. The political leadership of the country, on the other hand, refused to accept resolutions 706 and 712 because compliance with these resolutions would violate the country's sovereignty (Khadduri 1993: A1–A4). Rather than accept oil sales under resolutions 706 and 712 Iraq decided to push for the total lifting of the sanctions as provided under resolution 687. For this strategy to succeed Iraq had to convince the UNSC that it had fulfilled the conditions of resolution 687 on the elimination of weapons of mass destruction and expressed willingness to provide the names of foreign-arms suppliers as well as having accepted the provisions of resolution 715 of October 11, 1991 on the future monitoring of Iraq's military and industrial plants (*Middle East Economic Survey* 1993a, 1993b).

THE OIL-FOR-FOOD PROGRAM
UNDER RESOLUTION 986

Having forfeited the opportunity to sell limited amounts of oil under resolutions 706 and 712 and having failed to persuade the UNSC to lift the sanctions under resolution 687 Iraq was forced to live under difficult economic and social conditions.

In the meantime the United Nations found itself increasingly pressed for financial resources to fund its operations in Iraq and provide for the Compensation Fund. Attempts by the United Nations to raise funds through voluntary contributions and by tapping into Iraq's preembargo assets failed to provide the needed answer. To deal with these concerns the UNSC decided to revisit the issue of oil-for-food when it adopted resolution 986 on April 14, 1995. Some of the reasons that the UNSC listed for its decision to adopt the new resolution include its concern for the serious nutritional and health situation of the Iraqi population and the risk of a further deterioration in this situation and the need for equitable distribution of humanitarian relief to all segments of the Iraqi population throughout the country. The main change in the financial component of the plan was to authorize Iraq to export $2 billion worth of oil every six months as compared with $1.6 billion under the 706–712 plan. The other important parts of the 706–712 plan—30 percent deduction for the Compensation Fund, other deductions for U.N. operations, tight control over Iraq's exports and imports, and tight control over Iraq's revenue and expenditure through the U.N.–administered escrow account—were retained under the new scheme.

The government of Iraq, however, rejected the new scheme on the grounds that the resolution was no more than a public relations effort by the U.S government to jeopardize the prospects of lifting the whole economic sanctions and to infringe on the sovereignty and territorial integrity of Iraq. But the failure of Iraq to persuade the UNSC to lift the sanctions regime and its rejection of the partial relief provided under resolution 986 meant that economic conditions in Iraq would continue their decline as evidenced by the cutback in the food ration, the collapse of the value of the Iraqi dinar, and the widespread malnutrition throughout the country.

The deteriorating economic conditions in the country forced the government in January 1996 to introduce an austerity program which called for a halt to the printing of money, liberalization of foreign currency inflows, balancing the budget by curbing government expenditure, raising taxes and raising the costs of state-provided services, freezing government salaries, raising military service exemption fees, and sale of state-owned enterprises and government-owned durable goods. The depth of the economic crisis may be seen in a couple of economic indicators. First, the plummeting of the value of the dinar to 3,000 dinars to the dollar in January 1996 compared to 0.3 dinars to the dollar in August 1990. Second, food prices increased by 4,000 to 5,000 times between August 1990 and December 1995 (Economist Intelligence Unit 1996: 17–19; *Middle East Economic Survey* 1996a: A8). Given these dire economic conditions and the realization that the sanctions regime was not about to be lifted, the government of Iraq decided in January 1996 to reverse its position and enter into negotiations with the United Nations regarding the implementation of resolution 986.

The negotiations between Iraq and the United Nations dealt with several issues, some of which were considered fundamental while others were of a technical nature. The two fundamental issues relate to Iraq's oil export outlets and the handling of humanitarian supplies to the three Kurdish provinces in northern Iraq. As to the export outlets, Iraq felt that it should be free to decide on the volumes of its oil exports between the Turkish port of Ceyhan and the Iraqi port of al-Bakr at the Gulf. As to the question of providing supplies to the Kurdish area Iraq's position was that such distinction directly impinged on its sovereignty. This is so because the resolution decreed that between 13 percent and 15 percent of the proceeds from the sale of oil be provided to the U.N. Inter-Agency Humanitarian Programme for distribution of imported goods in the Kurdish areas. The position of the government of Iraq was that it should determine the humanitarian needs of the entire population of Iraq and that it should receive the imported supplies funded out of the U.N.–administered escrow account with the actual distribution of supplies carried out by U.N. agencies operating in the Kurdish areas.

The other issues to be negotiated include the elements of the cost of production, oil import equipment for the oil sector, oil transportation cost, purchase of supplies by Iraq, and the distribution and monitoring of goods purchased (*Middle East Economic Survey* 1996b: A1–A3). The negotiations lasted several months and were conclude when on May 29 a memorandum of understanding (MOU) was arrived at outlining Iraq's acceptance of the terms for the implementation of resolution 986. Given Iraq's dire economic plight the government had to agree to terms and conditions which it had for years refused to accept. Thus the division of oil exports between the Turkish pipeline and the Iraqi port of al-Bakr remained in the hands of the Sanctions Committee. Similarly, the United Nations retained for itself the power to procure goods for distribution in the Kurdish areas. In essence the country was to have two distribution systems administered by different authorities. This division was highlighted by the knowledge that there were no serious shortages of food and medicine in these areas and that humanitarian organizations operating in the north were recommending that the humanitarian relief funds allocated to these areas under resolution 986 should be spent to rehabilitate the infrastructure rather than to provide food and medicine. It should be noted also that all the restrictions regarding Iraq's imports and exports which resolutions 706 and 712 gave rise to were retained in this resolution. This meant that each and every oil sale and purchase of goods had to be submitted to the Sanctions Committee for approval. One reason for this tight control was to ensure that there were no loopholes that would allow the Iraqi regime to divert funds for other purposes and to make sure that the food distribution system will not be used by the regime to favor its supporters and punish its opponents (*Middle East Economic Survey* 1996c: 1–5). To help the Sanctions Committee with its tasks a number of oil overseers, monitors, observation personnel, inspection agents, and independent oil experts were appointed to ensure implementation and compliance.

But in order to put the terms of the MOU into effect the government had to prepare and submit to the secretary-general for his approval a distribution plan showing how the funds generated under the resolution will be spent on imported goods before any oil could be exported. Although the secretary-general approved the plan in July and oil was set to flow in August the U.S. government withheld its approval of the plan only to bestow it a week later. Then, toward the end of August one of the leaders of the two Kurdish factions invited the Iraqi army to help recover Arbil, a major urban center in northern Iraq, from the forces of the other faction which had overran it. As to the distribution plan and the sale of oil, President Bill Clinton announced that "the plan cannot go forward and the Iraqi Government will be denied the new resources it has been expecting" (*Middle East Economic Survey* 1996d: A2).

Finally, all outstanding issues over the plan were settled and Iraqi oil was reintroduced to the world oil market in December 1996—more than six years since the sanctions regime was imposed on Iraq in August 1990. And supplies under this program started to arrive in Iraq in March 1997. Commercial transactions under this scheme called for extensive monitoring. Thus receipts from Iraqi oil sales had to be deposited into a U.N.–controlled escrow account at the New York branch of the Banque Nationale de Paris (BNP), which would issue letters of credit at Iraq's request for suppliers of food, medicines, and other approved items. Funds would only be paid out when U.N. inspectors on the Iraqi border verify that the goods they have inspected correspond with the contract.

MODIFICATIONS OF THE RESOLUTION 986 PROGRAM

Between December 1996 and December 2000 the program went through eight 180-day phases following UNSC renewing resolutions. The first six-month phase, for example, lasted between December 10, 1996 and June 7, 1997 while the eighth phase ran between June 9 and December 5, 2000. It will be recalled that resolution 986 was adopted in April 1995 but was not put into effect until December 1996. The government of Iraq's initial rejection of the program was based on two reasons. First, the program relegated the government to the role of a mere recipient of humanitarian supplies which had been approved by the Sanctions Committee to be distributed by the government under the supervision of special U.N.–appointed observers. The same lack of independence applies also to its role as a seller of its own oil since all the steps and elements of any sale had to be approved by the overseers and by the Sanctions Committee. Second, the level of oil revenue that the government had access to was miniscule relative to the needs of the population, the infrastructure, and the economy. Moreover, Iraq received only 66 percent or $1.3 billion of the $2 billion of oil sale per phase allowed under this program.

One of the problems that Iraq had to contend with early in the program was its inability to calibrate its oil output to the level of oil revenue it was allowed to generate. Thus between phase one and phase four Iraq increased its oil exports by 157 percent, from 120 million barrels to 308 million barrels per phase, yet the revenue from the sales increased by 41 percent, or from $2.1

billion to $3 billion. The explanation for this lackluster fiscal performance was the fact that the price of exported oil declined from $17.92 per barrel in the first phase to $9.83 per barrel in the fourth phase. Iraq's inability to manage its oil production with reference to the market conditions manifested itself in phases four and five, May 1998 to May 1999, when Iraq's production capacity was not sufficient to produce enough oil to generate the $5.2 billion allowed under resolution 1153 of February 1998. Instead, it ended up selling $3 billion and $3.9 billion respectively. The change in the ceiling to $5.2 billion and the failure of Iraq's oil industry to avail itself of this opportunity brought to light the deteriorating conditions of that industry.

One of the major problems that had plagued the oil industry in Iraq in the 1990s had been the embargo placed on the import of necessary equipment and spare parts. A March 1998 report by a group of oil experts sent by the U.N. secretary-general to study the conditions of the oil industry in Iraq concluded that the industry was in a "lamentable state." Following the report of this group of experts, the UNSC adopted resolution 1175 in June 1998 authorizing, for the first time, the import of up to $300 million per six months of equipment and spare parts for the oil sector. In January 2000 another group of experts in yet another report concluded that the lamentable state of the Iraqi oil industry had not improved, the oil transportation sector had not been improved over the previous two years, insufficient spare parts and equipment had arrived in time to sustain production. In short, "decline of conditions of all sectors of the oil industry continues, and is accelerating in some cases. This trend will continue, and the ability of the Iraqi oil industry to sustain the current reduced production levels will be seriously compromised, until effective action is taken to reverse the situation" (United Nations 2000: 4).

Following this new report the UNSC adopted in March 2000 resolution 1293 which raised the cap on imports for the oil sector to $600 million for each six months. The problem, however, was not with the level of oil sector imports, although that was important; it was with the refusal of the Sanctions Committee to approve all the contracts that the U.N. secretary-general had already approved for Iraq's oil sector imports. The disruptive impact of withholding approval of such contracts was expressed by the U.N. executive director of the Office of the Iraq Program when he told the Security Council:

The Council last year doubled the allocation for oil spare parts and equipment. This was most welcome for the sector that is the lifeline of the humanitarian programme. However, that was the end of the good news—we continue to experience serious delays and the number of holds placed on applications has become unacceptably high.

On the one hand, everyone is calling on OPEC to increase the export of oil. On the other hand, the spare parts and equipment that are the minimum requirements of Iraq's oil industry, have been facing serious obstacles in the Security Council Committee. (Sevan 2000: 3)

For its part the government of Iraq believes that the holds on applications prevented it from reaching its goal of 3.4 MBD in 2000. But should the applications be approved the government expects oil output to reach that level of output in the Spring of 2001 (*Middle East Economic Survey* 2000: A3). In addition to allowing Iraq to import limited equipment for its oil sector other modifications were introduced over time. The early realization that the limited sale of oil authorized by the UNSC was miniscule relative to the needs of the economy persuaded the UNSC to raise the limit to $5.2 billion per phase effective with phase four (with $3.4 billion going to Iraq and $1.8 billion to UNSC–mandated programs). This ceiling on oil exports was lifted altogether under UNSC resolution 1284 of December 17, 1999. A year later on December 5, 2000 the UNSC adopted resolution 1330 which reduced, for the duration of phase nine, the allocation for the U.N. Compensation Fund from 30 to 25 percent of the oil revenue. Another modification was the expansion in the list of imports. In the initial phases of the program most of Iraq's revenue was allocated to foodstuffs and medicines. But as more revenue was placed at the disposal of the government due to the rise in oil prices it was able to finance a wider range of imports. Imports of oil industry spares and equipment, agricultural inputs and equipment, water and sanitation supplies, educational supplies, housing sector needs, and materials for transport and telecommunications sectors found their way to the import mechanism conducted and supervised by different bodies of the United Nations. Numerous import items were exempted from having to secure the approval of the Sanctions Committee. Instead, the Committee granted the U.N.'s Office of the Iraq Programme (OIP) the power to permit Iraq to import certain lists of goods eligible for the accelerated approval procedure.

Given the small amounts of imports that actually reached Iraq under this program the problem of holds for the economy cannot be overstated. Thus between December 1996, when the program was launched, and the end of October 2000 the OIP received $20 billion worth of contracts, of which $17 billion had been approved and $2.3 billion put on hold. In other words, the holds constituted 14 percent of the value of approved contracts. The problem becomes more serious when one realizes that the value of holds is 25 percent of the $9.3 billion worth of humanitarian supplies and oil industry equipment that had arrived in Iraq during this period.

The problem of holds is imbedded in the very nature of the Sanctions Committee, the composition of which mirrored that of the UNSC itself. It was observed that the meetings of the committee were closed, and neither vendors nor representatives of Iraq were permitted to appear before the committee for the purpose of addressing questions about a proposed contract. No criteria for approval or rejection were formulated, much less made available to Iraq or to companies seeking to sell goods to Iraq. This meant that when contracts were rejected no reasons were given to the potential exporter. Furthermore, this situation was not helped by the arbitrariness of the decisions since identical goods in identical quantity, by the same exporter, could be approved at one time and rejected six months later (Gordon 2001: 29).

An analysis of the impact of the sanctions will be undertaken in the following chapter.

REFERENCES

al-Anbari, A. (1996). "The UN Sanctions Regime: The Case of Iraq." *Middle East Economic Survey*, November 25, pp. D1–D5.

Economist Intelligence Unit. (1996). *Country Report, Iraq*. No. 1. London: EIU.

Gordon, J. (2001). "Chokehold on the World: Are Sanctions Ethical—or an Ill-Used Weapon of Mass Destruction?" *The Nation*, January 1, pp. 27–32.

Khadduri, W. (1993). "The Politics of Iraqi Oil Exports." *Middle East Economic Survey*, May 24.

Middle East Economic Survey. (1991). September 9.

———. (1993a). May 24.

———. (1993b). November 15.

———. (1996a). January 8.

———. (1996b). May 27.

———. (1996c). September 9.

———. (1996d). November 18.

———. (2000). September 25.

Sevan, B. V. (2000). Introductory Statement by Benon V. Sevan, *Report of the Secretary-General Pursuant to Paragraph 5 of Security Council Resolution 1302 of 8 June 2000*. New York: United Nations.

United Nations. (1996). *The United Nations and the Iraq–Kuwait Conflict*. New York: United Nations.

United Nations. (2000). *Report of the Group of United Nations Experts Established Pursuant to Paragraph 30 of the Security Council Resolution 1284 (1999)*. New York: United Nations.

CHAPTER 6

Sanctions and the Economy

Iraq has been under a United Nations comprehensive sanctions system since August 1990. Although the United Nations Security Council recognized in its resolution 666 of September 1990 the pending human suffering, it did not take the necessary steps to alleviate it. And when in subsequent resolutions it sought to relax the sanctions it failed to allow Iraq to export oil in order to import foodstuffs and other humanitarian supplies. And when the UNSC decided to allow Iraq to sell oil the conditions, as was noted earlier, were so stringent that the government of Iraq opted not to accept the offer. The tension between the government and the UNSC prevented Iraq's oil from reaching the world market for more than six years since the invasion of Kuwait. As a consequence Iraq's multiple social and economic crises intensified. Naturally, the human and economic losses that had occurred as a result of the confrontation between the government and the UNSC are irreversible. This means that Iraq's human and economic development in the future will, of necessity, be at lower levels.

SANCTIONS AND HUMAN WELFARE

The centerpiece of the sanctions system in its early phases was UNSC resolution 661 of August 1990. This resolution and subsequent sanctions resolutions created a set of conditions which virtually cut off Iraq from the world economy. As was stated earlier, the sanctions included a ban on all trade, an oil embargo, a freezing of Iraqi government financial assets abroad, an arms embargo, suspension of international flights, and a ban on financial transactions. The UNSC also called upon member states to enforce naval and air blockades against Iraq.

The blockade had immediate impact on food availability in Iraq and prices. To blunt the double impact of scarcity and inflation the government introduced a food rationing system effective September 1, 1990. This public rationing system saw to it that certain food items—wheat flour, rice, vegetable oil, sugar, tea, and baby milk—were provided on a monthly basis at preembargo prices. This diet was judged by the Food and Agriculture Organization to supply on a per capita basis 37 percent of the average calorie intake in 1987–1989 (FAO/WFP 1993: 3).There is really no more powerful testimony about the impact of the sanctions than the fact that ordinary people lost two-thirds of their caloric intake almost overnight. The impact of the initial sanctions was accentuated and aggravated by the Gulf War bombing, the dislocations caused by the internal uprising against the government, and the continued imposition of sanctions.

Iraq, as was stated earlier, had become totally dependent on imports and exports for the functioning of its economy, its state, and the welfare of its people. Foreign exchange earnings from a single export, oil, have been used to import foodstuffs, consumer goods, raw materials, inputs, and capital goods. The other side of this dependence is that once the oil flow is choked off it is only a matter of weeks before commodity shortages appear, inflation worsens, exchange rates fall, unemployment rises, economic dislocations occur, agricultural and industrial output declines, and the economy slides into stagnation. And this is precisely what happened soon after the embargo was imposed.

Some observers maintain that living standards and the levels of social services in Iraq prior to the war were comparable to those in some of the wealthier oil monarchies. That may be true so long as we remember that such living standards are imported and are unrelated to Iraq's non-oil economy. The outbreak of the Iraq–Iran War proved how a few bombing missions by the Iranian air force could deprive Iraq of a major portion of its oil income and expose its vulnerability to external shocks. Or take the 1991 bombing of electrical generating capacity as another illustration of Iraq's vulnerability. Iraq's inability to replace capacity was nothing short of catastrophe for the economy and society. Without electricity, hospitals cannot function, perishable medicines spoil, water cannot be purified, and raw sewage cannot be processed. In short, death rates would rise.

And this is precisely what happened in the aftermath of the Gulf War as the International Study Team (IST) showed in its report in October 1991:

1. Infant mortality increased by nearly 330 percent in January–August 1991 over the weighted average for the period 1987–1990.

2. Similarly the under-five mortality rate increased by 380 percent during the same period.

3. The nutritional status of children has been severely affected, especially those between one and two years. The team's estimates of height-for-age and weight-for-age show significant levels of malnutrition for the one to two-years age group which has lived most of its life under conditions of war, unrest, and sanctions.

4. All hospital laboratories were functioning at only a fraction, 30 percent, of their prewar capacity due to shortages and equipment failure (IST 1991: 1–9).

It should be stressed that there has been no shortage of warnings and appeals from international agencies and groups about the plight of Iraqis. Thus a Food and Agriculture Organization/World Food Program Crop and Food Supply Assessment Mission reported in its Special Alert of July 1993 the following:

• The mission noted the prevalence of the common prefamine indicators such as exorbitant prices, collapse of private incomes, soaring unemployment, drastically reduced food intakes, large-scale depletion of personal assets, high morbidity levels, escalating crime rates, and rapidly increasing numbers of destitute people.

• A massive starvation in the country has so far been averted by the provision of low-cost food under the public rationing system which meets one-half of the needed caloric intake. But a collapse of this system would spell a catastrophe for the majority of the Iraqi population.

• The nutritional status of the population continues to deteriorate at an alarming rate due to the embargo-induced hyperinflation and collapse of real income.

• Large numbers of Iraqis now have food intakes lower than those of the populations in the disaster-stricken African countries (FAO/WFP 1993: 1–3).

Delegates who participated in missions to Iraq both in 1991 and 1995 to report on nutritional status and mortality of children had these observations to make:

• The situation in the country had significantly deteriorated since our visit in 1991. Street children, a rare sight in 1991, were common now. Parents with severely malnourished children were begging on the streets.

• Among children under five there has been a fivefold increase in mortality compared to the period before the sanctions. The sustained mortality has resulted in a half-million child deaths related to the war and the sanctions occurring over the past five years.

• All sectors of society, aside from Saddam Hussein's inner circle, were affected.

• A civil engineer's monthly salary of ID 5,000 can purchase a little more than two pounds of chicken or one pound of red meat or about three dozen eggs.

• Government food rations which consists of flour, rice, sugar, tea, pulses, and cooking oil now meets one-third, instead of one-half, of the caloric need.

- At this level of malnutrition and excess mortality among children under the age of five Iraq is increasingly becoming a concentration camp with the economic sanctions imposed by UNSC effectively serving as the barbed wire (Fawzi and Zaidi 1996: 13–14).

The deterioration in living standards and health conditions could be gleaned from some of the observations and conclusions reported in the November 1995 FAO mission report:

- The monthly average of deaths of children under five years increased from 593 during the year 1989 to 4,475 in the January–July 1995 period. Selected causes of this dramatic rise in death include respiratory infections, diarrhea and gastroenteritis, and malnutrition (FAO 1995: 42).
- For Baghdad, a highly advanced city, the prevalence of underweight children, 29 percent, is comparable with children from Ghana at 27 percent and Mali at 31 percent. For stunting, prevalence rates are similar to estimates from Sri Lanka at 28 percent and the Congo at 27 percent. The prevalence of wasting in Baghdad is comparable with estimates from Madagascar at 12 percent and Burma at 11 percent (FAO 1995: 43).
- Major surgical operations have been reduced to 30 percent of presanction levels. Hospitals and pharmacies continue to suffer from lack of life-sustaining drugs, other medicine, medical equipment, and accessories (FAO 1995: 18).
- The health and nutrition situation in Kurdistan was made worse by the embargo that the government imposed on the three self-ruling governorates (FAO 1995: 19).
- Lack of spare parts and inputs inflicted further deterioration on the quality of water and sewage treatment plants, thus aggravating public health conditions in the country (FAO 1995: iii).
- Continued lack of spare parts and inputs in the agricultural sector compounded the difficulties of this sector causing decline in its productivity and output (FAO 1995: ii).
- The continued siege of Iraq and the collapse of its currency vis-à-vis the dollar caused prices to rise phenomenally. Thus the price of wheat flour in August 1995 was 11,667 times higher than in July 1990 and thirty-three times higher than in June 1993. The prices of other items increased in the order of 4,000 to 5,000 times compared to July 1990 and thirty to sixty times compared to June 1993 (FAO 1995).
- In contrast to this hyperinflation household incomes have collapsed for a large majority of the people—about 70 percent. The plight of the people may be gleaned from the fact that unskilled workers rarely find work and the average salary in the civil service is ID 5,000 per month (FAO 1995). This last figure could buy two pounds of chicken or three kilograms of flour (FAO 1995: ii–iii, 18–19, 25, 42).

Since the United Nations and its specialized agencies have been closely monitoring economic and social condition, one of their more recent observations and assessments is the following:

- Although the government of Iraq had planned to raise the caloric target in the eighth phase of the U.N.–organized oil-for-food program (June–December 2000) to 2,472 calories per person per day the target had to be scaled down by 11 percent. One of the reasons for the downward revision was the inefficient manner in which food imports are handled. This correctable condition prompted the U.N. secretary-general to appeal to the government of Iraq to take all necessary measures to improve its contracting and ordering procedures in order to ensure early arrival of the necessary supplies and effective distribution of the food basket, in full compliance with the targets set forth in the distribution plan (United Nations 2000: par. 69).

While the humanitarian situation in Iraq has somewhat improved since the inception of the oil-for-food program in December 1996, the lives of the vast majority of the people have not improved considerably (see Table 6.1). Among other things the U.N. secretary-general's report of November 29, 2000 provides the following:

• Four years into the implementation of the oil-for-food program, the vast majority of the Iraqi people still face a situation of decreasing income, thereby intensifying the

Table 6.1
Iraq: Planned per Capita Food Ration, 1990–2000

Year	Calories	Percent of 1987-89 Average Calorie In-take
1990	1199	37
1991	1372	42
1992	1423	44
1993	1705	53
1995	1093	34
1997	2030	63
1998	2115	66
1999	2175	68
2000	2401	75

Source: Food and Agriculture Organization and World Food Program, *FAO/WFP Crop and Food Supply Assessment Mission to Iraq, Special Alert No. 237* (Rome: FAO, July 1993), p. 3; FAO, *Assessment of the Food and Nutrition Situation: Iraq* (Rome: FAO, 2000), p. 12.

dependency of the poorer strata on the commodities and services provided through the program; that is, on the government (United Nations 2000: par. 3).

- The gap between those who have managed to maintain their living standards and the majority of the population who struggle to maintain themselves at or above subsistence level has also widened (United Nations 2000: par. 3).

- Vast numbers of highly trained professionals have emigrated due to the deterioration in their living standards as well as isolation from developments in their respective fields (United Nations 2000: par. 3).

- The program was never intended to meet all the humanitarian needs of the Iraqi population . . . and is not geared to address the longer-term deterioration of living standards or to remedy declining educational and health standards and infrastructure (United Nations 2000: par. 5).

Although the secretary-general maintains that the oil-for-food program has generally improved the humanitarian situation in Iraq he concludes that the lives of ordinary Iraqis have not improved commensurately. And although locally produced food items have become available throughout the country, most Iraqis do not have the necessary purchasing power to buy them. Unfortunately, the monthly food ration absorbs the largest proportion of their household income. They are obliged to either barter or sell items from the food basket in order to meet their other essential needs. This is one of the factors that partly explains why the nutritional situation has not improved in line with the enhanced food basket. Moreover, the absence of normal economic activity has given rise to the spread of deep-seated poverty (United Nations 2000: par. 125).

The combination of the consequences of the war and the sanctions gave rise to shortages and decline in every sector of the economy and society—food, health, agriculture, industry, housing, education, electricity, drinking water, sanitation and sewage treatment facilities, transportation, and communication. Again, some of the effects of these shortages may be seen in the following indicators:

- The rate of stunting of children less than five years old increased from 12 percent in 1991 to 28 percent in 1995.
- During the same period the underweight rate rose from 7 percent to 29 percent while that of wasting increased from 3 percent to 12 percent (WHO 1996: 5).

Other health indicators vividly illustrate the impact of the sanctions. According to UNICEF the under-five mortality rate which stood at 171 per 1,000 live births in 1960 declined to 50 in 1990, only to rise to 125 in 1999. Similarly, the infant mortality rate changed from 117 to 40 to 103 respectively (Pellet 2000: 161). It is clear from these indicators that several decades of improvement in mortality rates were nullified by the crisis. A study by the World Health Organization concluded that the quality of health care in Iraq, due to the six-week 1991 war and the subsequent sanctions, has been literally put back at least fifty years. Diseases that were once almost under control have rebounded since 1991 at epidemic levels, with the health sector as a helpless witness (WHO 1996: 17).

In a study of the unusual rise in child mortality in Iraq Richard Garfield draws a number of conclusions. In the first place he maintains that sustained increases in young child mortality were extremely rare in the twentieth century and that large increases in mortality rates of the kind that were found in Iraq are almost unknown in public health literature. Moreover, living conditions in Iraq represent the loss of several decades of progress in reducing mortality. Furthermore, Garfield asserts that the case of Iraq is the only instance of a sustained, large increase in mortality in a stable population of more than two million in the last two hundred years (Garfield 2000: 36). In its September 2000 *Assessment of the Food and Nutrition Situation in Iraq* the Food and Agriculture Organization made the following observations:

- The level of malnutrition among young children remains unacceptably high.
- 21.3 percent of children under five years of age were underweight.
- 20.4 percent were stunted, reflecting the prevalence of chronic malnutrition, while 9.3 percent were wasted, reflecting a high degree of acute malnutrition.
- The monthly food basket lasts less than a month for most people.
- All Iraqi citizens are entitled to a monthly food ration for which they pay ID 250 to the government; for those who are too poor to supplement the rations from other sources, nutrition problems continue.
- The proportion of household income spent on food was around 72 percent in 1994 and is likely to have increased as income decreased (FAO 2000: 8–14).
- Food basket targets were fully met in only six out of thirty-eight months of distribution cycles. The main reasons for shortfalls have been delayed submission of contracts by the government of Iraq, delays in the processing of contracts by the United Nations, and untimely delivery of goods by suppliers to Iraq (FAO 2000: 9).
- Food rations do not provide a nutritionally adequate and varied diet. Consequently a significant portion of the population requires special attention, particularly the most vulnerable population groups whose coping strategies are quickly being eroded (FAO 2000: 33).
- Reasons for the continued nutritional problems include prolonged reliance on inadequate and unvaried diet, inability of the agricultural sector to make up the shortfall, the dilapidation of the economy, underemployment and low incomes, poor quality of essential service delivery, and infection and disease (FAO 2000: 36).

In addition to the problems associated with the government of Iraq's food ration program or the U.N. oil-for-food program and the continued friction between the government and the United Nations there was also the lackluster performance of the agriculture sector in the decade of the 1990s. Although

this sector supplied about one-third of Iraq's food needs prior to the imposition of the sanctions any shortfall in domestic supplies were covered by imports as foreign exchange was available. But the sanctions regime closed off
the availability of foreign exchange and forced heavier reliance on domestic
production. The sudden exposure of the country to absence of food imports
forced the government to consolidate its precrisis food subsidies into one cen-
tralized food ration program and required farmers to sell all their production
of wheat, barley, rice, maize, and sunflower to the government at fixed prices.
But the agricultural sector's contribution to the food ration program was limited by the sector's own bottlenecks which included lack of farm machinery
and critical shortage of agricultural inputs. Moreover, after the embargo, all
irrigation and drainage programs had to be stopped and thus no new lands
could be reclaimed (FAO 1995: 4), thus keeping the contribution to food availability relatively small (FAO 1995: 4–12).

An important contributing factor to the humanitarian crisis conditions in
Iraq was government policy. Thus in the midst of the severe conditions of
humanitarian emergency that engulfed the overwhelming majority of the population the government of Iraq did not hesitate to single out certain groups for
special economic benefits and privileges. Thus in October 1994 it decided to
favor the military, the police and security, and other elite forces with special
monthly allowances and other privileges. Some of the privileges were extended to civil and military pensioners. While these benefits covered some 3.5
million people the other 17.2 million Iraqis, or 83 percent of the population,
were left out of the program of privileges (FAO 1995: 7–8, 19).

In addition to these discriminatory measures the government uses its fiscal
resources and the country's scarce supplies of food to extend favors to its
supporters or penalize its political opponents. While the Kurdish people of the
north were subjected to internal embargo the government interfered with the
flow of food to the inhabitants of the southern marshes as well (United Nations 1996: 401). In contrast, it was found that military officers and members
of the Baath Party enjoy their own food distribution network through special
cooperatives. In addition, government and Baath Party officials receive bribes
and "gifts" by virtue of the important administrative positions to which they
may be assigned. Moreover, the inner circle of the leadership does not appear
to be touched by any economic hardships affecting their access to food and
health care (United Nations 1996: 401). Furthermore, it is evident that there is
discrimination within the country on a regional basis. The central cities of
Iraq, especially Tikrit and parts of Baghdad, continue to enjoy preferred distribution of limited resources.

The government also enacted special measures designed to benefit certain
elite groups to ensure their continued loyalty to the regime. Individuals selected to receive state largesse include military personnel who had received
medals and citations in the Qadisiyyah of Saddam (the official name of the
Iraq–Iran War) and the Mother of all Battles (the official name of the Gulf

War); Baath Party officials who had received special citations; and police and security personnel and a special group of individuals designated as friends of the president (Tareeq Al-Shaab 1996). The decorated military personnel and party officials were granted salary increments ranging between 150 percent and 300 percent; they were offered to buy state land for home building at discounts ranging up to 80 percent of the price of the land; they were offered to purchase state agricultural land at discounts ranging up to 80 percent of the value of the land; and public sector assets may be bought by these individuals, their wives, and their children at discounts ranging up to 30 percent of the sale price. And in September 1995 an edict was issued which confined the sale of state and state-owned enterprise assets to those decorated individuals and the friends of the president and their families (Tareeq Al-Shaab 1996).

The practice of extending benefits and privileges to particular groups is in line with policies which the regime had followed since it came to power in 1968. As Charles Tripp observed, the clannish and personalized system constructed by the political leadership is based on patronage and inclusion of certain individuals and communities. Such a system means the exclusion and marginalization of other communities. Given the nature of sanctions-induced shortages it can be said that after 1990 the majority of the populations suffered under two sets of sanctions. One was imposed by the United Nations and the other had long formed the basis of the prevailing distribution and reward system. This meant that what in times of relative prosperity had been a social disadvantage became in times of absolute shortages a matter of desperation and destitution (Tripp 2000: 269).

ECONOMIC CONSEQUENCES OF THE SANCTIONS

The economic impact of the sanctions cannot be isolated, of course, from the economic consequences of the eight-year Iraq–Iran War which ended in 1988. The consequences of that war include the following: Iraq's major oil-exporting capacity was destroyed, blocked, or closed; Iraq's heavy industries were destroyed or in need of major repair; the infrastructure was extensively damaged; a major segment of the labor force (one-fifth) was drafted in the armed forces; agricultural and industrial growth was either stagnant or negative; rural workers had either been drafted into the army or drifted to the city; the large number of foreign workers who were encouraged to work in Iraq during the war had become a burden on the economy; dependence on food imports had increased due to natural population growth and a stagnant agricultural sector; inflation had become a structural problem; privatization was not succeeding according to expectations; foreign reserves (over $35 billion) which had accumulated in the 1970s were exhausted in the 1980s; Arab and foreign capital could not be enticed to flow into the economy; the value of the Iraqi dinar suffered from chronic depreciation; Iraq had become a major debtor country; levels of imports declined; development planning and spending had virtually ceased; the higher living standards that were promised during the war could not be delivered in the postwar period; staggering human losses; and unprecedented high levels of military spending. Suffice it to say that during the period of 1980–1988 military spending amounted to $120 billion or 36 percent of that period's GDP and 254 percent of the oil revenue which amounted to $47 billion during the same period. In addition to these structural problems the oil sector on which the entire economy had become more dependent could not generate the prewar levels of oil revenue that the state and the economy desperately needed. The economic crisis was further aggravated by the 1989 severe decline in GDP which prompted the government to adopt an ill-advised austerity program.

Needless to say the bombing-caused destruction of the infrastructure during the Gulf War and the continuation of the sanctions made the prospects for recovery rather bleak. These conditions were made worse by the fact that Iraq exported virtually no oil for more than six years.

Any attempt at a comprehensive analysis of the impact of the sanctions on the economy of Iraq is constrained by two factors. First, and unlike other countries, in the case of Iraq economic data are very difficult to come by since as far back as the mid-1970s the government adopted a policy of not publishing much data on the performance of the economy. Moreover, available published data even by the same sources are not always consistent. Second, it is difficult to separate the economic effects of the Iraq–Iran War from those of the Gulf War and the sanctions. It will be no exaggeration, however, to say that the longer the sanctions are in effect the more they are responsible for the difficulties of the economy. With these qualifications in mind the following paragraphs will attempt to study the impact of the sanctions on certain economic variables.

Gross Domestic Product

According to the U.N. *Statistical Yearbook* Iraq's gross domestic product (in constant 1980 prices) in 1989, the last full year prior to the invasion of Kuwait, was $26.9 billion. By 1991, the first year of sanctions, Iraq's GDP had declined to $12.3 billion. And by 1996, the last full year before the resumption of oil exports, the GDP reached a low of $6.5 billion (see Table 6.2). In these three years Iraq's population had increased from 17.5 million to 18.6 million and to 21 million respectively. Relating GDP to population, we find that per capita GDP was $1,537 in 1989 but declined to $661 in 1991 and further plummeted to $343 in 1996. Starting in 1997 GDP and GDP per capita started to assume an upward trend following the reintroduction of Iraq's oil to the world market.

Given the nature of the structure of the Iraqi economy, the oil sector suffered the worst rate of decline relative to the other sectors of the economy. Thus while Iraq's GDP, as measured in the constant prices of 1975, declined

Table 6.2
Iraq: Gross Domestic Product and GDP per Capita (1980 prices), 1950–2000

Year	Population (million)	GDP ($ billion)	GDP/PC $
1950	5.2	3.4	654
1960	6.9	8.7	1261
1970	9.4	16.4	1745
1980	13.2	53.9	4083
1985	15.3	31.7	2071
1990	18.1	16.4	906
1992	19.1	11.9	623
1994	19.9	6.8	342
1996	21.0	7.2	343
1997	21.6	11.5	532
1998	22.3	16.6	744
1999	23.0	28.0	1217
2000	23.7	46.0	1941

Source: Derived from the United Nations, *National Accounts Statistics: Analysis of Main Aggregates 1988–1989* (New York: United Nations, 1991); United Nations, *Statistical Yearbook* (New York: United Nations, annual).

by 66 percent between 1989 and 1991, the rate of decline in the mining and quarrying, which is dominated by the oil sector, was 97 percent during the same period. Economic activity in all other sectors declined drastically during this period. Thus the rate of decline in agriculture was 24 percent; manufacturing, 44 percent; construction, 79 percent; transport, 46 percent; finance, 33 percent; trade, 51 percent; and government services, 57 percent.

These rates of decline inform of the extent to which the Gulf War and the sanctions have impacted on the economy and on living standards. They also inform of the monumental task in the postsanctions era of attempting to put the economic pieces together for the purposes of reconstruction and development.

Inflation

The sharp decline in the national output gave rise, among other things, to two interrelated problems: inflation and unemployment. It should be stated that inflation was not a new phenomenon in the Iraqi economy. It actually started in the 1970s following the sharp rise in oil prices. The economy, however, was capable of dealing with the problem because of its relatively manageable magnitude and because of the availability of foreign exchange which provided the needed purchasing power to increase imports.

The inflation problem in Iraq started in the 1970s with the onset of the rise in oil revenue. In the first half of the 1970s inflation, as measured by the consumer price index, averaged 6 percent per year. By 1975 it was 18 percent and by 1979 it reached 68 percent using 1973 as the base year. Because of the sharp rise in government spending and the Iraq–Iran War the inflation rate jumped to 139 percent in 1981, and 369 in 1988 (Ali and Ganabi 1992: 91–113).

Following the invasion of Kuwait, the Gulf War, and the sanctions hyperinflation became a structural problem from which the Iraqi economy continues to suffer. There are several explanations for this phenomenon. First, and as was previously stated, the decline of all goods-producing sectors sharply reduced the supply of domestically produced goods and services and gave rise to all sorts of bottlenecks and shortages. Second, the embargo cut off imports of consumer goods and inputs, thus aggravating shortages in all sectors of the economy. Third, the collapse of the value of the Iraqi dinar from $1 = ID 0.3 prior to the crisis to $1 = ID 3,000 by the end of 1995 was reflected in price inflation. Fourth, in the absence of oil export-generated foreign exchange the government resorted to heavy borrowing from the central bank and to money printing, thus worsening the problem of inflation. The following data will illustrate the severity of the problem.

A Food and Agriculture Organization's market survey carried out in both rural and urban Iraq showed the extent of food price inflation. Compared to preembargo (July 1990) levels, the average price of wheat flour (the most important food staple in Iraq) increased in June 1993 by 355 times; rice, 71 times; vegetable oil, 106 times; and sugar, 149 times. Such price increases led inevitably to the collapse in personal-income purchasing power. Thus it was found that in June 1993, average monthly wages or salaries which have increased for most occupations twofold to threefold since 1990, were found to be in the range of ID 250 for an unskilled worker to ID 775 for a senior civil servant (or $3.00 to $9.00 at the unofficial exchange rate at the time). By comparison, the cost of the average monthly food basket for a family of six which was ID 100 in July 1990 had jumped to ID 5,400 in June 1993. Even after factoring in the low-cost food provided under the food rationing system, a family of six will still need ID 3,000 per month to make up the shortfall in food consumption. Obviously, these income levels are beyond the reach of the overwhelming majority of Iraqi families. It is worth noting that prior to the onset of the crisis expenditure on food accounted for about one-half of total household expenditure. But with average incomes in 1993 insufficient to cover even the minimum food requirements of a large section of the population, spending on other goods and services such as medical and health care, rent, clothing, and so forth had to be reduced drastically (FAO/WFP 1993: 3–5).

In a 1995 study of the food and nutrition situation in Iraq the FAO reported that prices of basic foodstuffs have risen sharply from their levels in 1993. For example, the price of wheat flour in August 1995 was thirty-three times higher than in June 1993. In the case of other items increases were in the range of thirty to sixty times compared to June 1993. In the meantime household incomes have collapsed for about 70 percent of the people, forcing them to sell household effects and personal items to buy food. Moreover, the food basket which earlier provided 53 percent of the 1987–1989 food energy availability was reduced from September 1994 to provide 34 percent (FAO 1995: ii). The same report notes that the government granted certain groups of the population special supplementary income of ID 2,000 per month. These groups comprise military, police and security forces, civil servants, certain war veterans, and pensioners. This allowance covered some 3.5 million people with the remaining 17.2 million left uncovered by the program (FAO 1995: 7) (see Table 6.3).

SANCTIONS AND THE EXCHANGE RATE

One of the structural features of an oil-based economy like Iraq's is the lack of symmetry between national income and the composition of national output. The root of the problem is that in generating between one-half and two-thirds of the GDP the oil sector was absorbing no more than 2–3 percent of the labor force. Since the goods-producing sectors, agriculture and industry, contribute less than one-fifth of the national output, it follows that any domestically spent portion of the income generated by the oil sector is bound to exert an upward pressure on domestic prices. Since government development spending to increase national output has failed to show serious results then the only avenue left to policy makers was to increase imports. But this rising dependence on imports reduced the economy to a mere mechanism that exports oil in exchange for imports. Increases in living standards may be attained but such increases become a hostage to the availability of imports.

In the case of Iraq the problem was made even worse by a series of decisions by the government in the 1970s to invest heavily in the oil sector thus perpetuating and deepening the phenomenon of an oil-based economy.

The government could mask its failure to increase non-oil output and also give the appearance of a growing economy so long as oil revenues were rising so it could finance the cost of imported consumer and other goods.

Table 6.3
Iraq: Open Market Prices of Selected Basic Food Items, August 1995 over July 1990

Food Item	July 1990 ID/kg	End August 1995 ID/kg.	Increase in August 1995 Over July 1990 Prices (times)
Wheat	0.060	700	11,667
Rice	0.240	1,000	4,767
Vegetable Oil	0.600	2,700	4,500
Lentils	0.400	800	2,000
Potatoes	0.500	750	1,500
Sugar	0.200	1,100	5,500
Tea	2.000	3,000	1,500
Baby Milk	1.600	8,900	5,562

Source: Food and Agriculture Organization, *Evaluation of Food and Nutrition Situation in Iraq* (Rome: Food and Agriculture Organization, 1995).

Unfortunately, the Iraqi government's decision to plunge the country into a devastating war with Iran revealed the basic weakness of the economy and its utter dependence on imported goods and on outside help and foreign loans. The problem was made worse when the abnormal cost of the war was superimposed on the economy at a time when its sole foreign-exchange earner, oil, was shrinking. This is more or less what happened in Iraq and caused inflation rates to jump beyond control.

The destruction of the infrastructure during the Gulf War, the decline in domestic output, and the tight system of sanctions were among the forces which caused severe shortages of all kinds of goods, thus forcing their prices up. The government for its part made matters worse by printing, and indeed even photocopying, money to pay for its ordinary budget expenditure. Given this chaotic situation it is no wonder that inflation rates reached unprecedented levels as was noted earlier.

If not curbed such structural inflation tends to create its own spiral. Unless the government curbs its own spending it will be forced to increase the supply of money to meet its expenditures targets. Since the supply of goods and services cannot be increased under the present conditions in Iraq this increase in the supply of money will be translated into higher prices, setting the stage for another round of larger money supply and higher prices and so on. Since only few people in Iraq, such as top party and government officials, importers, sanctions profiteers, contractors, and so forth can be expected to see their incomes rise at the same rate of inflation and even higher, it follows that the burden of inflation in the form of further loss in purchasing power and living standards had to be endured by the overwhelming majority of the population.

Then there is the impact of the problem of structural inflation on the value of the currency. As the currency purchasing power declines people tend to convert their liquid assets, such as currency and deposits, into other assets such as land, buildings, goods, and gold whose real values tend to increase in times of inflation. Another way to protect the value of one's wealth is to convert it into foreign currency to be deposited abroad, giving rise to the phenomenon of capital flight.

Regardless of whether holders of wealth convert their monetary assets (dinar balances) into real assets in Iraq or into foreign assets abroad the dinar loses its function as a store of value and in many cases its function as medium of exchange. This simply means that the people have lost confidence in the dinar and prefer to conduct their transactions in another currency, which in the case of Iraq happens to be the American dollar. The loss of confidence in the dinar is one of the explanations for the constant decline in its value against the dollar (see Table 6.4). There were other factors at work, of course, as will be seen in the following paragraphs.

In 1972 the Iraqi dinar was valued at $3.00. The strength of Iraq's balance of payments made it possible to revalue the dinar to $3.31. Its value was raised again in 1974 to ID 1 = $3.38. When the Iran–Iraq War turned Iraq's balance-of-payments surplus into deficit and forced it to incur heavy foreign debt the dinar was devalued in 1983 to ID 1 = $3.21. While in the 1970s there was proximity between the official rates and the market rate of exchange this was not the case in the 1980s when the open-market rate started to decline under the impact of the war conditions. This problem was magnified in the 1990s under the conditions of sanctions.

One reason for this decline was the war-generated uncertainties that prompted many people to transfer their currency holdings into dollars and to a lesser extent nondollar deposits abroad. Another reason was the emigration of those who could do so which entailed the conversion of their wealth to other currencies. Another reason was the failure of the economy to generate employment or sustain living standards, hence pushing people to emigrate. In either case

Table 6.4
Unofficial Exchange Rate Changes: Selected Months (Iraqi dinar per U.S. dollar)

Month/Year	1994	1995	1996	1997
January	--	640	700	1137
March	--	1020	--	1250
May	--	1180	--	1258
July	460	1670	--	--
September	525	2020	1140	--
November	550	2530	1740	--
December	560	2900	850	--

Source: Food and Agriculture Organization and World Food Program, *Special Report: FAO/ WFP Supply and Nutrition Assessment Mission to Iraq* (Rome: Food and Agriculture Organization, 3 October 1997).

such acts increased the supply of dinars on the international market and caused its value to decline.

Another factor was the austerity measures of the war and the shortages under sanctions which curtailed consumer goods imports and prompted the smuggling of the currency to neighboring countries to buy such goods for sale in Iraq at exorbitant prices. The increase in the supply of the dinar in these countries forced its value or exchange rate down vis-à-vis these countries' currencies as well as other currencies. The practice of exporting dinars to import goods for sale at inflated prices in Iraq gained momentum in 1984 when the government removed the licensing requirement for imports provided that importers use their foreign-held assets to finance their imports. The smuggling of local currency in large quantities depressed its value vis-à-vis other currencies in the international currency market.

The decline in the exchange rate in the 1980s proved in retrospect to have been mild by comparison to what happened to the value of the dinar in the aftermath of the invasion of Kuwait. The freezing of Iraqi assets, the sanctions, shortages of goods of all kinds, the emigration of large numbers of professionals, high rates of unemployment, the collapse of the economy, the hyperinflation, the feverish speculation in currency, the continued printing of money, and the general fear and uncertainty about the future were among the factors that contributed to the collapse in the value of the dinar to $0.05 or $0.02 or at one time to only $0.01 when the official rate was still $3.21 to the dinar. The longer the sanctions were in place and the longer Iraq was not exporting its oil the more depressed the value of the Iraqi currency was. This can be seen in the decline in the value of the Iraqi dinar from $1.00 = ID 460 in July 1994 to $1.00 = ID 2,900 in December 1995. But as soon as the government announced in January 1996 that it was willing to enter into negotiations with the United Nations over the implementation of UNSC resolution 986 (the oil-for-food program) the value of the dinar improved dramatically to $1.00 = ID 700 in that month in anticipation of the return of Iraqi oil to the market.

CIVILIAN IMPORTS

Another indicator of the impact of sanctions relates to the drastic fall in the level of imports in the aftermath of the invasion of Kuwait and the imposition of sanctions. Iraq imported $127.7 billion of goods during the period 1980–1989. Out of this arms imports amounted to $52.4 billion leaving $75.3 billion for civilian imports or $495 per person per year. By contrast, during the period 1990–2000 Iraq's civilian imports were $10.6 billion or $60 per person per year or 12 percent of the presanctions level (see Table 6.5).

In a country like Iraq where no sector of the economy is free from import dependency, such a drastic decline had a profound effect on the economy. This is so because not only the major part of food consumption is dependent on imports but all sorts of inputs, capital goods, and spare parts had to be imported, without which the economy cannot function for any length of time.

THE UNSC ASSESSMENT OF CONDITIONS IN IRAQ

In 1999 the UNSC decided to create a panel to study humanitarian issues in Iraq in the context of increasing concern over social and economic conditions in Iraq. The panel's report dated March 30, 1999 compared conditions in Iraq prior to the sanctions and the consequences of the sanctions on these conditions. The importance of the document warrants the following extensive citation of some of the relevant paragraphs of the report:

11. According to the information presented to the panel, at the end of the last decade Iraq's social and economic indicators were generally above the regional and developing country averages. GDP in 1989 stood at [$]75.5 billion for a population of 18.3 million. GDP growth had averaged 10.4% from 1974 to 1980. By 1988 GDP per capita totaled $3510. The concerted push for economic growth from the mid-seventies onward had benefited the country's infrastructure.

   With oil accounting for 60% of the country's GDP and 95% of foreign currency earnings, Iraq's economy was heavily dependent on the external sector and sensitive to oil price fluctuations. Such dependence on oil exports would subsequently

Table 6.5
Exports, Imports, and Arms Imports, 1980–2000 (billions of dollars)

Year	Exports	Civilian Imports	Arms Imports	Total Imports
1980	28.4	11.3	2.4	13.7
1982	9.8	14.1	7.1	21.2
1984	9.1	0.5	9.3	9.8
1986	7.4	3.8	4.9	8.7
1988	9.7	3.6	5.6	9.2
1990	10.4	2.8	3.7	6.5
1992	0.6	0.6	0	0.6
1994	0.4	0.5	0	0.5
1996	0.5	0.6	0	0.6
1998	5.1	1.0	0	1.0
2000[e]	19.3	1.5	0	1.5

Source: International Monetary Fund, *Direction of Trade Statistics*; U.S. Arms Control and Disarmament Agency, *World Military Expenditures and Arms Transfers* (Washington, D.C.: U.S. Arms Control and Disarmament Agency, annual).

[e] = estimate.

expose Iraq to a high degree of vulnerability to sanctions. In the early 1980's Iraq had been producing as many as 3.5 million barrels per day (MBD), but that amount declined to 2.8 million by 1989.

12. Up to 1990, domestic food production represented only one third of total consumption for most essential food items, with the balance covered by imports. As highlighted by FAO, at that time Iraq had one of the highest per capita foods availability indicators in the region. Dietary energy supply averaged 3120 calories per capita/per day. Due to its relative prosperity Iraq had the capacity to import large quantities of food, which met up to two thirds of its requirements at an average estimated cost of $2.5 billion a year, although in poor production years the food bill could rise to $3 billion.

13. According to WHO, prior to 1991 health care reached approximately 97 percent of the urban population and 78 percent of rural residents. The health care system was based on an extensive expanding network of health facilities linked up by reliable communications and a large fleet of service vehicles and ambulances. Health care emphasized curative aspects, but a set of active public health programs complemented it through immunization and control of insect borne diseases. A major reduction of young child mortality took place from 1960 to 1990, with the infant mortality rate at 65 per 1000 live births in 1989 (average for developing countries was 76 per 1000 live births).

14. As described by UNICEF, the Government of Iraq made sizable investments in the education sector from the mid-1970s until 1990. According to UNESCO, educational policy included provision for scholarships, research facilities and medical support for students. By 1989 the combined primary and secondary enrollment ratio stood at 75 percent (slightly above the average for all developing countries at 70 percent). Illiteracy had been reduced to 20 percent by 1987. While Iraq's indicators were inferior to that of other Arab countries such as Egypt, education accounted for over 5 percent of the state budget in 1989, above the developing country average of 3.8 percent.

15. Before 1991 the South and Center of Iraq had a well-developed water and sanitation system, as well as an extensive distribution network. WHO estimates that 90 percent of the population had access to an abundant quantity of safe drinking water. There were modern mechanical means of collection and sanitary disposal.

16. The brutal campaign waged by the Iraqi Government against the Kurdish rebels in the North, had constituted the main issue of humanitarian concern in Iraq prior to the events of 1990–91. Aspirations among the Kurdish population of Northern Iraq for autonomy had already resulted in periods of open revolt in 1960–75 and 1983–88. Landmines had been used as early as 1965. According to figures provided by UNOPS [United Nations Office for Project Services], the conflict and the forced depopulation of over 4800 rural villages and the subsequent mining of a majority of the villages or their surroundings resulted in a known mined area which would come to reach over 212 square kilometers in the 1990s.

17. After the Gulf War and under the effect of sanctions it is estimated that Iraq's GDP may have fallen by nearly two-thirds in 1991, owing to an 85 percent decline in oil production and the devastation of the industrial and services sectors of the economy. Agricultural growth has since been erratic and manufacturing output has all but vanished. According to figures provided by UNFPA per capita income fell from $3416 in 1984 to $1500 in 1991 and has decreased to less than $1036 in 1998. Other sources estimate a decrease in per capita GDP to as a low as $450 in 1995.

18. As mentioned by UNFPA, the maternal mortality rate increased from 50/100,000 live births in 1989 to 117/100,000 in 1997. The under-five child mortality rate increased from 30/1000 live births to 97/1000 during the same period. Although figures for infant deaths are based on estimates that may involve a margin of error, the trend is one of sharp increases. The Population Division of DESA [Department of Economic and Social Affairs] calculates that the infant mortality rate rose from 64/1000 births in 1990 to 129/1000 in 1995 (the latest Human Develop-

ment Report sets the average infant mortality rate for Least Developed Countries at 109/1000). Low birth weight babies (less than 2.5 kg) rose from 4 percent in 1990 to around a quarter of registered births in 1997, due mainly to maternal malnutrition. UNFPA and other sources such as the International Federation of the Red Cross and Red Crescent Societies believe that as many as 70 percent of Iraqi women are suffering from anemia.

19. The dietary energy supply had fallen from 3120 to 1093 calories per capita/per day by 1994–95. The prevalence of malnutrition in Iraqi children under five almost doubled from 1991 to 1996 (from 12 percent to 23 percent). Acute malnutrition in Center/South rose from 3 percent to 11 percent for the same age bracket. Results of a nutritional status survey conducted on 15000 children under 5 years of age in April 1997 indicated that almost the whole young child population was affected by a shift in their nutritional status towards malnutrition (Nutritional Status Survey of Infants in Iraq, UNICEF November 7 1998). WFP indicates that according to estimates for July 1995, average shop prices of essential commodities stood at 850 times the July 1990 level.

20. In addition to the scarcity of resources, malnutrition problems also seem to stem from the massive deterioration in basic infrastructure, in particular in the water-supply and waste disposal systems. The most vulnerable groups have been the hardest hit, especially children under five years of age who are being exposed to unhygienic conditions, particularly in urban centers. The WFP estimates that access to potable water is currently 50 percent of the 1990 level in urban areas and only 33 percent in rural areas.

21. Since 1991, hospitals and health centers have remained without repair and maintenance. The functional capacity of the health care system has degraded further by shortages of water and power supply, lack of transportation and the collapse of the telecommunications system.

22. School enrollment for all ages (6–23) has declined to 53 percent. According to a field survey conducted in 1993, as quoted by UNESCO, in Central and Southern governorates 83 percent of school buildings needed rehabilitation, with 8613 out of 10344 schools having suffered serious damage. The same source indicated that some schools with a planned capacity of 700 pupils actually have 4500 enrolled in them. Substantive progress in reducing adult and female illiteracy has ceased and regressed to mid-1980 levels, according to UNICEF. The rising number of street children and children who work can be explained, in part, as a result of increasing rates of school drop-outs and repetition, as more families are forced to rely on children to secure household incomes. Figures provided by UNESCO indicate that drop-outs in elementary school increased from 95,692 in 1990 to 131,658 in 1999.

23. The accelerating decline of the power sector has had acute consequences for the humanitarian situation.

25. Increase in juvenile delinquency, begging and prostitution, anxiety about the future and lack of motivation, a rising sense of isolation bred by absence of contact with the outside world, the development of a parallel economy replete with profiteering and criminality, cultural and scientific impoverishment, disruption of family life. WHO points out that the number of mental health patients

attending health facilities rose by 157% from 1990 to 1998 (from 197,000 to 507,000 persons).

26. The cumulative effect of the sanctions regime and economic decline on the social fabric of Iraq was particularly evident to the first hand observers who addressed the panel either orally or in writing. While WHO mentioned the extreme isolation of the Iraqi scientific community and its outdated expertise, the ICRC observed that medical training is no longer guaranteed and skills are being lost. UNICEF spoke of a whole generation of Iraqis who are growing up disconnected from the rest of the world. UNESCO commented that children between 5 and 15 years of age were the most affected. According to the Humanitarian Coordinator in Iraq, unemployment and low salaries were forcing Iraqis with higher levels of education to abandon jobs as teachers or doctors and to either emigrate or search for employment as taxi drivers or security guards etc. adding to the problems in the areas of health and education.

27. The dependence of the Iraqi population on humanitarian supplies had increased government control over individual lives to the detriment of personal initiative and self-reliance.

29. The adoption of the "oil for food" program has played an important role in averting major food shortages in Iraq.

30. Results of a nutritional status survey of infants attending routine immunization sessions at primary health centers throughout Central and Southern Iraq conducted in October 1997, and again one year later, reveal little change in the nutritional status since the beginning of the program established by Security Council resolution 986 (UNICEF November 7, 1999). According to the FAO, the survey showed signs that infant feeding patterns may have deteriorated, and that children and younger male adults remained subject to significant levels of malnutrition. As mentioned by WFP, the introduction of the resolution 986 food ration in 1997 led to a decrease in prices of food items found in the ration. Prices of non-ration food items such as meat and eggs, however, remain prohibitively high.

31. The collapse of the irrigation system and the introduction of the oil-for-food program have prompted the government to withdraw from agriculture.

32. The flow of medicines and medical supplies under Security Council resolution 986 as from May 1997 increased availability of such supplies to health institutions and people. As a result the quality of health has improved somewhat, but the insufficiency of funds has not allowed for significant improvement in the environment in which health care is provided nor has there been a renewal of basic equipment. Preventive activities are suffering from lack of communication and transport. The environmental risks of water borne communicable diseases, primarily diarrhea, but also malaria and leishmaniasis continue to be of great concern. There is a continuing threat of typhoid and cholera outbreaks.

37. While there is agreement that the Government could do more to make the "oil for food" program work in a better and more timely fashion, it was not clear to what extent the problems encountered could be attributed to deliberate action or inaction on the part of the Iraqi Government. It is generally recognized that certain sectors such as electricity work smoothly while drug supplies suffer from delays in distribution. But mismanagement, funding shortages (absence of the so called

"cash component") and a general lack of motivation might also explain such delays. While food and medicine had been explicitly exempted by Security Council resolution 661, controls imposed by resolution 986 had, at times, created obstacles to their timely supply.

39. Information reviewed by the panel indicated that while the humanitarian program established by resolution 986 had clearly contributed to prevent a steadier decline in certain indicators than would have otherwise been the case, particularly in terms of nutrition, written submissions and oral presentations to the panel converged in recognizing the inherent limitations of such efforts in the medium term. The WFP considers that food imports alone could not address the problem of malnutrition in the absence of a drive to rehabilitate the infrastructure, especially as regards health care and water/sanitation.

40. Although Iraq is exporting more oil than ever since 1991, revenue remained insufficient due to a negative correlation linking low oil prices, delays in obtaining spare parts for the oil industry and general obsolescence of oil infrastructure.

42. It was acknowledged that factors independent from the effectiveness of the humanitarian efforts to assist the Iraqi population could help to improve the situation, such as a sustained rise in international oil price levels. However, in order for Iraq to aspire to social and economic indicators comparable to the ones reached at the beginning of the decade humanitarian efforts of the kind envisaged under the "oil for food" system alone would not suffice and massive investment would be required in a number of key sectors, including oil, energy, agriculture and sanitation. Finally, it was pointed out that if and when sanctions are lifted, it will take a long time before the infrastructure is repaired and the economy recovers.

43. The data provided to the panel point to a continuing degradation of the Iraqi economy with an acute deterioration in the living conditions of the Iraqi population and severe strains on its social fabric. As summarized by the UNDP field office, "the country has experienced a shift from relative affluence to massive poverty." In marked contrast to the prevailing situation prior to the events of 1990–91, the infant mortality rates in Iraq today are among the highest in the world, low infant birth weight affects at least 23 percent of all births, chronic malnutrition affects every fourth child under five years of age, only 41 percent of the population have regular access to clean water, 83 percent of all schools need substantial repairs. The ICRC states that the Iraqi health-care system is today in a decrepit state. UNDP calculates that it would take $7 billion to rehabilitate the power sector country-wide to its 1990 capacity.

44. The North of Iraq is clearly doing better than the Center/South for a variety of reasons. The per capita allocation of funds under the 986 program is higher, distribution of food and medicine through U.N. agencies is comparatively more efficient than distribution by the government, and the Northern border is more permeable to embargoed commodities than the rest of the country.

45. Although Member States should not shun their collective responsibility in the face of acute Iraqi humanitarian needs, this does not exempt the Government of Iraq from its own responsibilities in providing relief to its citizens, given its unsatisfactory performance in certain areas—as noted in Section III of this report—

nor can Iraq's original responsibility for the current situation be ignored. At the same time, it is the panel's view that, under current conditions the humanitarian outlook will remain bleak and become more serious with time. Even if not all suffering in Iraq can be imputed to external factors, especially sanctions, the Iraqi people would not be undergoing such deprivations in the absence of the prolonged measures imposed by the Security Council and the effects of war.

47. In light of the near absolute dependence of Iraq on oil exports to generate foreign exchange, the precarious state of the oil industry infrastructure, if allowed to deteriorate further, will have disastrous effects on the country's ability to cover the costs for basic humanitarian needs. Irrespective of sanctions, low oil prices remain an important constraint on the availability of funds, further underscoring the importance of exploring alternative sources of funding.

48. The fact that basic humanitarian needs are being met through hand-outs does not contribute to stimulate the economy and has an indirect negative impact on agriculture, while increasing state control over a population whose private initiative is already under severe constraints of an internal and external nature.

49. The gravity of the humanitarian situation of the Iraqi people is indisputable and cannot be overstated. Irrespective of alleged attempts by the Iraq authorities to exaggerate the significance of certain facts for political propaganda purposes, the data from different sources as well as qualitative assessments of bona fide observers and sheer common sense analysis of economic variables converge and corroborate this evaluation (United Nations 1999: ¶11–49).

OBSERVATIONS ON THE PANEL'S REPORT

The panel's report codified what has long been recognized—that the oil-for-food program was designed to be of limited importance. As was noted earlier imports under the program supplied only a fraction of what the Iraqi economy was accustomed to import prior to the eruption of the crisis in 1990. One of the major shortcomings of the program is its depressing effect on the domestic economy, especially agriculture since the program did not allow the spending of any oil revenue on locally produced foods and services.

In short, the program was not designed as a vehicle for the rehabilitation and development of the economy or to provide the necessary funding to safeguard against economic and social disintegration.

REFERENCES

Ali, A.M.S., and Al-Ganabi, A.H.J. (1992). "Political Economy of Inflation in Iraq." *Arab Economic Journal* 1 (1): 91–113 (in Arabic).

Fawzi, M.C.S., and Zaidi, S. (1996). "Sanctions, Saddam and Silence: Child Malnutrition and Mortality in Iraq." *The Washington Report on Middle East Affairs*, January, pp. 13–14.

Food and Agriculture Organization. (1995). *Evaluation of Food and Nutrition Situation in Iraq*. Rome: Food and Agriculture Organization.

———. (2000). *Assessment of the Food and Nutrition Situation: IRAQ*. Rome: Food and Agriculture Organization.

Food and Agriculture Organization, and World Food Program. (1993). *FAO/WFP Crop and Food Supply Assessment Mission to Iraq*. Rome: Food and Agriculture Organization.

Garfield, R. (2000). "Changes in Health and Well-Being in Iraq during the 1990s: What Do We Know and How Do We Know It." In Campaign Against Sanctions on Iraq, *Sanctions on Iraq: Background, Consequences, and Strategies*. Cambridge: The Campaign.

International Study Team. (1991). *Health and Welfare in Iraq after the Gulf Crisis: An In-Depth Assessment*. Washington, D.C.: Wagner Communications.

Pellet, P. (2000). "Sanctions, Food, Nutrition, and Health in Iraq." In *Iraq under Siege: The Deadly Impact of Sanctions and War*, ed. A. Arnov. Cambridge, Mass.: South End Press.

Provost, R. (1992). "Starvation as a Weapon: Legal Implications of the United Nations Food Blockade Against Iraq and Kuwait." *Columbia Journal of Transnational Law* 30 (3): 577–639.

Tareeq Al-Shaab. (1996). "General Attack on the Citizens' Livelihood and Numerous Privileges to the Followers" (in Arabic) June, pp. 6–8.

Tripp, C. (2000). *A History of Iraq*. Cambridge: Cambridge University Press.

UNICEF. (1999). *Child and Maternal Mortality Survey 1999: Preliminary Report*. New York: UNICEF.

United Nations. (1996). *The United Nations and the Iraq–Kuwait Conflict*. New York: United Nations.

———. (1999). *Report of the second panel established pursuant to the note by the president of the Security Council of 30 January 1999 (S1999/100), concerning the current humanitarian situation in Iraq, Annex II of S/1999/356—30 March 1999*. New York: United Nations.

———. (2000). *Report of the Secretary-General Pursuant to Paragraph 5 of Resolution 1302 (2000)*. New York: United Nations.

World Health Organization. (1996). *The Health Conditions of the Population in Iraq Since the Gulf Crisis*. Geneva: World Health Organization.

CHAPTER 7

Oil under Sanctions

In an oil-dependent country like Iraq the imposition of sanctions in 1990 was a serious external shock of unprecedented proportion. Since the emergence of Iraq's oil industry, but especially since the 1950s, Iraq's dependence on the oil sector continued to rise with the rise in Iraq's oil exports. More significantly the rise in oil exports was not accompanied by any serious increase in Iraq's non-oil exports (see Table 7.1). This meant that over time export earnings were generated almost exclusively by oil exports. Thus in most of the 1980s oil exports amounted to 99 percent of Iraq's total exports. This meant that the entire economy was affected whenever Iraq's oil exports were affected. In the following pages the relationship between the sanctions, in their various configurations, and the oil industry will be explored.

In December 1996 Iraq's oil was reintroduced to the world market following an agreement between the United Nations and the government of Iraq over how oil exports were to be conducted and over how Iraq could spend the revenue from oil sales. Since this agreement was an important landmark in the history of the sanctions the analysis in this section will focus on the period of 1990–1996 while the next section will be devoted to the period since 1996. The final section will be devoted to an exploration of likely developments in the oil industry in the postsanctions era.

Table 7.1
Iraq: Total Exports and Oil Exports, 1972–1990 (billions of dollars)

	Total Exports	Oil Exports
1972	1.1	1.0
1974	6.6	6.5
1976	9.3	9.2
1978	11.1	10.9
1980	26.5	26.3
1982	10.1	10.1
1984	9.4	9.4
1986	7.0	6.9
1988	11.1	11.0
1990	9.5	9.5

Source: OPEC, *Annual Statistical Bulletin* (Vienna: OPEC, various years).

THE UNITED NATIONS AND THE OIL SECTOR
UP TO DECEMBER 1996

Between 1991 and 1996 several attempts were made to utilize the oil sector to provide funds to finance civilian consumption, to provide a source of income to pay for war reparation and to fund various U.N. operations in Iraq. Since no agreement could be reached between the United Nations and the government of Iraq over the modalities of oil sales, Iraq's oil industry remained confined mostly to producing oil to meet local consumption needs.

ASSESSING IRAQ'S CIVILIAN NEEDS

In July 1990 Iraq's oil production was 3.3 MBD and averaged 2.1 MBD for the whole year. For the entire year of 1991 production was 0.3 MBD. The decline in oil exports was even more pronounced since exports in 1991 were a mere 50,000 barrels per day or 2 percent of the 1989 level of exports of 2.4 MBD. Iraq's oil exports remained low until the latter part of the 1990s when they reached 0.7 MBD in 1997 to rise to around 2 MBD in 1999 and 2000. In spite of the drastic decline in the oil sector in terms of output and export levels, Iraq's oil figured prominently in all United Nations actions and policies toward Iraq soon after the adoption of the March 2, 1991 cease-fire resolution.

The first U.N. mission was sent to Iraq only a few days after the adoption of that resolution to report on Iraq's humanitarian conditions. It noted that the bombing campaign has wrought near-apocalyptic results upon the economic infrastructure of what had been, until two months earlier, a rather highly ur-banized and mechanized society. The mission concluded that Iraq has, for some time to come, been relegated to a preindustrial age, but with all the disabilities of postindustrial dependency on an intensive use of energy and technology. Given the scope of the devastation the mission stressed the need for a major mobilization and movement of resources to deal with aspects of the deep crisis in the field of agriculture and food, water, sanitation, and health. But these immediate humanitarian needs could not be addressed without si-multaneously considering the need for a reliable source of energy which was not available at the time. To remedy this particular shortcoming it was recom-mended that emergency oil imports had to be resorted to and that rapid patch-ing up of a limited refining and electricity production capacity be undertaken with essential supplies imported from other countries. Although the report prompted the Sanctions Committee to declare that humanitarian conditions apply with respect to the entire population of Iraq it chose not to relax the sanctions on oil exports (United Nations 1996: 186–189).

In July 1991 another U.N. mission was sent to Iraq to assess "current needs for humanitarian assistance and recommend measures for meeting those needs." The mission focused on the need to rehabilitate the oil sector, power-generat-ing sector, water and sanitation systems, and the costs of food and medicines imports and came up with a total cost of $22 billion. It also provided cost figures for a one-year reduced level of rehabilitation. These costs were com-puted to be $6.8 billion. A third option to provide funding for a four-month program that would cost $2.63 billion was also presented by the mission. In all cases the mission argued that the costs of these programs were simply far beyond what is, or is likely to be, under any U.N.–sponsored programs. More-over, any additional requests for aid to Iraq must compete with a list of other emergency situations around the world with very compelling needs (United Nations 1996: 273–278).

Given these considerations the mission argued strongly in favor of allow-ing Iraq to sell its oil in order to fund its needs. Indeed, the mission pointed out that UNSC resolution 687 of April 1991 provided for exemptions to the em-bargo on oil sales by allowing the government of Iraq to sell enough oil to assure enough financial resources to procure medicine and health supplies, foodstuffs, and materials and supplies for "essential civilian needs." The mis-sion pointed out that the oil sector was capable of generating 1 MBD of oil exports yielding at the prevailing prices some $5.5 billion over one year. And in order to increase oil production and export the mission recommended that Iraq be allowed to import over a four-month period $1 billion worth of equipment, spare parts, and consumable materials to start restoration of the oil sector (United Nations 1996: 273–278).

THE FIRST ATTEMPT TO SELL OIL

Instead of accepting any of the three funding alternatives that the mission had outlined, the U.N. Security Council passed in August 1991 resolution 706 which authorized the sale of $1.6 billion worth of oil over a six-month period or $3.2 billion over one year. This last figure fell way below the $6.8 billion that the mission had recommended. Not only that but the UNSC recommended figure of $1.6 billion was $800 million below what the U.N. secretary-general had deemed to be necessary to meet the humanitarian and essential civilian requirements so desperately needed by the people of Iraq, as the international community fully recognizes (United Nations 1996: 299).

Oil was central not only to the U.N. position vis-à-vis the predicament of the people of Iraq, but it became an integral part of the other activities of the United Nations such as payment of compensation through the U.N.–created Compensation Fund for loss, damage, or injury to foreign governments, nationals, and corporations. Oil also became the source of funding of U.N. operations for the disarmament of Iraq and other U.N.–mandated programs and operations.

It is important to reiterate that the $1.6 billion was subject to several deductions including 30 percent to be transferred to the U.N. Compensation Fund, funding a variety of U.N. operations in Iraq or related to Iraq and oil transit fees payable to Turkey. These deductions had the effect of reducing the authorized figure to less than $1 billion available to Iraq.

It should be reiterated that all funds generated by the oil sales were to be deposited in a special escrow account to be administered by the U.N. secretary-general. Also, all payments out of this account must be preapproved by the secretary-general.

It is not clear how the UNSC arrived at the figure of $1.6 billion (actually $1 billion after the deductions) at a time when it acknowledged in the preamble of resolution 706 that it was concerned by the serious nutritional and health situation of the Iraqi civilian population and by the risk of a further deterioration of this situation. In other words, if the authorization was to mitigate deteriorating human conditions, why limit the sales to any fixed amount?

There is also the question as to the dilution of an already small amount of oil sale by the considerable deductions established by the resolution. The most important deduction, 30 percent, was for the Compensation Fund. This ratio was arrived at by the U.N. secretary-general by estimating that imports and debt service would absorb 70 percent of Iraq's estimated 1993 oil revenue of $21 billion, leaving a balance of 30 percent to be transferred to the Compensation Fund. One of the most interesting points in the calculation was the estimate by the secretary-general that $8 billion may be required to sustain a level of civilian imports in 1991 consistent with the needs of the Iraqi economy. Yet resolution 706 provided for merely $2 billion of imports in that year. For its part the government of Iraq rejected the resolution on the grounds that its provisions impinged on its national sovereignty and imposed a foreign guardianship on its people.

The Iraqi government's rejection of this scheme did not prevent the UNSC from pursuing Iraqi oil sold after the invasion of Kuwait. In the first action of its kind the UNSC passed in October 1992 resolution 778 which stipulated that all states in which there were funds from sale of Iraqi oil paid for since the sanctions had been imposed should transfer those funds to the escrow account. And if certain states had in their possession Iraqi oil such oil should be sold at fair market value and the proceeds were to be transferred to the escrow account (United Nations 1996: 103). This confiscation of Iraqi assets by the UNSC did not result in any appreciable transfer of funds into the escrow account, leading the UNSC to adopt a new resolution for the sale of Iraqi oil.

THE SECOND ATTEMPT TO SELL OIL

Not surprisingly, the failure to activate resolution 706 worsened economic and social conditions in Iraq on the one hand and left the Compensation Fund and other Iraq-related U.N. programs without the necessary financial resources for their functioning.

It was not until 1995 that the UNSC decided to revisit the issue of oil sales when it adopted on April 14 resolution 986 allowing Iraq to sell $2 billion worth of oil every six-month period to provide funding for the Compensation Fund, various UNSC mandated operations in Iraq, and to enable Iraq to purchase food and medicine. Except for the increase in oil sales—from $1.6 billion under the 1991 resolutions to $2 billion under this resolution—the core of the scheme remained the same. The UNSC retained the necessary mechanisms to monitor all sales, all purchases, and all funds were to move in and out of a U.N.–administered escrow account. With 30 percent of the proceeds to be diverted to the Compensation Fund and other deductions to pay for U.N.–mandated operations in Iraq it is estimated that Iraq would get $1.3 billion every six months to finance its imports of food, medical supplies, and other essential civilian needs. Although the UNSC–authorized sale of oil was insignificant relative to civilian needs the income from the sale of oil, however, would have provided much needed economic and social relief. Yet the Iraqi government decided to reject resolution 986, thus plunging the country in a deeper crisis. One indicator among many of the depth of the economic crisis was the collapse of the value of the Iraqi dinar vis-à-vis the dollar, which declined from ID 706 in January 1995 to nearly ID 3,000 in January 1996. The resulting hyperinflation and further collapse in what remained of personal-income purchasing power forced the government in January 1996 to reverse its position and agree to enter into negotiations with the UNSC over the implementation of resolution 986. An agreement was reached in May 1996 over the implementation of the resolution. But it was not until December 1996 when Iraqi oil was finally exported to the world market.

Soon after the flow of Iraqi oil to the world market it became clear that the authorized $2 billion every six months was far from sufficient to meet Iraq's minimum needs. To increase oil revenue the UNSC decided in February 1998 to raise the ceiling on oil sales to $5.26 billion every six months. And in December 1999 the UNSC decided to remove the ceiling on oil exports altogether but kept all other parts of the program (see Table 7.2).

One of the structural problems of the oil-for-food program prior to the removal of the ceiling on oil exports was that it set a dollar ceiling on Iraq's oil exports. Since Iraq did not have unlimited production capacity a fiscal ceiling meant that Iraq would not be able to reach its allowable ceiling if the price of oil was too low. The failure of Iraq to actually reach its allowable target prompted the UNSC to raise the ceiling from $2 billion per six-month phase under resolution 986 to $5.3 billion under resolution 1153 which was adopted on February 20, 1998. When Iraq launched its exports under the oil-for-food program in December 1996 the price of OPEC oil was $23.51 per barrel. But by the time the new ceiling was established in February 1998 the price of the OPEC basket has fallen to $13.45 per barrel and continued its downward slide to reach $9.67 per barrel in December 1998. Iraq in 1998 simply did not have the production capacity to produce enough oil to reach the target allowed by resolution 1153. During that year Iraq was able to export $5.1 billion worth of oil—far below what the UNSC had allowed at $10.5 billion.

The disparity between what the UNSC wanted Iraq to produce and what Iraq actually was capable of producing led the UNSC to decide in resolution 1153 of February 1998 to send a group of oil-industry experts to study the conditions of the oil industry to determine whether Iraq was able to export enough oil tb meet the new target of $5.26 billion.

The report of the experts that the secretary-general transmitted to the UNSC on April 15, 1998 had, among other things, these findings:

1. The oil industry of Iraq is in a lamentable state and the developed oil fields have had their productivity seriously reduced, some irreparably over the last twenty years.

2. The oil processing and treatment facilities, refineries, and storage terminals in the country have been severely damaged and continue to deteriorate, and this deterioration will accelerate until significant action is taken to contain and relieve the problems.

3. The experts have strong doubt that the production profile of 3 MBD envisaged by the government will be sustainable and a sharp increase in production without concurrent expenditures on spare parts and equipment would be against accepted principles of good oil-field husbandry.

Table 7.2
Oil Revenue of Iraq and OPEC, 1960–2000 (billions of dollars)

Year	Iraq	OPEC	Ratio of Iraq to OPEC (%)
1960	0.3	--	--
1970	0.8	14.8	5.4
1975	8.2	104.9	7.8
1980	26.3	282.6	9.3
1982	9.9	205.3	4.8
1984	8.9	148.9	6.0
1986	6.9	77.0	9.0
1988	9.3	86.6	10.7
1990	9.6	147.1	6.5
1992	.5	132.1	0.4
1994	.4	120.2	0.3
1996	.7	165.4	0.4
1998	5.1	110.1	4.6
2000[e]	19.3	224.7	8.9

Source: OPEC, *Annual Statistical Bulletin* (Vienna: OPEC, various years); *Middle East Economic Survey*, various years.
[e]estimate.

4. Should the current export capacity of 1.6 MBD and the average price of $10.50 per barrel for Iraqi crude oil remain unchanged then Iraq would be able to generate revenues in the amount of $3 billion in a six-month period.

5. It was estimated that the expenditure of $1.2 billion was necessary in order to ensure the gradual increase in production to 3 MBD.

6. The Iraqi oil industry is really in desperate need for spare parts in order to comply with the provisions of resolution 1153 which allowed $5.2 billion of oil exports (*Middle East Economic Survey* 1998: A1–A3).

This report prompted the U.N. secretary-general to recommend to the UNSC that it authorize Iraq to import $300 million of spare parts and equipment for its oil industry over a six-month period. On June 19, 1998 the UNSC adopted resolution 1175 which authorized the export to Iraq of $300 million of oil-sector spare parts to enable it to increase its oil exports in order to reach the allowable ceiling of $5.26 billion set in resolution 1153. But to authorize the allocation of a given sum of money for the import of oil equipment to increase oil export to meet a given target will not be actualized unless the equipment actually reaches its destination in the various sectors of the oil industry. Although Iraq may submit to the Sanctions Committee a list of needed equipment for approval it does not mean that such a list will receive approval. Thus, while the UNSC has approved the import of $300 million of spare parts for the oil sector, Iraq, by the end of 1998, received only a fraction of what it had applied for. Obviously, such delays defeat the very purpose for which the original authorization was provided with the consequent continued deterioration of the oil industry. The U.N. secretary-general himself warned that the pace of approval of applications for spare parts by the Sanctions Committee has been slow and that unless Iraq is expeditiously provided with the essential oil spare parts and equipment, it may be difficult to sustain even the current level of production and export of oil (*Middle East Economic Survey* 1999: A3–A5).

To avoid dealing with the problem of delays, which is symptomatic of political differences between the permanent members of the UNSC toward the question of sanctions on Iraq, another group of oil experts was sent to Iraq and reported, unsurprisingly, that Iraq's oil industry remains in a lamentable state and oil production continued to decline (*Middle East Economic Survey* 1999: A3–A5). Since it was inevitable that political differences would continue to plague the oil industry import program the UNSC decided in resolution 1284 adopted on December 17, 1999 to establish yet another group of experts to report on Iraq's existing oil production and export capacity and to make recommendations on alternatives for increasing Iraq's production and export capacity and on the options for involving foreign oil companies in Iraq's oil sector.

The report of this latest group of experts concluded, unsurprisingly, that the country's oil industry was still in a lamentable state and the level of oil exports during the first half of 2000 will decline from 2.2 MBD achieved in the second half of 1999 to 1.8–1.9 MBD. In addition, a further production decline of 5–15 percent will occur unless the delivery of spares and equipment is accelerated immediately. The report added that the decline in the conditions of all sectors of the industry will continue and the ability of the Iraqi oil industry to sustain the current reduced production levels will be seriously compromised until effective action is taken to reverse the situation. The experts noted that since the launching of the oil-for-food program in December 1996 Iraq has produced 2 billion barrels of oil but invested around $1.2 billion in the industry or $0.30 per barrel per year compared with the annual norm for onshore production in the Middle East of around $1.50 per barrel. Given the holds on contracts by the Sanctions Committee and other delays in delivery the group recommended a review of the procedure controlling spares and an increase in the value of parts authorized for purchase to $600 million per phase. The group calculated the annual investment requirements of the oil industry to be $1.3 billion to sustain an average daily production of 2.5 million barrels. The experts went on to warn that the oil industry is degrading, safety is below conventionally accepted standards, the environment is endangered, the ultimate recovery potential is jeopardized, and the current situation, if left unchanged, will lead inexorably to the demise of the oil industry (Townsend 2000a: 64–65).

Although the UNSC decided in its resolution 1293 adopted on March 31, 2000 to increase the allocation for the Iraqi oil industry import program to $600 million per phase the problem of holds at the Sanctions Committee level continued to compromise the effectiveness of the oil imports program. Needless to say that the oil sector is the foundation upon which the entire oil-for-food program rests and that any time this sector is compromised or weakened the consequences will be felt throughout the country by all sectors of society. The continued practice of delays and holds was articulated by the executive director of the U.N. Iraq Program. In a September 2000 presentation before the UNSC Benon V. Sevan pointed out that the Sanctions Committee was taking too long in its review of lists of items to be imported and that despite the commendable efforts by the Iraqi authorities to increase their production and export of oil, under very difficult conditions and without the supply of spare parts he feared the current volume of production and export levels were not sustainable, unless the necessary spare parts and equipment were delivered. Iraq is producing and exporting oil at the expense of the future, by destroying some oil fields, some irreparably. Sevan pointed out that the oil sector is the lifeline of the humanitarian program. He also pointed out the contradiction between calling upon OPEC to increase oil exports and Iraq not being supplied with the minimum requirements of its oil industry by the Sanctions Committee (Sevan 2000: 1–3).

For the period of December 1996 to December 2000 Iraq submitted $1.95 billion worth of contracts of oil spares and equipment. The Sanctions Committee approved $1.3 billion but only $0.62 billion worth of imports arrived in Iraq by March 2001. The value of contracts placed on hold during this period was $0.4 billion or 22 percent of the value of contracts submitted. It should be stressed that the value of contracts placed on hold is a serious obstacle to the oil sector program not only because it is high in absolute terms but also because of the complementary nature of such goods.

As to the performance of the entire oil-for-food program, a quick look at the financial data reveal its inadequacy. As of December 31, 2000 the cumulative total proceeds from the sale of Iraqi oil under the program amounted to $38.6 billion. These funds were distributed as follows: $22.9 billion was the value of contracts for imports which Iraq had submitted to the United Nations and out of which $18.8 billion worth of imports was approved, leaving 17.9 percent or $4.1 billion worth of contracts frozen or placed on hold by the Sanctions Committee. Out of what was approved only $10.3 billion worth of imports actually reached Iraq during this period. By comparison, the Compensation Fund received $11.6 billion during this period (OIP 2001b: 1–3). The balance went to fund U.N.–mandated operations related to Iraq or remained as a deposit for Iraq in the escrow account to be used in the future.

Relating Iraq's imports under this program to the total population of the country we find that the program enabled Iraq to import $116 per person per year during the period 1997–2000 compared with preembargo (1980–1989) civilian imports of $495 per person per year.

IRAQ OIL AND OPEC IN THE 1990s

On August 2 the government of Iraq decided to invade and occupy Kuwait. And on August 8 the Iraqi government announced the annexation of Kuwait. The ensuing imposition of blockade against any exports from Iraq and Kuwait gave rise to demands that OPEC member countries be allowed to increase output beyond their quotas. Initially, OPEC was of the opinion that its July 1990 resolution should be adhered to and stressed that individual initiatives should be avoided so as to preserve OPEC unity and not hamper its capacity to collectively play its role as a major factor of market stability. But on August 29 OPEC decided to suspend quota allocations so that member countries may expand their output without restrictions. In the same announcement OPEC reiterated its commitment to the July 27 resolution by asserting that the new arrangement shall not in any way compromise the provisions of that resolution which was still valid and once the current crisis is considered to be over, OPEC shall return to it (OPEC 1996: 9).

The decision to suspend the quotas was described as having been adopted by OPEC under considerable pressure by the United States, a pressure which amounted to a direct order (Ibrahim 1990). The involvement of the United States in the decision to suspend quotas is not surprising since close cooperation on oil issues such as price and production between the U.S. government and the Saudi government has been going on for a long time. Indeed, U.S. State Department documents have shown that the Saudis have informed the United States in advance of key moves they planned to make at meetings of OPEC and have consulted U.S. officials about marketing initiatives. In addition, it was revealed that U.S. officials have often discussed the price of oil, not asking for any particular price but emphasizing the negative consequences if prices were to move outside a certain range. Thus when in the early 1980s prices were above $30.00 per barrel the United States leaned on the Saudis to bring them down and when they bottomed out at almost $10.00 per barrel the Reagan administration conveyed to the Saudis its concern about the threat posed by the price crash to U.S. banks involved in oil projects and to oil-exporting allies such as Mexico and Egypt (*Middle East Economic Survey* 1992: A3).

The removal of the ceiling on member country output meant that those countries with excess capacity production were in a position to raise output, increase their share of the market, and have higher levels of revenues. Being the country with the largest excess capacity, Saudi Arabia was in a position to raise its output from 5.43 MBD in July 1990 to its peak production capacity of 8.46 MBD by December 1990, an increase of 56 percent. Relative to OPEC, Saudi Arabia's share in the group's output increased from 25 percent in 1989 to 36 percent in 1991. And, together with the crisis-induced rise in oil prices, Saudi Arabia's oil revenue increased from $24.1 billion in 1989 to $43.7 billion in 1991, an increase of 81 percent (see Table 7.3).

As the crisis continued and as the economies of OPEC member countries became increasingly dependent, especially Saudi Arabia, on the new levels of production and revenue it became obvious that a return to the July 1990 output shares was unlikely when Iraq started to export oil again. In the meantime OPEC had no plans for dealing with the eventual return of Iraq's oil to the world market. Instead, OPEC took the position that it would face the situation when the time came for it to do so. And when Iraq finally started to export oil OPEC had no contingency plan to deal with this important development. The absence of such a plan, in retrospect, seems to have been part of a general inability by member countries to manage their quota system.

OPEC's inability to manage its own supply, most of which is exported, is ultimately determined by the level of oil exports from other oil sources. These non-OPEC sources of supply received a major boost in the 1970s from OPEC's own decisions to increase prices in 1973–1974. In other words, non-OPEC high-cost oil reserves became commercially profitable as a result of those price increases. In 1974 OPEC supplied 27. 3 MBD or 87 percent of the world crude-oil exports of 31.1 MBD. By 1989 OPEC managed to export 14.9 MBD or 58 percent of a world total of 25.9 MBD. Along the way OPEC cohesion was saved by such external shocks as the Iranian revolution, the Iraq–Iran War and the Gulf crisis. This trend continued from 1991, the first full year of the Gulf crisis, to 1997, when Iraq's oil reached the world market. During this period world exports increased by 7.3 MBD, out of which OPEC managed to capture 2.2 MBD or 35 percent.

The weak rise in OPEC's crude oil exports in the post–Gulf crisis period prompted certain member countries to disregard their quotas and increase output at the expense of other producers. OPEC's predicament in the 1990s would have been much worse had it not been for the embargo on Iraq's oil exports, which in 1989 were 2.3 MBD or 15 percent of OPEC's total crude oil exports.

Following the July 1990 decision by OPEC that the reference price of the OPEC crude basket be set at $21.00 per barrel the price, under the Gulf crisis conditions, increased to $24.68 per barrel in August and peaked at $34.32 per barrel in October, then declined to $26.16 per barrel in December. For the year

Table 7.3
Oil Output of OPEC, Saudi Arabia, and Iraq, 1988–2000

Year	OPEC (MBD)	Saudi Arabia		Iraq	
		Output MBD	Percent of OPEC	Output MBD	Percent of OPEC
1988	18.9	5.1	27.0	2.7	14.3
1989	20.5	5.1	24.9	2.8	13.7
1990	22.1	6.4	30.0	2.1	9.5
1991	22.3	8.1	36.3	0.3	0.01
1992	23.9	8.3	34.7	0.5	0.02
1993	24.2	8.0	33.1	0.7	0.03
1994	24.6	8.0	32.5	0.7	0.03
1995	24.6	8.0	32.5	0.7	0.03
1996	24.8	8.1	32.7	0.7	0.03
1997	25.4	8.0	31.5	1.4	5.5
1998	27.8	8.3	30.0	2.2	7.9
1999	26.5	7.7	29.1	2.5	9.4
2000	28.1	8.3	29.5	2.5	8.9

Source: OPEC, *Annual Statistical Bulletin* (Vienna: OPEC, various years); *Middle East Economic Survey*, various years.

1990 the price had increased to $22.26 per barrel but declined to $18.66 and $18.43 in 1991and 1992 respectively. This downward trend in price continued for the next three years, making it unlikely for certain countries to observe their quotas. Under these circumstances it can be safely said that OPEC member countries had no interest in seeing Iraq's oil returning to the world market.

In addition to the rise in OPEC's output and exports and as a result of Iraq's resumption of oil exports, the rules that the UNSC established for this resumption added to OPEC's difficulties. Resolution 986 of April 1995 stated that Iraq may export $2 billion of oil over a six-month period. This meant that Iraq may lower or raise its exports depending on the price of oil at the time of export. In other words, if the price declined Iraq must export more oil to meet the revenue target and consequently adding to OPEC's supply woes. Similarly, when the market is tight and prices are rising Iraq is required to lower its oil exports, therefore causing difficulties in the other direction.

In 1996 disagreement among OPEC member countries was observed at different levels. In the first place, OPEC had no plan to deal even with a limited resumption of Iraqi oil exports. The leading beneficiary from the embargo on Iraqi oil exports, Saudi Arabia, was not willing to relinquish part of its quota to make room for Iraqi oil. Instead, it advocated that countries, such as Venezuela, that were producing above their quotas should observe them in order to ease the reentry of Iraq's oil (*Middle East Economic Survey* 1992: A3). In the absence of an agreement among OPEC's major producers the organization chose not to restructure the quota system or change its level. But in anticipation of the return of Iraqi oil, at its June meeting the organization decided to give Iraq a target output of 1.2 MBD as part of the organization's overall supply ceiling of 25.03 MBD. This official allocation remained in effect until the end of 1997 when allocations were significantly changed for the fist time since the end of 1993.

The 25.03 MBD target which OPEC set for itself for 1997 was surpassed by actual production which reached close to 28 MBD. This overproduction took place at a time when the Asian economic crisis caused a decline in the demand for oil. Instead of striving to lower output OPEC decided to set allocations for the first half of 1998 at 27.5 MBD (Saudi Arabia's share was raised by 8.8 MBD). Even this new higher level of allocation was exceeded when actual output reached 28.7 MBD in February 1998.

This inexplicable decision to increase OPEC quotas led, unsurprisingly, to a decline in prices. Thus the price of the OPEC crude basket which was $23.19 per barrel in January 1997 fell to $12.41 per barrel by March 1998. This price collapse forced OPEC to reexamine its earlier decision and conclude that output targets had to be revised downward. In order to ensure that its new levels of output would arrest the slide in prices, OPEC decided to lower its output and also ask some non-OPEC oil producing countries such as Mexico, China, and Norway to lower their output in order to stabilize oil prices. For its part, OPEC decided to cut output by 1.245 MBD for the period of April 1 to December 31, 1998. Iraq, because of its exceptional circumstances, was not called upon to lower its output (OPEC 1998a: 7). These decisions to cut output failed to improve oil prices as the pledged cuts by OPEC member countries did not materialize in full. This failure was compounded by a significant rise in Iraq's output from 1.4 MB in 1997 to 2.1 MBD in 1998 and the continued weak demand for oil.

To stabilize prices and revenue OPEC found itself once more having to resort to further cuts. And so it was decided that effective July 1, 1998 output be cut by 1.355 MBD on top of the previous 1.245 MBD cut, bringing the total cut to 2.6 MBD to be augmented by more than 0.5 MBD cuts by non-OPEC countries such as Russia and Mexico (OPEC 1998b: 6–7). The newly adopted levels of output were to remain in effect for one year ending June 30, 1999. Once again Iraq was excluded from the latest quota system.

The new cutback measures, however, failed to stem the decline in prices since these measures were not fully implemented by member countries. Again, Iraq was in a position to expand its output and exports and the demand for oil remained weak. This resulted in a further decline in the price of the OPEC crude basket from $12.05 per barrel in July 1998, when the new cutbacks were supposed to be implemented, to $9.67 per barrel in December of that year. For the year 1998 the price averaged $12.28 per barrel, or 34 percent lower than the average price in the previous year.

The failure of member countries to comply with their own decisions to lower output was reflected in the rise in output and decline in oil revenue. Thus OPEC crude oil output in 1998 rose by more than 9 percent to 27.8 MBD from 25.4 MBD in 1997. And although OPEC's oil exports increased by 5 percent between these two years its revenue from these exports declined by nearly 37 percent, from $166 billion in 1997 to $110 billion in 1998.

It is rather clear from this brief review that OPEC had committed two major strategic errors over the course of 1997–1998. First, it should have started the process of output cutback in early 1997 when prices started their downward descent instead of waiting until 1998. Second, OPEC should have included Iraq's production in its quota system instead of allowing it to produce and export any volume it deemed necessary. Interestingly, the leading oil-producing country, Saudi Arabia, acknowledged the existence of a linkage between Iraq's oil output and OPEC's inability to contain the price decline when its oil minister said that when the decision to reduce output took place, Iraqi production was around 1.2–1.4 MBD and now it is around 2.5 MBD. But to include Iraq in the calculation would have required that member countries accept lower quotas in order to accommodate Iraq. This was something that certain countries, especially Saudi Arabia, were not willing to do. Thus when the Saudi oil minister was asked about the position of his country on the issue whether OPEC should have returned to the July 1990 agreement in order to accommodate Iraq's comeback to the market he answered that such thoughts were rather simplistic thoughts and lacked any profundity of understanding the market. And as far Saudi Arabia was concerned the July 1990 decision had been superseded by recent events and was dead and buried (*Middle East Economic Survey* 1999: A1–A5). It is worth recalling that Saudi Arabia was the premier beneficiary from the demise of Iraq's production since it allowed it to increase its output by almost 3 MBD. In addition to Iraq's production the Saudi oil minister maintained that OPEC's problem was not a supply problem, rather it was a demand problem. It was the drop in demand, which refused to go away, and the uncertainty regarding world economic growth (*Middle East Economic*

Survey 1999: A1). But how can one not have a supply problem when there is a demand problem?

Since the drop in demand and Iraq's rise in production refused to go away OPEC had no choice but to try to regulate the supply again. This regulation took the form of another reduction in production of 1.7 MBD for one year ending March 31, 2000. Iraq, again, was not party to the agreement. This projected reduction of nearly 7 percent of the pre-April OPEC quota was smaller than the rise in OPEC's output in 1998 over 1997. This latest reduction brought the total of the three reductions that OPEC had approved between March 1998 and March 1999 to 3.3 MBD.The March 1999 production cuts were complied with by member countries. This compliance and the change in demand conditions resulted in the price to rise from $9.96 per barrel in February 1999 to $26.84 per barrel in February 2000. The success of OPEC in lowering production coincided with lack of growth in refining capacity to meet the rising demand for refined products. In addition, demand for oil increased due to particularly cold weather conditions which accentuated the effects of the OPEC-induced supply cuts. These developments pushed the price to a peak of $31.45 per barrel in September 2000 (see Table 7.4).

This persistent increase in the price led OPEC to adopt two sets of decisions in 2000. First OPEC decided on three occasions in 2000—effective April, July, and October—to raise output. These three increases amounted to 3.2 MBD, thus negating the output cuts which the organization had instituted in the previous year.

The other decision that the organization adopted in 2000 relates to a price-triggered output adjustment mechanism. According to this mechanism OPEC production will be automatically raised or lowered by 0.5 MBD on a pro-rata basis among member countries (except Iraq) in order to keep the OPEC basket crude price within a range of between $22.00 and $28.00 per barrel. Output will be increased if the basket price rises above $28.00 per barrel for twenty trading days and output will be reduced if the price remains below $22.00 per barrel for twenty days, later changed to ten days. (*Middle East Economic Survey* 2000a: A2; 2000b: A2). This new price mechanism was actually put into effect on October 31, 2000 when output was raised by 0.5 MBD in line with OPEC's price band mechanism.

The series of output cuts that OPEC embarked upon in 2000 and which contributed to the price decline gave way to a reversal of policy in the first part of 2001 when output was reduced by 1.5 MBD in February and by another 1 MBD in April in the hope of being able to stabilize the OPEC basket price at $25.00 per barrel.

As far as Iraq was concerned, its own special case set it in a category all by itself. Thus while OPEC was increasing its output Iraq was doing the same for most of 2000 when its production rose from 2.2 MBD in at the beginning of the year to 3.1 MBD in August and was projected to rise to 3.4 MBD in the following year pending arrival of oil spare parts and equipment.

Table 7.4
Oil Revenues of OPEC, Saudi Arabia, and Iraq, 1988–2000

Year	OPEC $ bn	Saudi Arabia Revenue $ bn	Percent of OPEC	Iraq Revenue $ bn	Percent of OPEC
1988	86.6	20.2	23.3	9.3	10.7
1989	107.5	24.1	22.4	11.9	11.1
1990	147.1	40.1	27.3	9.6	6.5
1991	127.4	43.7	34.3	.4	n
1992	132.1	44.8	33.4	.5	n
1993	120.1	38.6	32.1	.4	n
1994	120.2	38.1	31.7	.4	n
1995	133.2	43.5	32.7	.5	n
1996	165.4	54.3	32.8	.7	n
1997	166.0	52.1	31.4	4.3	2.3
1998	110.1	33.4	30.3	5.1	4.6
1999	132.2	38.8	29.3	11.4	8.6
2000[e]	224.7	66.0	29.4	19.3	8.6

Source: OPEC, *Annual Statistical Bulletin* (Vienna: OPEC, various years).
[n]negligible; [e]estimate.

OPEC, IRAQ, AND THE FUTURE DEMAND FOR OIL

It is obvious that the sanctions regime, which has been in place since 1990, has placed Iraq in a special relationship vis-à-vis OPEC and its member countries. While Iraq continued to be a full member of the organization its impact on the decisions of the organization is constrained by the fact that for most of the 1990s its oil production and exports were negligible. It was in the last two years of the 1990s that Iraq's oil weight became significant. Yet Iraq could influence oil prices as an outsider since its oil output was in the final analysis determined not by its relationship to OPEC but by decisions made by the United Nations, especially the Sanctions Committee.

But the United Nations was not the only agency that complicated Iraq's interaction with OPEC. OPEC itself bears a major share of responsibility in what has taken place and in what will transpire in the future. First, OPEC's or at least certain member countries' rush to abrogate rather than suspend the July 1990 quota decisions weakened OPEC's attempt to stabilize OPEC and will do so when Iraq regains and improves its production capacity. Saudi Arabia, as was noted earlier, took the position that those decisions were overshadowed by recent events and now dead and buried. But the case for a return to that pattern of quota distribution, or something similar to it, is rather strong given Iraq's production record, its oil reserves, and the size of its population. The Saudi position of influence within the organization is directly related to the relative importance of its output within that of the organization. Second, whatever losses of market share or loss of oil revenue that may have occurred in the 1990s can be fairly attributed to the way OPEC made its decisions. It would be no exaggeration to say that in arriving at its decisions OPEC lacked both vision and strategy. How else can an outsider assess OPEC's lack of any policy toward the eventual return of Iraqi oil to the market? Indeed, one can argue that OPEC seems to have denied the importance of over 2 MBD of Iraqi oil when it sat down to distribute the quotas for 1998 with the disastrous results of overproduction, lower prices, and loss of revenue. OPEC's unwillingness or inability to declare its readiness to readjust quotas to allow for the reentry of Iraq is rather astonishing.

Even in 2001 OPEC still refused to face the eventuality of the full return of Iraq's oil to the world market and the implications of such return for OPEC's own future. This is particularly puzzling given the well-known fact that Iraq, in the postsanctions era, will be in a position to increase its production well beyond the current 3 MBD. Given Iraq's considerable oil reserves and given the projected increase in the demand for oil there is no reason to assume that capital investment to develop these resources will not be forthcoming. What makes the development of these resources attractive is the ever-declining development costs due to technological advances. Thus current estimates indicate that applying new technology to Iraq could reduce finding costs by 50 percent, while applying complex well drilling and completion technology could reduce development costs to 55 percent of their current levels (Townsend 2000b: 3).

In a recently released study the International Energy Agency (IEA) forecasts that world demand for oil will rise from 75 MBD in 1997 to 96 MBD in 2010 and to 115 MBD by 2020, assuming an average annual rate of growth in the demand for oil of 1.9 percent. To meet this demand for oil the IEA forecasts that non-OPEC oil supply will increase from 42 MBD in 1997 to 46 MBD in 2020, while that of OPEC will have to rise from 30 MBD to 62 MBD between these two years. Out of this 32 MBD increase by OPEC, 27 MBD will have to come from the Middle East, overwhelmingly from Saudi Arabia, Iraq, Iran, Kuwait, and the United Arab Emirates. In other words, the Middle East oil-producing countries will be called upon to provide 68 percent of the increase in the world's oil demand by 2020 (*Middle East Economic Survey* 2000: A3–A6). This means that not only will the sanctions on Iraq have to be lifted soon but foreign investment will have to be made available if these resources are to be developed.

If OPEC is called upon to increase its output by 14 MBD in 2010 and by another 18 MBD by 2020 then OPEC must have a long-term strategy which is nowhere to be found at present. It was OPEC's lack of strategy or even a policy towards the resumption of Iraqi oil exports that caused prices and consequently oil revenues to decline in 1997, 1998, and part of 1999. In order to avoid a disorderly growth of output and ruinous price cutting Iraq's oil will have to be a prominent component of that strategy.

REFERENCES

General Accounting Office. (1982). *The Changing Structure of the International Oil Market*. Washington, D.C.: U.S. Government Printing Office.

Ibrahim, Y. M. (1990). "OPEC Members Close to Raising Output Ceiling." *The New York Times*, August 20, p. A1.

Middle East Economic Survey. (1992). July 27, A3.

———. (1998). April 20, A1–A5.

———. (1999). March 1, A1–A5.

———. (2000a). April 3, A2.

———. (2000b). June 26, A2.

———. (2000c). November 27, A3–A6.

OPEC. (1996). *OPEC Official Resolutions and Press Releases 1990–1996*. Vienna: OPEC.

———. (1998a). *OPEC Bulletin*. April, p. 7.

———. (1998b). *OPEC Bulletin*. July, pp. 6–7.

Sevan, B. V. (2000). *Introductory Statement by Benon V. Sevan, Report of the Secretary-General Pursuant to Paragraph 5 of Security Council Resolution 1302 of 8 June 2000*. New York: United Nations.

Townsend, D. (2000a). "A State of Disrepair." *Petroleum Economist*, May, pp. 64–65.

———. (2000b). "Hope Springs Eternal." *Petroleum Economist*, August, pp. 3–4.

United Nations. (1996). *The United Nations and the Iraq–Kuwait Conflict*. New York: United Nations.

United Nations Office of the Iraq Programme. (2001a). *Basic Figures*. New York: United Nations. January 19, pp. 1–3.

———. (2001b). *Basic Figures*. New York: United Nations. March 21, pp. 1–3.

CHAPTER 8

Burdens in the Future

In attempting to look into the future course of development of any country one is normally called upon to trace past developments, relate them to current conditions and projected changes in order to formulate some ideas about the future direction of the economy. In the process a wealth of variables must be analyzed. Such variables and magnitudes include population trends, gross domestic product, infrastructure, the changing structure of the economy, the labor force and its skill structure, the relative importance of public and private sectors, structure of public finance, nature and scope of the pattern of relationships with the world economy, savings and investments, and foreign debt, among others. While the availability of data on these and other variables will not ensure the validity of projection such availability will, without a doubt, improve the prospects for better policy recommendations. Iraq, on the other hand, is a whole different and rather a special case among developing countries.

One of the very serious obstacles which faces any inquiry into the future of Iraq is the lack or absence of data. The government of Iraq, for reasons of its own, decreed in the 1970s that economic data, especially those related to the oil sector and government spending, not be made public. Given the overwhelming importance of both sectors in the economy it is easy, therefore, to appreciate the difficulties which one faces in attempting to address some of the problems associated with past and future trends. Another major obstacle is the sheer anomaly of the Iraqi economy. Here is a country that was in the upper rungs of middle-income developing countries and had every prospect to continue its upward growth, only to reverse course and sink into underdevelopment and stagnation with per capita GDP falling to levels displayed by some of the least developed countries in the world. Although Iraq may share some of the severe features of underdevelopment and de-development with most low-income countries it, however, differs from them in several important respects.

Unlike many low-income countries, Iraq has accumulated in most of the second half of the twentieth century vast experience in economic development which yielded a considerable infrastructure. In the process of its economic development Iraq was also able to expand and improve its human capital formation in virtually every field of human endeavor. To be certain some of this national human wealth was lost to foreign countries or utilized below capacity due to the sanctions-induced condition of stagnation, poverty, and unemployment. Another difference that will work in favor of Iraq is the fact that it will be in a position to restart the process of development from a relatively higher threshold of physical assets—a condition that will help in the process of economic rehabilitation and growth. Another important fact which favors Iraq is its vast wealth of oil reserves. If managed effectively and rationally Iraq's oil wealth should enable it to shorten the period of recovery, rehabilitation, and return to normalcy.

It is very difficult to classify Iraq in any one particular grouping of developing countries for any length of time since its GDP and consequently its per capita GDP change depending on the contribution of the oil sector to the economy. Thus its per capita GDP in 1996 was 8 percent of what it was in 1980 but climbed to 48 percent of that year's level in 2000 due to the reintroduction of its oil to the world market. Another measure of Iraq's special case is that 55 percent of the population in 1997 lived below a poverty line of $9.00 per month per person.

Clearly, if the economy were to be on the road to rehabilitation and development it will have to deal with two distinct but interrelated sets of challenges: internal and external. Internal challenges include the relationship between the private and public sector, efficient and rational utilization of human and physical resource endowments; depth and breadth of poverty, economic diversification, a widening gap in income distribution, malnutrition and rising child mortality rates, population policy, high unemployment rate, and the problem of the educated unemployed.

As to external obstacles to development that are specific to Iraq these include, among other factors, the U.N.–imposed economic sanctions, the Compensation Fund, the special case of Iraq foreign debt, and the world future demand for oil. These and other internal and external obstacles to development will be explored in the following sections.

ROLE OF THE STATE IN THE ECONOMY

The new state of Iraq which was set up in 1921 under the control of Britain was led by an administration composed of local elites who in addition to the Britain-installed monarchy included a new class of landowners created by the colonial power as well. As government functions expanded, so did the size of its military and civilian labor force, which meant that new recruits had to be drawn from outside the ranks of traditional elite groups. It also meant that the government had become the largest employer in the economy. As import-substitution industrialization gained a place in the economy in the decades of the 1930s and the 1940s a new class of urban proletariat emerged together with another class of petit bourgeoisie encompassing bankers, exporters, importers, shippers, and insurance agents who were tied to the international economy. By the time World War II ended the new classes were challenging the status quo and advocating a new social and economic order. This challenge culminated in the overthrowing of the monarchy in July 1958.

The new republican regime under the leadership of Abdel-Karim Qasim proceeded to destroy the economic and political power base of the landed classes, enact agrarian reform, expand the public sector, provide more social services, broaden Iraq's foreign economic relations, and restrict the scope of the activities of the foreign-owned oil companies.

The military–civilian alliance that overthrew the Qasim regime in 1963 was itself overthrown in 1968 by a military–Baath Party alliance. Between 1968, when the Baath Party seized power, and 1979, when the current president of Iraq assumed the presidency, the regime succeeded in consolidating its power through a mixture of rewards and repression. Two important developments that helped the Baath Party stay in power were its success in nationalizing the foreign oil companies operating in Iraq and the phenomenal rise in oil revenue in the decade of the 1970s which gave the government unprecedented control over the economy.

Iraq had a long history of government involvement in the economy through the provision of social services, infrastructure, and regulation. Several reasons can be cited for this involvement. In the first place, when the modern state of Iraq was created the new government found itself facing a legacy of social and economic backwardness left by the Ottoman Empire—the previous colonial power which had controlled the country since the early part of the seventeenth century. This state of backwardness required the newly installed government to provide for health, education, training, welfare, and all that was needed to usher the new state into the modern world. Second, the availability of oil revenue prompted the government to involve itself in the building of the infrastructure at an early phase in the history of the country. Following the revolution of 1958 there was a shift in the configuration of the country's political and economic forces in favor of a wider role for the state in the economy and society. This orientation was helped by the sharp rise in oil revenue in 1950 as the government found itself in a position of being able to increase its spending and influence in the economy without having to resort to new taxes to fund its programs.

Another factor that moved the government in the direction of expanding its role in the economy was the influence of the slogans of what came to be known as Arab socialism which constituted a challenge to the well-entrenched monarchies in the Arab world. This trend of Arab socialism, which in fact was no more than an advocacy of state-led development was a policy that was common in most developing countries in the 1960s and 1970s. And in the case of Iraq, Arab socialism meant the continued expansion of the role of the state in the economy through the nationalizing of privately owned enterprises in industries such as banking and insurance and by keeping government control in fields that were already being controlled such as transportation, communication, major industrial activity, and foreign and domestic trade.

The war with Iran in 1980s, however, forced the government to reexamine its role in the economy and allow various degrees of freedom to the private sector before its adoption of a policy of privatization in 1987. Prior to 1987 the government sought to ride the economic crisis brought about by the war and the decline in oil revenue by resorting to economic retrenchment and austerity measures. When such measures proved to be inadequate to the task, the government found itself forced to reorient its policy by narrowing the scope of its involvement in the economy relative to the private sector.

In a state-run economy where the government was the recipient of over 60 percent of GDP and where its management of the economy involved every segment of its oil production and export, agriculture and land distribution, foreign and domestic trade, industry, construction, banking, insurance, transportation, and communication, the scope of the private sector, of necessity, was influenced by the state's pattern of spending as well as by its policies toward it. Thus, while the private sector contributed in 1981 one-third of GDP and one-fifth of gross fixed capital formation its sectoral contribution varied considerably, ranging from 1.3 percent of the mining sector to 45 percent of manufacturing, 49 percent of agriculture, 72 percent of transport and communication, and 95 percent of construction (Alnasrawi 1994: 96–99).

Although the war with Iran and the collapse of the oil economy provided the context for the shift toward the private sector it was the agricultural sector that led the change in 1979 when the government decided to increase the role of the private enterprise in that sector. This decision was driven by political and economic embarrassment at the failure of the government to achieve its major goals in food self-sufficiency, the rising food-import bill, decline in agricultural labor, rise in the number of foreign agricultural workers and technicians, and the acknowledgment that the massive infusion of capital into agriculture had failed to result in the hoped for gain in agricultural productivity (Springborg 1986: 33–52). Prior to deciding to expand private sector agriculture the political leadership had already acknowledged that after ten years of promises that agricultural development was a priority in the government program of modernization and after billions of dollars of investment, agriculture continued to be in a depressed state with a generally declining level of cultivation in most parts of the country. And underlying this neglect of agriculture was the regime's drift toward a largely oil-based economy (Economist Intelligence Unit 1989: 12). Evidence of the depressed state of agriculture can be seen in the rise in Iraq's cereal import from 0.87 million tons in 1974 to 3.5 million tons in 1983 (The World Bank 1985: 185).

The collapse of the oil economy under the impact of the war with Iran and the decline in oil prices in the 1980s forced the government to decide in 1982 that it was time to allow the private sector to expand its role in the economy. This shift in policy was articulated in 1987 by the Iraqi president when he stated that "our brand of socialism cannot live without the private sector now, or after the war" (*Middle East Economic Digest* 1987: 18). To translate this shift in ideology into policy the government decided in 1987 to adopt an ambitious program of economic liberalization and privatization. The main features of the new program include the sale by the government of state lands, farms, and factories to the private sector. Other measures were announced to expand the role of the private sector in the banking industry, deregulation of the labor market, creation of a stock exchange, and opening up of the economy to foreign investment. The government decided also to reduce subsidies to state-owned enterprises and to relax its policy of setting price ceilings on a wide range of goods.

But the economy's structural problems of stagnant agriculture and industry, aggravated by the war conditions, could not be solved by a policy of privatization that was driven by political expediency. Instead of solving these problems the new policy led to higher inflation and speculation. The resulting decline in purchasing power caused further decline in the living standards of the overwhelming majority of the people. In the face of such failure the government found it necessary to retreat from its policies of economic liberalization when it decided to lower prices, decree a price freeze on many consumer goods, increase agricultural subsidies, renationalize some enterprises, and set lower profit margins for state and joint enterprises (*Middle East Economic Survey* 1989a: B3–B4; 1989b: B1–B2).

This vacillation in drawing clear lines of demarcation did not help the economy to adjust to the post-Iraq–Iran War conditions, a fact that ultimately led to the invasion of Kuwait, the Gulf War, and the present system of economic sanctions.

Under the current system of economic sanctions neither the government nor the private sector are independent agents capable of making their economic decisions free of the control which is exerted by the administrators of the sanctions. It can be said that under the current system of sanctions the economy has to respond to decisions and signals emanating from three centers of decision-making power. These are the private sector, the government, and the United Nations, with the latter divided between the Office of the Iraq Program and the Sanctions Committee.

Economic decisions taken by the private sector regarding levels of output must receive the approval of the government since, most likely, such decisions involve the import of some inputs. Such imports must be reconciled with the government's own import program and must receive the approval of the Office of the Iraq Program. Following such approval the program will have to clear the Sanctions Committee. Any objection by any member of the Sanctions Committee to any import contract will cause delay or derailment of the import of that particular commodity. Given the complementarity between inputs the delay in the approval of any one input will jeopardize output.

Government output of goods and services is similarly dependent on the United Nations import-approval system. Under these hierarchical conditions there is a great deal of delay, uncertainty, waste of time and resources, and inability to engage in planning for one production cycle, not to mention short-term or long-term planning. What is oppressive about this system is that the ultimate decisions about the economy are made by diplomats and international civil servants who have no association with the Iraqi economy yet their decisions have serious and long-term implications for it.

As to the future it is very difficult to analyze the respective roles of the private sector and the public sector so long as the sanctions are in place. But in postsanction Iraq the government will be the leading force in rehabilitating the economy and launching it along the path of economic growth. This will have to be the case for at least four reasons. First, the government is expected to continue the provisioning of food at low cost for a long time to come. Second, the scale of the problem is so daunting that only the government will be in a position to mobilize the necessary resources. Third, the reconstruction process cuts across the entire economy and the country that only the government can be entrusted with the task for reasons of regional balance and equity. Fourth, more foreign capital will be forthcoming if the process is being undertaken by the government than by a large number of private sector entities.

Following the completion of the initial phase the government will have to draw clearly defined spheres of economic activity for the private sector and the public sector. The experience of the economy over the last three decades does not bode well for the kind of administrative and political stability necessary for economic decision making. In a country like Iraq the government cannot be expected to relinquish the oil sector and continue to provide for health, education, and other social services, invest in infrastructure, and agricultural and rural improvement and development. The manufacturing industry, service sector activities, and agriculture could be left to the private sector. Regardless of the relative importance of either sector the most important factor is the stability of the relationship between the two sectors.

ECONOMIC DIVERSIFICATION

Iraq, for all intents and purposes, is a one-crop economy. The oil rent was utilized over the last half century in such a way as to deepen the phenomenon of this dependence rather than to attempt to overcome it. In other words, economic policy failed to achieve economic diversification. This failure is dramatically manifested in the agricultural sector which was transformed under the impact of the oil rent from an exporter of modest amounts of cereals to a massive importer of such commodities when between 1974 and 1989 Iraq's cereal imports increased from 0.87 million tons to 4.9 million tons. The country had to pay a heavy human and economic toll for this transformation in the aftermath of the Gulf crisis which triggered the imposition of embargo on trade with Iraq.

Public policy could play a supporting role in steering private sector investment in those lines of industry that would help the diversification process. Of particular importance, especially in the early years of the postsanctions era, will be the development of rural and agriculture-based industry in rural Iraq. Agricultural development should top the list of priorities in order to increase the contribution of this sector to the economy, to discourage further rural–urban migration, and to help in the process of economic diversification and food self-sufficiency. Looking at the rural–urban migration in Iraq over the last four decades it was found that in 1965 the ratio of urban population to total population was 50 percent but increased to 76 percent in 1998 and that over 70 percent of the urban population lived in three cities.

Economic policy in the postsanctions era must induce more investment in rural Iraq to offset the built-in urban bias common in all developing economies and stabilize and hopefully increase the ratio of rural population to total population and improve rural resource utilization to enhance the prospects for economic diversification.

POPULATION, POVERTY, AND UNEMPLOYMENT

Iraq's population increased from 11 million in 1970 to 22 million in 1998 and is projected to rise at an average annual rate of 2.7 percent during the period of 1998–2015 to reach 34 million in 2015. Labor participation and female participation rates in the labor force are expected to continue to rise as more people enter the labor force. Annual rates of growth of the labor force increased from 3 percent in 1965–1983 to 3.1 percent in 1980–2000. Rates of growth of both the population and the labor force are too high for an economy that has been moving from one crisis to another over the last twenty years while the proceeds from its main export have not been under its control since 1990 and its economy is still laboring under the impact of sanctions.

These high rates of growth of population and labor force will be magnified by the rising flow of female workers as time goes on. If the population growth rate is projected to rise by nearly 2.7 percent then the rate of economic growth must increase by more than this rate in order to allow for some increase in GDP per capita and in living standards. Raising GDP by that rate will require, of course, considerable investment which will ultimately be determined by how much resources Iraq will have at its disposal after making U.N. Security Council–mandated payments.

One of the major problems that will have to be dealt with and is affected by the GDP and population growth rates is the depth and breadth of poverty in Iraq. The Human Development Index (HDI) could be taken as a relatively acceptable measure of economic development. This measure, which had been developed by the United Nations Development Program, is a composite index based on three indicators: longevity, as measured by life expectancy at birth; educational attainment; and standard of living as measured by GDP per capita. According to this measure Iraq's HDI rank was 85 in 1990. This meant that there were 84 countries with higher human-development levels. By 1998 Iraq's human development ranking had collapsed to 126. This drastic decline in Iraq's ranking reflected the depth of the decline in Iraq's economic and social conditions with poverty reflecting the emergence of a number of new phenomena in the country.

It has been recognized early on in the sanctions decade that within a short time the quality of life changed from that of an emerging modern country or an upper middle-income country to one of a poor country affected by disaster. Having these sanctions in place for such a long time led the vast majority of people to a state of poverty and trapped them in conditions that could not be escaped without changing the forces that led to these conditions in the first place. And the longer these forces rule over the people the more difficult it will be to escape their impact. This is so because of the deep impact of poverty and poor environmental conditions, poor water quality, spread of malnutrition and disease, lack of quality and essential health care, disruption of family structures and relationships, diminished opportunity for work, high inflation, postponement of marriage for economic reasons, and increase in mental and psychological disorder.

But in order to alleviate poverty and its consequences, GDP must grow. While Iraq enjoyed significant growth in its GDP in the 1960s and 1970s, such growth turned into historical decline in the 1980s and 1990s. This decline in the economy plunged the population into unprecedented conditions of poverty, unemployment, and a generalized economic collapse.

These changes caused the commodity sectors to lose major segments of their traditional shares of the economy. It was estimated that in the period of 1991–1996 the construction sector lost 82 percent of its share in the economy while the industrial sector lost 52 percent and the combined loss of the commodity sectors was 43 percent. Such changes and losses were reflected in the enormous hidden unemployment which had been estimated at 50 percent while the open employment rate was estimated at 20 percent (United Nations Security Council Panel on Humanitarian Issues 1999: 9).

EDUCATION AND HUMAN CAPITAL INVESTMENT

Under normal economic and social conditions human capital formation in the form of education and skill acquisition is a prerequisite for economic development. This linkage between education and economic development had been recognized early on in the history of modern Iraq. Such recognition could be found in the free provisioning of formal schooling at all levels and in the effort to combat illiteracy. Available data indicate that by 1990 the enrollment rate for the age group of six to twenty-three years had reached 56 percent. Similarly, the adult literacy rate reached 89 percent in 1985. Under the impact of sanctions the enrollment rate had dropped to 26 percent in 1994 while the adult literacy rate declined to 59 percent in 1995. Moreover, the quality of education has deteriorated as many qualified teachers were driven out of their jobs due to low salaries (United Nations Security Council Panel on Humanitarian Issues 1999: 10). In addition, the length and severity of the sanctions era left a major portion of the educational infrastructure in need of rehabilitation. As the U.N. secretary-general noted in his May 2001 report, shortages of educational materials and equipment, substandard institutional resources, and pronounced disincentives to the academic cadres continue to inflict greater structural damage than the oil-for-food program can address. In addition to lack of resources under the program the secretary-general noted other contributing factors. First, there was the noticeable rise in the number of contracts for imports which the Sanctions Committee placed on hold. Second, there was the decision by the government of Iraq not to avail itself of funds available under the program for the education sector. In addition to these difficulties it was pointed out that the absence of a viable cash component coming from the program for this sector meant that program rehabilitation materials still had not been installed two years after their arrival in Iraq (United Nations 2001: ¶ 97, 98). It should be noted that the problems which plagued the education sector; that is, the combination of lack of resources, holds placed on contracts by the Sanctions Committee, and the failure of the government of Iraq to use available funds, were common to all other sectors of the economy.

Two particular challenges will face education and economic planners in postsanctions Iraq. First, how to allocate scarce resources to education in such a way as to meet the requirements of the economy. This means that the country will not be in a position to indulge in patterns of wasteful spending that were made possible in the oil-boom era of the 1970s. Education, in other words, will have to be narrowed to meet the specific requirements of the economy and employment opportunities, help reduce income inequality and alleviate poverty, and to help accelerate the process of economic growth.

The other challenge to education in postsanctions Iraq is the rectification of the loss of educated cadres to internal migration and brain drain. Professionals and skilled workers resorted to internal migration in the sanctions era in order improve their economic status or to protect against its erosion.

To the extent that such internal migrants are willing to return to their previous jobs, assuming a narrowing of the gap in compensation, then the task of the planners will be to invest heavily to upgrade and restore the skills of these professionals in their "new" jobs. As to those who left the country in search of better economic opportunities, the main task of planners would be to provide enough incentives to entice them to return to their original professional pursuits.

THE IMPERATIVE OF AGRICULTURAL DEVELOPMENT

In 1975 the urban population was 61 percent of Iraq's total population but increased to 76 percent in 1998 and projected to rise to 82 percent in 2015. This depopulation of rural Iraq was accompanied by a decline in the percentage of labor force in agriculture from 42 percent in 1981 to 11 percent in 1998. And the contribution of agriculture to GDP declined from 18 percent in the 1960s to a mere 6 percent by 1989. These changes in the structure of Iraq's population, labor force, and output indicate that economic planners have neglected the most important sector of Iraq's non-oil economy—agriculture.

There are several important considerations which dictate that a change in policy in the postsanctions era is necessary. In the first place the low level of the contribution of agriculture to GDP reflects agriculture's low productivity which tends to perpetuate rural–urban income inequality and the rural–urban migration that has been going on for decades. One of the consequences of the neglect of agriculture was Iraq's rising food-import dependency. And such dependency proved to be catastrophic once sanctions were imposed and Iraq was denied the freedom to import its food needs. Moreover, the manner in which the sanctions regime was organized and implemented continued the trend of agricultural neglect since Iraq is not allowed to spend oil revenue on domestic output, thus causing serious disincentives to agriculture.

Given Iraq's basic agricultural resources of land and water and given the anticipated multiplicity of claims on its oil revenue Iraq really cannot afford not to develop its agriculture. The development of this sector will, among other things, reduce Iraq's dependence on food imports and enable it to conserve considerable amounts of foreign exchange. Agricultural development can be undertaken in a context of rural and industrial growth policy that may provide incentives for migration in the opposite direction from urban centers to rural areas. Such development will also have the effect of relieving some of the pressures associated with urban unemployment.

But Iraq's prospects for rehabilitation and redevelopment of its agriculture and other sectors will be constrained by external factors such as foreign debt, compensation, and the sanctions regime itself.

THE DEBT AND COMPENSATION PROBLEMS

Iraq was a debt-free country until the 1980s when the length and the cost of the war with Iran exceeded all expectations. Iraq, sometime in the 1980s, changed status from a creditor to a debtor country. The decline in the oil sector and the massive financial requirements of the Iraq–Iran War forced the change in status.

Although there are no precise figures on the size of Iraq's foreign debt or what constitutes debt there are estimates of magnitudes. According to one such estimate Iraq's debt by the end of 1990 was $86 billion—$35 billion to Western governments and banks; $11 billion to the former Soviet Union and East European countries; and $40 billion to Arab countries (Bradsher 1991). But the government of Iraq had taken the position that the funds it received in the 1980s from the Arab Gulf states—Saudi Arabia, Kuwait, and the United Arab Emirates—were grants that were given to Iraq for its war effort. This position was made clear to the United Nations when the government stated that "Iraq total external debt and obligations" amounted as of December 13, 1990, to ID 13.1 billion, the equivalent of $42.1 billion, excluding interest (*Middle East Economic Survey* 1991: D6–D9). In the same submission to the United Nations the government projected total payment of installments and interest to be $75.1 billion at the end of 1995.This last figure should be more than $120 billion by now, assuming an annual interest rate of 8 percent. No other debtor country in the world has Iraq's debt burden in terms of the relationship of the debt to GDP or to exports.

Given the many claims on Iraq's financial resources in the postsanctions era it is difficult to see how Iraq will be in a position to pay the debt. Moreover, Iraq's freedom of action with respect to its foreign debt is constrained by UNSC resolution 687 of April 1991 which stated "that all Iraqi statements repudiating its foreign debt are null and void, and demands that Iraq scrupulously adhere to all its obligations concerning servicing and repayment of its foreign debt." Indeed, without the cancellation of all or most of the debt Iraq's economic crisis will be perpetuated.

The reiteration by the UNSC of Iraq's obligations to service its debt was made in the context of establishing in the same resolution Iraq's liability for any direct loss, damage, including environmental damage and the depletion of natural resources, or injury to foreign governments, nationals, and corporations. To effect payment for war damage the UNSC created a Compensation Fund to be administered by a Compensation Commission and decreed that 30 percent (25 percent effective 2001) of all oil sales be earmarked to the fund. As of April 30, 2001 the sum of $12.3 billion was transferred to the fund which had allotted $10.7 billion for payment of various claims (United Nations 2001: annex I).

The burden of compensation is far more serious than that of foreign debt if all claims to compensation, which have been estimated to be over $300 billion, were to be approved. A recently approved claim of $15.9 billion was awarded to Kuwait to compensate it for oil revenue which had been lost and for oil reserves which had been burnt off. It is worth noting that this one single award exceeds the combined sum of all the claims which the Compensation Commission has awarded so far. Leaving the size of the award aside, its validity was challenged on the grounds that the Compensation Commission seriously overstated the amount due to Kuwait to the extent that it challenges the integrity of the commission and the credibility of the process (Stauffer 2001: 20–22). If a major portion of the outstanding claims is to be approved by the commission and given Iraq's limited oil revenue a simple calculation seems to indicate that Iraq will be forced to pay these claims for a good part of this century if not the next century as well. The burden of compensation together with the burden of foreign debt will make the prospects for rehabilitation and development rather bleak. Without some serious relief from these two external burdens, the Iraqi economy will be condemned to stagnation for a long time to come.

THE BURDEN OF SANCTIONS

Iraq will not be able to do much by way of rehabilitation and development so long as any sanctions regime is in place. This is so because sanctions rob the country of its freedom to make decisions regarding resource allocation and macroeconomic and growth policies. The regime of sanctions that was imposed on Iraq was unusually restrictive, distortive, and punitive. From its very inception the sanctions regime failed to allow for the importation of sufficient food and medicines as the UNSC disregarded the recommendations of the U.N. secretary-general for higher allocation. The negative consequences of sanctions for the health and well-being of the population and the economy were extensively documented by U.N. specialized agencies. And there was a repeated reiteration of the fact that the oil-for-food program was not a program of rehabilitation, not to mention development.

Dealing with the program on its own terms, one is struck by a number of rigidities which diluted its effectiveness. The complicated and cumbersome import procedure did not allow for the effective utilization of inputs. The practice by the Sanctions Committee of placing holds (blocking) on so many complementary imports rendered other allowed imports useless, thus defeating the purpose for which a particular import contract was drawn up in the first place. Imports of equipment and spare parts for the oil industry that were placed on hold played havoc with the projected growth of oil output. The absence of cash component to be spent on the installation of imported equipment rendered such imports useless. The absence of cash flow to be spent in Iraq, especially on agricultural commodities, caused that sector to stagnate.

The biggest drawback of the sanctions regime was its failure to provide a predictable stream of cash flow into the economy. Such cash flows would have helped spur economic activity, increased employment, and helped start the process of rehabilitation. What happened instead was the opposite as sanctions stifled economic activity, increased unemployment, and created a high degree of uncertainty regarding the future. Moreover, the net effect of the oil-for-food program was that the well-being and even the survival of the population has become increasingly dependent on decisions of the UNSC that were to a considerable extent guided by political considerations.

This new form of dependency and the pivotal intermediary role that the government had to play between its own people and the UNSC resulted in yet another form of dependence on the government that the people found themselves having to cope with. This is so since physical survival became dependent for the majority of the people on the food-ration system, the content and the level of which are determined by the government on the one hand and the UNSC on the other.

The significance of this new form of dependency derives from the fact that it is rooted in a system of scarcity of the basic necessities of life in a country where the central government is the sole provider of these basic necessities for most of the people. In depriving the people of the means of their economic activity the sanctions regime contributed to the undermining of political freedom. The implication of this is that sanctions narrowed the room for political action to challenge government policies, let alone attempting to change the government.

Another important implication of the sanctions regime for the future of the country is its reinforcement of the relative importance of the oil sector in the economy. It was indicated in earlier chapters that contrary to proclamations by successive regimes in Iraq that oil should be utilized to diversify the economy such statements were not translated into concrete development policies. On the contrary and as the analysis in Chapter 3 has shown all development plans had the ultimate effect of expanding rather than contracting the role of the oil sector in the economy. The rising importance of the oil sector in the economy reached its peak in the decade of the 1970s when the phenomenal increase in oil revenue corrupted development planning by increasing allocations to projects without having determined their economic feasibility or benefits.

The series of decisions that the UNSC took in the context of relaxing the sanctions were all based on the revenue which the oil sector was assumed to be able to generate. The oil sector was called upon to provide funds to import food, medicine, and meet some of the needs of the infrastructure. Iraq's oil was also looked upon as the provider of funds for the Compensation Fund, the U.N. Special Commission as well as the various mushrooming U.N. administrative agencies and structures dealing with the Iraq question. The oil sector was also tapped to provide funds for itself in order to ensure the flow of oil in order to meet the various claims on Iraq. In order to achieve all these goals the United Nations created several groups of oil experts whose task is to keep the UNSC well informed of oil sector developments.

Such preoccupation with the oil sector was unavoidable once the UNSC made the decision in 1991 that Iraq should not be allowed to start the process of rebuilding its infrastructure and return the economy to some resemblance of normal activity. With this decision in place oil became the sole source of funds. Yet even this vital source of funds for Iraq and the United Nations was not allowed to function like other oil sectors in the region.

In order for the oil sector to function normally a certain amount of investment is necessary for maintenance and expansion. In the absence of expansion and in the absence of investment for normal repair, maintenance, and replacement, the oil sector is bound to decline. And this is precisely what happened to the oil sector under sanctions.

As was stated earlier the UNSC must have made the decision in the early stages of sanctions not to allow the Iraqi economy to return to a state of normalcy. And for the first six years of the sanctions disputes between the government of Iraq and the UNSC prevented the country from exporting its oil. This near closure of the oil sector for such a long time led to serious deterioration in all facets of this sector. Following the resumption of oil export in December 1996 the country was not in a position to invest in the oil sector, thus allowing the deterioration to continue with actual output remaining below capacity production.

An important outcome of this state of affairs was Iraq's inability to produce enough oil to generate enough revenue to meet the ceiling set by UNSC. This happened in the fourth and fifth phases (May 1998–May 1999) of the oil-for-food program when oil prices had fallen to such levels that Iraq could not export enough oil to meet the ceiling of $5.2 billion per phase of six months. It was clear at the time that assigning a ceiling for oil exports was not a viable policy in light of the deepening crisis in Iraq and the need of U.N. programs such as the Compensation Fund for ever-higher levels of revenue.

The need for funds forced UNSC to reexamine its policy of continuing the export embargo on oil equipment and spare parts to Iraq. It was not until 1998 that UNSC decided to allow Iraq to import up to $300 million of oil industry equipment per phase (raised to $600 million in 2000) in order to increase production of oil for export but only after a U.N.–appointed group of oil industry experts noted the lamentable state of Iraq's oil industry and recommended that Iraq be allowed to import spare parts and equipment for the oil sector. But the degradation of Iraq's oil industry did not end as the UNSC's own Sanctions Committee placed holds on some of the contracts to import such equipment.

The actions which the UNSC and the Sanctions Committee took vis-à-vis Iraq's oil industry meant that the oil industry could never reach its full potential so long as its performance is externally determined. By first refusing and then delaying the import of the necessary capital goods for the industry's maintenance and expansion meant that the industry continued to be mired in its lamentable state.

But the oil industry was not the only sector that had to function under such extraordinary conditions. Its plight is illustrative of what happened to all other importing sectors, except for food, that were either denied the import of necessary inputs or had some of their import contracts placed on hold. Thus, during the period from December 1996 to April 2001, the percentage of the value of contracts placed on hold by the Sanctions Committee to the value of contracts approved by the committee was 33 percent for oil spares; 26 percent for food-handling equipment; 19 percent for health; 31 percent for electricity; 36 percent for water and sanitation; 31 percent for agriculture; 27 percent for education; and 80 percent for telecommunication and transport. For the entire import program the amount was 20 percent (United Nations Office of the Iraq Programme 2000: 1–3).

It is worth noting that the imports contracts which the Sanctions Committee had placed on hold had already been approved by the U.N. specialists both in Baghdad and New York. This meant that the infrastructure and the economy of Iraq were subject to more than one level of external approval, both located in the United Nations, that had no direct contacts with the realities of the Iraqi scene. In other words, the sanctions had the effect of creating more than several command centers of decision making without the benefit of coordination among these decision makers, not to mention the government of Iraq. The consequences of such disjointed and contradictory policy making for the economy cannot be underestimated in terms of wasted resources and missed economic opportunities.

Moreover, the absence of a cash component to be spent in Iraq and the UNSC refusal to allow the purchase of Iraqi-produced agricultural commodities illustrate the dilemma of Iraq. It has been recognized by the UNSC that in addition to the import program Iraq needed also a certain amount of cash flow to install imported equipment and provide training and maintenance. Yet the government of Iraq and the UNSC have failed to agree over modalities for the utilization of such a cash component. In the education sector, for instance, the absence of a viable cash component meant that 27 percent of program rehabilitation materials had not been installed two years after their arrival. This problem was recognized by the U.N. secretary-general as a serious impediment to the implementation of the program when he said that an increasing range of equipment is being imported with insufficient local resources available to undertake installation, training, and maintenance. This makes the arrangement for local procurement of goods and services and the provision of a cash component more necessary than ever, as it is essential for the efficient use of imported commodities (United Nations 2001: ¶ 98, 127).

This admission by the secretary-general of the program's glaring deficiency combined with his recommendation is a clear invitation that a drastic overhaul of the entire program is rather overdue.

THE BURDEN OF OIL

Iraq's economic and social crisis cannot be attributed solely to the deficiencies of the oil-for-food program or the sanctions regime. The sanctions regime and the program had the effect of aggravating and perpetuating the crisis with long-term implications for the society and the economy. It is important to remember that the crisis emerged as a result of certain economic and noneconomic policies which successive governments in Iraq implemented over the last two decades.

One of the most serious failures of public policy in the oil era was the failure to develop the country's considerable agricultural resource endowment. Up to the early years of the oil era Iraq was a net exporter of cereals. But the nature of the land tenure system and the landlord-biased agricultural development policies drove large segments of the poor peasantry to urban Iraq. This, together with the failure to actually invest what had been appropriated to the agricultural sector, led to decline in productivity and output. The agrarian reform which changed the structure of land ownership in favor of landless peasants was not followed by enabling policies such as agricultural credit, extension service, proper irrigation, and marketing. This failure combined with the urban-biased development policies further accelerated the migration of peasants to Iraq's urban centers.

The pressure of urban population growth and the rise in personal income increased food consumption and therefore the demand for agricultural commodities. Since domestic production could not keep up with the rise in demand Iraq had to resort to importing increasing amounts of food items. Since Iraq's foreign exchange earnings continued to increase, the rise in food imports did not present a balance-of-trade problem. Indeed, Iraq was, prior to 1981, in the enviable position of being able to meet its rising food-imports bill and see its foreign reserves rising at the same time. A case can be made to the effect that because of the availability of the oil income Iraq did not find it necessary to increase its agricultural sector productivity and output to meet its rising food requirements. The relative decline of the agricultural sector was matched by a similar decline in manufacturing industry in spite of the impressive high rate of growth that this sector exhibited in the decade of the 1970s over that of the previous decade. But here again the combination of larger population and higher oil-generated personal income led to higher level of demand for manufactured imports which domestic output could not meet.

As was shown in Chapter 3, successive governments allocated increasingly larger amounts of funds for investment in the industrial sector but failed to actually spend these allocations. The net effect of this failure was the failure to diversify the economy away from the oil sector and the rise in Iraq's dependence on imported consumer goods, industrial inputs, and capital goods. It is safe to say that in the absence of easy access to the oil income Iraq would have followed a different policy of industrialization that would have helped in the direction of economic diversification.

Another aspect of Iraq's economy that was deeply affected by the availability of oil revenue was taxation. The tendency on the part of the state to spread the benefits of oil revenue affected the working of the fiscal system. The state in the oil era could increase spending on social programs such as health, education, subsidies, income maintenance, and the like without having to raise taxes to cover the expanded spending. This policy derives from at least two elements. The first is the recognition that the oil wealth and the revenue from it belongs to the nation as a whole. The second element is the desire of the state to ensure the allegiance of its citizens, especially when the country is run by an authoritarian system.

One of the implications of this state of affairs is that the government can now commit itself to all forms and levels of spending without the need to secure the approval of its citizens. In other words, the government does not need its citizen as tax payers. The state, thanks to oil revenue, can now expand social programs, and increase the size of its civil bureaucracy and the military at will. The government under this revenue arrangement can even take the country to war, as it actually did, without having to ask its citizens to contribute to the cost of executing the war.

The evolution of military spending in Iraq prior to the Gulf War illustrates this point. In 1970 the ratio of Iraq's armed forces to its labor force was 2.9 percent but increased to 13.4 percent in 1980 to rise again to 21.3 percent by the time the war with Iran ended in 1988. By the same token the country's military spending increased from less than $1 billion in 1970 or 19 percent of that year's GDP to $3.1 billion or 22.8 of GDP in 1975. By 1980, the government raised military spending more than sixfold of the 1975 level to close to $20 billion, 38.8 percent of that year's GDP. Between 1980 and 1988 military spending continued to rise with its share of GDP rising up to close to 60 percent in 1984. In relation to oil revenue during 1980–1988 Iraq received $98.4 billion in oil revenue but spent $178.2 billion on its armed forces. In other words, Iraq's military spending during that period amounted to 181 percent of its oil revenue (Alnasrawi 1994: 92–96).

But there are other implications for the economy as a result of the relationship between oil revenue and military expenditures. As the size of the armed forces increases, so does the size of support workers in the civilian economy who are called upon to supply the nonmilitary requirement of the military. This in turn leads to the unavoidable diversion of workers from the nonmilitary sectors of the economy and consequently creating problems for the civilian sectors. This may be seen in the decline of the ratio of agricultural employment to labor force from 42 percent in 1975 to 12.5 percent in 1985–1988 (Alnasrawi 1994: 92–96). As the war continued and as the size of the armed forces continued to increase the government was forced to recruit large numbers of workers from other Arab countries, thus creating a new set of problems associated with the influx of foreign workers that had to be dealt with during and after the war.

The decline in oil revenue in the 1980s combined with heavy government spending on the military and the weakening of the economy set in an unprecedented inflationary spiral as the consumer price index rose from an average annual rate of 5 percent in the decade of the 1960s to 18 percent in 1975; 95 percent in 1980; 139 percent in the following year and all the way up 369 percent in 1988 (Ali and Al-Ganabi 1992: 91–113).

But while the oil sector provided the financial resources to go to war it also proved to be Iraq's burden during the war. One of the earliest economic victims of the war was the oil sector that suffered extensive damage from the bombing which caused Iraq's oil output to decline from 2.6 MBD in 1980 to 0.9 MBD in 1981. The decline in output was accompanied by a decline in oil revenue from $26 billion to $10 billion respectively. The combination of lower demand for oil in general and the continued war conditions pushed Iraq's oil revenue to $6.9 billion in 1986. The decline in oil revenue was partially offset in the initial stages of the war by loans from Arab and non-Arab countries and by drawing down on Iraq's own foreign-held reserves. But as the war dragged on the government had no choice but to introduce austerity measures, start the privatization process, and suspend development planning. Paradoxically, in spite of its lower contribution to the national economy the oil sector became the one sector that could have provided the means to solve Iraq's economic crisis. Against the lower level of oil revenue the government had to balance a number of important and urgent claims, including the need for more civilian imports, expenditure on reconstruction and development, financing ordinary government programs, funding an ambitious military industrialization program, and foreign debt. In the meantime inflation had become a serious structural problem, as was noted earlier.

And this is precisely what the government of Iraq found itself faced with in the post-Iraq–Iran War period. The dilemma for the government was the disparity between its need for high levels of oil income and its lack of ability to generate those incomes since world oil market conditions have changed to such an extent that OPEC was too marginalized to influence them in its favor. The lack of discipline on the part of some OPEC member countries such as Kuwait and the changing market conditions in favor of non-OPEC oil-producing countries led to a severe decline in the price of oil which in turn set in motion certain developments that resulted in Iraq's invasion of Kuwait.

OIL AND THE FUTURE OF IRAQ

It has been shown in Chapter 3 that successive governments in Iraq had pledged themselves to certain common development goals and strategies. To be certain there were differences in emphasis reflecting the ideological inclinations of a particular political leadership but by and large governments had similar objectives. The one major difference between the pre-1958 monarchy and the post-1958 republican regime was the land-reform system which changed the configuration of political and economic power away from large landowners.

Iraq's economic goals were shaped by the continued rise in oil revenue and tended to focus on improving living standards. This was not surprising since the oil wealth belongs to the nation as a whole. The extent of sharing by the government of this income from oil took several forms and was achieved through different channels.

The first and most significant way of sharing was for the government to increase its spending in the local economy, thus generating new oil-based employment and income. The provision of free or subsidized social services such as health care, education, income security, housing, and food subsidies was another way to spread the benefits of the oil income. The extent of the redistribution of oil income in this fashion was governed by the economic and political beliefs of this or that political leadership which happened to be in power. Thus the monarchy was less inclined to have the same welfare programs as the republican regimes that followed it. There was also the constituency which any given government was inclined to serve. Again, under the monarchy large landowners and tribal sheikhs were thought to have provided the legitimacy it needed to rule the country. By contrast post-monarchy regimes tended to secure their legitimacy among urban middle classes, workers, farm workers, and small landowners. Another reason for spreading the oil wealth and income was the simple desire of the government to remain in power which would be enhanced through targeted government spending.

A second objective of policy was simply to develop the country by developing its human and natural resources. An important first step in this direction was the creation of a network of infrastructure projects that protect, facilitate, and increase national output. Investment of the oil revenue in flood control and dam projects was looked at as an important way to protect people and assets and to generate hydroelectric power thus contributing to economic growth. Along the same lines investment in ports, transportation, communication, and in power and water plants was looked at as improving the country's economic and geographical cohesion and enhancing its prospects for economic growth.

Another objective of economic development was to lessen the dependence of the country and its economy on one sector—oil. This was an avowed goal that all regimes committed themselves to yet they all failed to attain. There are several explanations for this failure. First, government policy in general had the effect if not the design of encouraging consumption. As employment opportunities and personal income grew so did the demand for a whole array of consumer goods that the domestic economy was not prepared to supply. To meet this rise in demand and expectation imports were allowed to increase. The availability of foreign exchange made the decision to increase imports rather easy since the country had a very healthy balance of payments. To continue this rising level of consumption in both the private and the public sector required the continued increase in oil revenue. And by sheer coincidence of historical forces such increase actually occurred.

Iraq was helped by two important changes in the oil industry. The first such change was Iraq's successful nationalization in 1972 of the bulk of its oil sector which was foreign-owned. The second was the oil price explosion of

1973–1974. The combined effect of these two changes pushed Iraq's oil revenue from $0.8 billion in 1970 to $26.1 billion in 1980. This in turn allowed Iraq to increase its imports from $0.5 billion to $13.8 billion during the same period. By contrast Iraq's non-oil exports during the same period increased from a negligible $63 million to a negligible $212 million. As oil revenue continued to rise during the decade of the 1970s it had the effect of overwhelming and distorting the economy. The availability of oil revenue allowed the government to increase its spending without having to raise tax revenue. The problem with such a policy stance is the fact that it is not sustainable since it is dependent on what happened to the oil sector.

In addition to the general economic factors that are associated with oil revenue, income, windfall, or rent there is also the uniquely Iraqi factor which played a crucial role in the demise of the economy and society and which turned oil from a national asset into a national burden. In summing up Iraq's experience with its oil income Amuzegar concluded that the oil bounty brought Iraq a stagnant agriculture, high-cost manufactures and rising dependence on foreign food, foreign labor, and foreign skills (Amuzegar 1999: 137).

It can be said that between the time oil revenue started its upward trend in the early 1950s and the implementation of the oil nationalization measures and the oil price increases of the early 1970s, Iraq by and large made the correct decisions regarding the exploitation of this wealth. In those two decades a development machinery was set up, plans were drawn up and implemented, studies were made and consultant advice was sought. One may disagree with the pattern of appropriations and with the level of spending but policy makers attempted to rectify problems and drawbacks as time went by. It is important to recall that in the early years of its experimentation with development planning the country lacked many of the prerequisites for development, not the least of which was technical expertise and cadres. But as time went on many of these shortcomings were rectified and the country was able to utilize and build on its accumulated experience.

But the drastic changes in the oil sector in the 1970s combined with the changing nature of the political leadership in the country changed every thing in Iraq and led to the kind of collapse from which the country is attempting to escape. This sudden change placed at the disposal of the government unprecedented amounts of funds to pursue multiple policy objectives without having to worry about the availability of funds to accomplish these objectives.

The prospects for economic growth in the future are hampered by several factors including the sanctions themselves, size of oil revenue, and external claims and the nature of the political regime that will rule in postsanctions Iraq.

As was indicated earlier sanctions initially exacerbated Iraq's economic crisis and then perpetuated it. Clearly, a two-tier decision-making process by the government of Iraq and by the United Nations cannot be conducive to the functioning of any economy, let alone the Iraqi economy which has been in crisis for more than two decades. Simple economics dictates that such a decision-making process regarding the level of output, consumption, investment, exports, imports, and resource allocation will end up causing waste, uncertainty, and stagnation.

As to external claims, they arise from two sources. Iraq entered the decade of the 1990s with a heavy burden of external debt due mainly to the war with Iran and the oil price collapse of the mid-1980s. This debt has ballooned now to more than $120 billion. The second source of external claims is related to decisions by the UNSC that a certain percentage of Iraq's oil revenue be marked to the UNSC–created Compensation Fund to make payment to those who were entitled to reparation as a result of Iraq's invasion of Kuwait. Although individual claims have been settled corporate and government claims against Iraq are still standing and have been estimated to be in excess of $250 billion.

The biggest challenge that will face Iraq in the postsanctions era is the nature of the political system that will determine the pattern of allocating scarce resources for the benefit of the broader population. Serious questions regarding the future of the country will have to be debated and eventually formulated into concrete economic and social policies. This in turn requires the creation of a civil society capable of influencing and shaping policies. In other words the first and most important task would be to create genuine democratic institutions that would provide for accountability and transparency and the peaceful transfer of political power through elections.

In the absence of such political and cultural overhaul Iraq's economic and social conditions are bound to remain stagnant and crisis-ridden since there is no reason to believe that the catastrophes of the 1980s and the 1990s will not be repeated again. After all, given the oil money and the nature of the present political establishment one is compelled to conclude that there will be an external crisis along the lines of the historical pattern of the last two decades. It is also significant to note that the regime never hesitated to use its economic resources to benefit its supporters at the expense of the majority of the population in times of sanctions and scarcities.

An example of income discriminatory measures may be found in the series of economic decisions which the government took at various times in the 1990s. Thus, in the midst of the severe conditions of humanitarian emergency that engulfed the overwhelming majority of the population the government did not hesitate to single out certain groups for special economic benefits and privileges. Thus in October 1994 it decided to favor the military, the police and security, and other elite forces with special monthly allowances and other privileges. While these privileges cover some 3.5 million people the other 17.2 million Iraqis, or 83 percent of the population, were left out of the program of privileges (FAO 1995: 7–8, 19).

In addition to these discriminatory measures the government uses its fiscal resources and the country's scarce supplies of food in other forms to extend favors to its supporters or penalize its political opponents. While the Kurdish people of the north were subjected to internal embargo the government interfered with the flow of food to the inhabitants of the southern marshes as well (United Nations 1996: 401). In contrast, it was found that military officers and members of the Baath Party enjoy their own food distribution network through special cooperatives. In addition, government and Baath party officials receive bribes and gifts by virtue of the important administrative positions to which they may be assigned. Moreover, the inner circle of the leadership does not appear to be touched by any economic hardships affecting their access to food and health care. Furthermore, it is evident that there is discrimination within the country on regional basis. The central cities of Iraq, especially Tikrit and parts of Baghdad, continue to enjoy preferred distribution of limited resources. According to a July 1995 UNICEF–sponsored report it was found that 50 percent of the rural population of the central and southern part of Iraq (and 90 percent in one southern governorate) have no access to potable water (United Nations 1996: 401).

The government also enacted special measures designed to benefit certain elite groups to ensure their continued loyalty to the regime. The decorated military personnel and party officials were granted salary increments ranging between 150 percent and 300 percent; they were offered to buy state land for home building at discounts ranging up to 80 percent of the price of the land; they were offered to purchase state agricultural land at discounts ranging up to 80 percent of the value of the land; public sector assets may be bought by these individuals, their wives, and their children at discounts ranging up to 30 percent of the sale price. And in September 1995 an edict was issued which confined the sale of state and state-owned enterprise assets to those decorated individuals and the friends of the president and their families ("General Attack on Citizens' Livelihood" 1996).

It would be no exaggeration to say that in Iraq the regime is based on the personal rule of the president who exercises his rule using a combination of fear and rewards. In this predatory state power is concentrated in this single ruler who occupies the apex of a clientele-list pyramid. In such a predatory system public and private resources are melded and public office serves as a means for the creation of private wealth. (Holsti 2000: 250–253).

Given this state of governance decision making tends to be concentrated in the hands of one person who is the president of the state, the prime minister, the chairman of the Revolution Command Council, the commander in chief, among other important positions. Clearly, this is a dangerous state of affairs since there is an absence of accountability, transparency, and periodic transfer of power as the ruling political party has been in power since 1968.

The danger of this form of concentration of power was seen in the decisions to initiate the war with Iran and to invade Kuwait with all the catastrophic consequences which flowed from them. It can be said that it was the oil wealth that provided the means for the building and expanding of the military which in turn set the stage for the Iraq–Iran War. In other words, if the government of Iraq did not have the access to oil revenue which it had and the form of government was democratic rather than authoritarian the brutal and destructive war of the 1980s could have been avoided.

Similarly, it was oil that dominated the course of events which led to the invasion of Kuwait. It was the decline in the price of oil in the late 1980s coupled with Kuwait's noncompliance with OPEC's output decision and Iraq's insistence that Kuwait was resorting to diagonal drilling to pump oil from the Iraqi side of the Rumaila oil field that eventually led to the fateful decision to invade Kuwait.

While the rise of oil revenue was responsible for Iraq's higher rates of economic growth in the 1970s, the decline in this important source of income was a contributing factor to the low and negative rates of growth that characterized the economy in the 1980s and 1990s. This nullification of growth pushed per capita GDP in the 1990s to the levels that prevailed in the 1940s.

Under these conditions an argument can be made that in the particular context of Iraq oil proved to be a burden in this particular phase of Iraq's history.

REFERENCES

Ali, A.M.S., and Al-Ganabi, H.A.J. (1992). "The Political Economy of Inflation in Iraq, 1988–1992." *Arab Economic Journal* 1 (1): 91–113 (in Arabic).

Alnasrawi, A. (1994). *The Economy of Iraq: Oil, Wars, Destruction of Development and Prospects, 1950–2010*. Westport, Conn.: Greenwood Press.

Amuzegar, J. (1999). *Managing the Oil Wealth: OPEC's Windfalls and Pitfalls*. London: I. B. Tauris.

Bradsher, K. (1991). "War Damages and Old Debts Could Exhaust Iraq's Assets." *The New York Times*, March 1.

Economist Intelligence Unit. (1989). *Country Report, Iraq* 4. London: Economist Intelligence Unit.

Food and Agriculture Organization. (1995). *Evaluation of Food and Nutrition Situation in Iraq*. Rome: Food and Agriculture Organization.

"General Attack on Citizens' Livelihood and Numerous Privileges to the Followers." (1996). *Tareeq Al-Shaab*. June (in Arabic).

Holsti, K. J. (2000). "Political Causes of Humanitarian Emergencies." In *War, Hunger, and Displacement*, ed. E. W. Nafziger, E. Wayne Nafziger, Frances Stewart, and Raimo Vayrynen. Oxford, U.K.: Oxford University Press.

Middle East Economic Digest. (1987). March 28.

Middle East Economic Survey. (1989a). January 23.

———. (1989b). September 18.

———. (1990). February 12.

———. (1991). May 13.

Springborg, R . (1986). "Infitah, Agrarian Transformation, and the Elite Consolidation in Contemporary Iraq." *The Middle East Journal* 40 (1): 33–52.

Stauffer, T. (2001). "Compensation to Kuwait: Multi-Billion Dollar Miscalculation." *Middle East International*, February 9, pp. 20–22.

United Nations. (1996). *The United Nations and the Iraq–Kuwait Conflict 1990–1996*. New York: United Nations.

CHAPTER 9

Conclusions and Prospects

Following the end of World War II European colonial powers were forced to abandon their colonies in many parts of the world. As the former colonies became independent states they found themselves faced with, among other things, the monumental task of economic development as centuries of foreign rule had distorted and bankrupted their economies. Yet these newly independent states were in need of foreign capital since the inherited low level of national income made it virtually impossible to generate the necessary saving for investment in infrastructure and industrial and agricultural development. Yet in the vast grouping of countries, which came to be known as the Third World, few countries had natural resource endowments, the demand for which proved to be inexhaustible. Iraq was one such country that was endowed with a considerable amount of oil reserves. Although Iraq's oil was discovered and exported in the first half of the twentieth century it was not until the second half of that century that oil became the central force in the economic life of the country and the life of its people. Thus in the span of four short decades culminating in 1990 one can make the case that oil, or more precisely, the management of the oil wealth was responsible in varying degrees for all the major changes that engulfed Iraq, be it economic development, the Iraq–Iran War, or the invasion of Kuwait and the economic sanctions under which the country is still laboring. In the following pages a summary review will be undertaken of the forces that transformed Iraq from a relatively prosperous country to a country with a failed economy struggling to regain its promising recent past.

OIL AND THE STATE

In Iraq oil and all other subsoil minerals belong to the people of Iraq. This means that the state is called upon to obtain, on behalf of the people, the maximum possible benefits from exploiting this natural resource. For a good part of the twentieth century Iraq and its government were under direct or indirect British rule. This fact and the fact that Iraq was ill-equipped to develop its oil reserves paved the way to a consortium of multinational oil companies to be given a long-term concession to develop the country's oil reserves. Under these arrangements and for a good part of the last century, the government was a passive recipient of a fixed sum of revenue per barrel of oil export.

The second half of the last century, especially in the decade of the 1970s, brought about fundamental changes in the oil industry, including a significant increase in the share of the government in the oil rent, the nationalization of the oil industry, the OPEC-led increase in the price of crude oil, and the transformation of the Iraqi economy to an oil-dependent economy.

The first-stage increase in oil revenue, from a mere $20 million in 1950 to $521 million in 1970, was brought about by changing the fiscal terms in favor of all oil-producing countries. This change prompted the government to utilize the revenue to build a modern infrastructure and improve the performance of other sectors of the economy. Toward this end a development board was created and was tasked to see to it that the oil income was spent according to a series of development plans. And as oil revenue continued to rise the development board responded by revising its plans by adding new projects without having analyzed the feasibility of implementing these plans. This in turn led to the constant failure of plans to invest their appropriated funds. This failure to spend budgeted funds and the rising needs of the current budget led policy makers to divert funds from capital spending to ordinary expenditure. This diversion was also made necessary as a response to the rising discontent that development spending tended to benefit those who were already well-off, especially the landed classes.

As the revenue from oil continued to rise in the decades of the 1960s and the 1970s and as political changes brought new leaderships from the middle classes to power the role of oil in government finance continued to rise. This phenomenon was accentuated by the desire on the part of new leaders to expand the military on the one hand and to fund social welfare programs, especially in the ever-growing urban centers, on the other hand.

The decade of the 1970s witnessed major qualitative and quantitative changes in the oil sector and the relationship of the government to it. The first major change was the success of the government in nationalizing the oil sector in

1972. This act completed the initial steps taken in 1961. This nationalization which gave the government the full amount of the oil rent was followed by the 1973–1974 OPEC-led price increases. Suffice it to say that Iraq's income from oil jumped twenty-sixfold from $1 billion in 1971 to $26 billion in 1980.

This sharp increase in the revenue from oil transformed the political economy of Iraq in many ways. The most important change was the belief on the part of the government that the new levels of income would continue into the future. The newly found income overwhelmed the absorptive capacity of the economy and development plans and mechanisms.

The state under the leadership of the ruling Baath Party, which came to power in 1968, was quick to utilize the windfall in many directions and at many levels. In the first place the state no longer needed its citizens as a source of necessary revenue to meet ordinary budget requirements. On the contrary, the state was now in a position to embark on all sorts of social and welfare programs to distribute the oil income. In the meantime the government found itself in a position to vastly expand the civil service, the military and the security services, and other instruments of coercion. Similarly, the state increased spending on the infrastructure, thus increasing the control of the central authority over the economy and at the same time facilitating the movement of goods and persons in the context of its development plans. As to the traditional neglect of the agricultural sector the availability of foreign exchange made it easy to resort to imports to meet any deficit in food requirements.

The availability of foreign exchange made it easy to increase all sorts of imports of consumer goods, inputs, and capital goods and services as the balance of trade was registering surplus year after year, leading to a sizeable accumulation of foreign reserves.

Another consequence of this new oil order was the ability of the state to award large numbers of lucrative contracts to existing or yet to be created Iraqi firms to build infrastructure and other projects. This policy led to the rise of an entrepreneurial social class that became dependent on the government and the continued flow of oil for its survival and growth.

Having established full control over the oil sector and having entrenched itself in the economy and in all state institutions the Baath leadership turned to the armed forces to increase their numbers and to lavish on them all sorts of modern military equipment imported mainly from France and the former Soviet Union. In all these developments decision making was concentrated in the hands of a small number of individuals in the Revolution Command Council who were not accountable to any other institutions in the country.

By all accounts the decade of the 1970s was the best decade in Iraq's modern economic history. All economic indicators, except for agriculture, registered impressive gains not likely to be repeated for a long time to come. The country was on the verge of another decade of growth when in September 1980 a handful of men under the leadership of the Iraqi president decided to take the country to war with Iran, a war that lasted eight years and changed everything for Iraq for a long time to come.

The other side of the sharp rise in oil revenue was the very highly risky conditions of dependency on the international economy. The volumes of oil exports and the price at which oil is exported are variables which in the final analysis are determined by forces of supply and demand in the world oil market. This meant that the viability of Iraq's economy as well as the viability of the state itself has become highly dependent on the international economy and in some cases on political decisions made outside its borders. Equally serious, Iraq's loss of its food self-sufficiency in the oil era increased the risk of exposure to embargo and boycott. No less serious is the fact that most of Iraq's industrial output has become dependent on imported inputs, capital goods, technology, and services. Such dependency proved to be devastating once the United Nations Security Council imposed sanction on all trade with Iraq in 1990.

The price Iraq had to pay for not diversifying its economy and for not developing its agriculture proved to be exorbitant in the context of the Iraq–Iran War. While Iraq was able to coast along for the first two years of the war its ability to withstand the pressures of the war proved to be limited as Iraq found itself unable to fund social programs and execute the war at the same time. Once Iraq's income from oil plummeted from $26 billion in 1980 to $10 billion in 1981 it had to revise all its spending plans. Running down foreign reserves and becoming a debtor country may help but only up to a point. Thus the government found itself reducing the scope of social programs, abandoning or curtailing development projects, imposing austerity measures, and resorting to foreign loans and supplier credit after having exhausted its reserves of foreign currency. In short, Iraq emerged from the inconclusive war of the 1980s with vast human casualties, all kinds of social problems, a smaller economy, heavy foreign debt, and an oil sector in need of heavy investment. Moreover, the good times which the government had told the people would return after the war were far from being attained any time soon. Furthermore, Iraq's economic woes were not helped by the drastic change in the international oil industry.

The decade of the 1980s, especially its second half, witnessed a drastic decline in the demand for OPEC oil as oil from other producing regions was competing with OPEC oil and as economic conditions were stagnant in many countries throughout the world. In short, at the end of the decade Iraq found itself forced to cope with a weak economy suffering from high inflation and high unemployment, a smaller oil sector, and a heavy debt burden. In the meantime the population had increased by one-third during the decade of the 1980s. The prospects of extricating itself from the combination of such forces were dim indeed. Yet the government had nowhere to go but to the oil sector in the hope that it could provide at least a temporary solution to the crisis.

But the contribution of the oil sector itself was ultimately determined by forces outside the control of the Iraqi government. This was made painfully clear when some fellow members of OPEC such as Kuwait among others chose to produce above their allotted production quotas which in turn deprived Iraq of billions of dollars in oil revenue.

Kuwait's wealth, oil reserves, and oil industry must have been on top of the list of factors that persuaded the government of Iraq to invade and annex its neighbor to the south in August 1990. This proved to be a catastrophic blunder since instead of acquiring Kuwait's wealth and assets Iraq found itself under a comprehensive U.N. system of economic sanctions that is still in effect.

It can be seen from this narrative that oil was central to several important changes in Iraq. Given the fact that the state was the primary recipient of the income from oil and given the necessity of having to distribute this income throughout the country and to all social classes through different mechanisms it follows that the economic and political fortunes of the country were tied more than ever to what affects the oil sector. But the war against Iran exposed the bankruptcy of the government's economic and political policies which depended almost exclusively on the oil sector. Moreover, the war with Iran forced the government to exhaust the country's foreign reserves and forced it also to contract massive amounts of foreign debt as military spending exceeded the amount of the oil revenue of the war period.

The war-induced fiscal bankruptcy was compounded by the steep decline in oil prices. To solve its economic and political predicament the government thought that an easy solution may be found in invading and annexing the state of Kuwait. The act of the invasion prompted the U.N. Security Council to impose the most comprehensive set of economic sanctions under which Iraq is still laboring.

SANCTIONS, WAR, AND THE ECONOMY

The sanctions system imposed by the U.N. Security Council was comprehensive in its scope and in the degree of compliance which U.N. member countries observed. Its impact was felt almost immediately as Iraq had grown dependent on the outside world for three-fourths of its food consumption. The access to Kuwait's oil and other assets which the government of Iraq had hoped for was denied to it under the sanctions regime.

Given the fact that Iraq had become dependent for three-fourths of its food requirements on foreign sources the sanctions-induced sharp rise in food prices was immediate and forced the government to introduce a system of food rationing to stave off starvation. The inflation that ensued in this period had the effect of destroying personal-income purchasing power and forced those with savings to use them to forestall a major collapse in their living standards.

The effects of the sanctions on the economy and living standards were compounded by the six-week bombing campaign that started in the middle of January 1991. The bombing targeted Iraq's infrastructure, industrial plants, and civilian structures in a campaign that was designed to accentuate the effects of the sanctions regime. The bombing, in addition to its destruction of assets vital for the working of the economy, had other consequences which had particular impact on society and the economy. The first such impact was related to the fact that most of Iraq's infrastructure such as transportation and communications were built by foreign firms which meant that the repair and replacement of destroyed assets had to await the removal or the modification of the sanctions system. Even in those cases where Iraq had the professional and technical manpower to rebuild destroyed assets, as was the case in the oil sector, Iraq still needed the foreign-manufactured capital goods and inputs for it to complete the task.

The other effect of the bombing was its destruction of water purification and sanitary systems which Iraq could not repair without input from abroad. This failure led in turn to the massive spread of water-borne diseases which had severe impact on the health conditions of children under five years of age, causing a sharp rise in their mortality rates, thus nullifying the progress made in the decades prior to the Gulf War.

The catastrophic state of the economy and the people was observed and documented by the missions the U.N. secretary-general sent to Iraq immediately after the war. These missions came up with estimates of Iraq's fiscal requirements to rebuild its infrastructure and rehabilitate its economy. Such recommendations were not acted upon. Instead, the UNSC passed a resolution in 1991 recommending the sale by Iraq of small amounts of oil to finance the import of food and medicines to deal with what the UNSC acknowledged to be a serious nutritional and health situation of the Iraqi civilian population. Yet the UNSC authorized the sale of only $1.6 billion of oil per six months to be reduced to some $1 billion after deductions for war reparations and the funding of Iraq-related U.N. activities. It is worth noting that the $2 billion per year that was to finance the purchase of foodstuffs, medicines, and materials and supplies for essential civilian needs for the purpose of providing human relief was much smaller than what the secretary-general had recommended for this purpose and was less than 14 percent of Iraq's oil sales in 1989.

The government of Iraq took the extraordinary step of rejecting the offer of the UNSC on the pretext that it would compromise its sovereignty, thus deepening the crisis of the economy and compounding the difficulties of ordinary people. Although the technocratic side in the government argued in favor of acceptance it was the political leadership which had the final say, of course. As the difficulties of the people continued to mount and as the U.N. need for funds to finance its Iraq-related programs such as war reparations and Iraq disarmament programs became greater the UNSC decided in 1995 to revisit the issue by passing resolution 986 in April which authorized the sale of $2 billion of oil per six months. Again, the government of Iraq rejected the new offer on the same old grounds of sovereignty causing the country's economic and social crises to further deepen. Eventually, the government had no choice but to accept the resolution, thus allowing Iraq's oil to be reintroduced to the world market in December 1996 after more than six years of absence from the market. A few months later food and medical supplies started to arrive in the country. The cap on the value of oil exports was raised to $5.2 billion, then removed altogether in 2000.

During the five-year period (as of the end of October 2001) of the oil-for-food program Iraq was able to export a total of $47.7 billion of oil under the program. The revenue from oil was deposited in an escrow account in New York and administered by the United Nations. Iraq is denied access to this account since all deposits into and payments from this account must be authorized by the secretary-general. The $47.7 billion was distributed as follows: $31.6 billion went to Iraq to cover its imports under the program; $14 billion was transferred directly into the U.N. Compensation Fund; $1.3 billion to cover the operational and administrative expenses of the United Nations associated with the implementation of the oil-for-food program and the expenses of the two commissions in charge of disarming Iraq; and $0.9 billion to Turkey for the transportation cost of Iraqi oil through that country. It is worth noting that by the end of this period some $16.8 billion of goods had arrived in Iraq while the value of contracts that remained on hold amounted to over $4 billion with the balance being the value of contracts still in production and shipping phases.

It can be seen from the data that the economy of Iraq received—by the end of 2001—some $17 billion of goods, with 62 percent of those goods going directly to the food and health sectors, and the balance of $6.4 billion going to meet the needs of all other sectors including oil, electricity, transport, telecommunications, agriculture, education, housing, and water and sanitation.

In addition to the low levels of imports, holds, and other delays the program suffers from other drawbacks as far as the Iraqi economy is concerned. One of the most serious shortcomings of the program is that it denied Iraq the ability to spend some of its oil revenue on domestically produced products and services. This meant that Iraq's own agricultural sector was sidelined in favor of imported wheat, rice, and other agricultural commodities. This was so because the program was designed to provide for imports and not for domestic production. Second, the very nature of the way in which the program was structured did not require transparency and accountability as far as the decisions of the Sanctions Committee were concerned. Nor were there time limits as to when the committee's holds might have to be lifted. Nor did the government have any say in how the program was implemented since the UNSC did not find a role for the government regarding the implementation phases of the program, thus reducing the government to a mere protesting spectator.

Another major problem with the program was its neglect of the oil sector. Early on in the history of the program oil industry experts commissioned by the U.N. secretary-general reported more than once that Iraq's oil industry was in a lamentable state and it needed a massive infusion of funds for investment to stave off stagnation and decline. The centrality of the oil sector to the humanitarian program cannot be overstressed. If output continues to be at the current low levels then any serious decline in the price of oil will mean a decline in oil revenue and with that the levels of imports.

It is clear from these observations that the program has failed to stem the deterioration of the economy, not to mention helping it to resume a degree of normalcy. Instead, the program has altered the society into becoming a hand-out society whose survival has become dependent on decisions made by external institutions driven largely by political considerations. Furthermore, the way the program was structured tends to increase the dependency of the Iraqi people on their government. People living under authoritarian regimes are never free, of course, in their dealing with their repressive governments. In Iraq people are doubly handicapped in their dealings with their government because of the importance of the government-supplied essential goods under the food-rationing system. It is a matter of physical survival for the overwhelming majority of the people that they continue to receive the commodities provided by the food-rationing system. In short, one is compelled to conclude that the Iraqi people have become victims of internal repression and the externally imposed system of sanctions.

PROSPECTS

Between 1968, when the current regime seized power, and 1990 Iraq received some $200 billion in oil revenue. Yet by 1991 Iraq was a heavily indebted country with a shattered economy, a nearly worthless currency, and a population on the verge of starvation. Moreover, the country was laboring under conditions of economic sanctions with the major economic decisions being made by U.N. diplomats and bureaucrats. Major segments of its professional classes either left the country or moved to jobs for which they were overqualified, or remained unemployed. After nearly twelve years of economic sanctions it is still difficult to speculate on the time of their removal. The mutual tension that has characterized relations between the U.N. Security Council and the government of Iraq does not seem to be on the verge of change. Under these conditions one can do no more than speculate about the prospects for the economic future of Iraq, assuming the removal of sanctions.

In the postsanctions era Iraq will have to contend with three major kinds of financial claims on its financial resources: the need for reconstruction and development, foreign debt service, and war reparations.

It is rather self-evident that Iraq must rebuild its infrastructure and restart the long process of reconstruction and development in order to enable the economy and its various sectors to function in a normal fashion. Needless to say, the process will require a long time and considerable effort since a great deal of capital goods, equipment, and inputs will have to be imported. Iraq's ability to push ahead with its program of rehabilitation and development will be constrained by the other two sets of financial claims as reparations and debt payments will have first claim on Iraq's foreign-exchange earnings.

As to reparation payments UNSC resolutions are clear on this issue since reparations have been given priority over the needs of the economy of Iraq by having 25 percent of Iraq's oil earnings transferred to the Compensation Fund. There is no reason, of course, that this particular arrangement will continue to be adhered to in the postsanctions era. It is conceivable that the UNSC may decide to set a lower deduction ratio or leave it up to Iraq to settle such claims with the claimants or forgive payments altogether. But in the absence of new modalities Iraq may find itself making payments for a long time to come.

Similarly, servicing Iraq's foreign debt will cut deeply into the financial residual available for investment in the economy. Iraq's creditors can, of course, restructure or reduce or forgive their claims on Iraq. To a certain extent changing the terms of Iraq's war reparations and foreign debt burdens become in the postsanctions era a political question as much as an economic one. The question that Iraq's creditors, especially its regional Arab ones, will have to answer is whether from the viewpoint of the region's economic and political stability it would be better to forgive Iraq its debts and let it rebuild and develop its economy or continue to force it to lead the life of a defeated regional power with the possibility of periodic adventurous and destructive political and military outburst.

Regardless of the position of creditors and claimants Iraq will have no choice but develop its oil reserves and increase its production. Paradoxically, instead of lessening the dependence of the economy on the oil sector this sector has become the single most important source of finance for the economy and its future viability. The problem with developing the oil sector rests not with whether Iraq has the reserves to expand production but with whether Iraq will have access to financial resources to develop its oil reserves. Given the fact that Iraq has the second largest oil reserves after Saudi Arabia and given the relatively low cost of development it can be safely assumed that foreign capital will be available to develop Iraq's oil resources. The question will be one of terms and conditions. Iraq will be further integrated in the world economy and its dependence on that economy will be deepened.

Looking back at Iraq's recent history it seems that the country's political and economic developments were driven almost exclusively by what happened to the oil sector and the implications of that for the economy and society. This dependence narrowed the range of options for policy makers and the people. By the same token the oil sector contributed enormous amounts of easily generated economic rent which pushed the political leadership into destructive adventures that ruined the economy and saddled it with a very heavy burden of debt. From this perspective oil cannot be considered anything but a burden on the economy and society. As to sanctions it is rather self-evident that they are the other burden under which the economy and the people have suffered for long time and will continue to suffer into the future.

Selected Bibliography

Abdulghani, J. M. (1984). *Iraq and Iran: The Years of Crisis*. Baltimore: Johns Hopkins University Press.

Adelman, M. A. (1972). *The World Petroleum Market*. Baltimore: Johns Hopkins University Press.

al-Anbari, A. (1996). "The UN Sanctions Regime: The Case of Iraq." *Middle East Economic Survey*, November 25.

Al-Chalabi, F. J. (1989). *OPEC at the Crossroads*. Oxford: Pergamon Press.

Al-Chalabi, I. (2001). "Future Prospects of Iraq's Oil Industry." *Middle East Economic Survey*, February 19, pp. D1–D7.

Ali, A.M.S. (1991). "Evaluation of the Role of the State in Arab Countries." In *The Role of the State in the Arab Countries*, ed. Ali Nassar (in Arabic). Kuwait: Arab Planning Institute.

Ali, A.M.S., and Al-Ganabi, A.H.J. (1992). "The Political Economy of Inflation in Iraq, 1988–1992." *Arab Economic Journal* 1 (1): 91–113 (in Arabic).

Alnasrawi, A. (1975). "The Petrodollar Energy Crisis: An Overview and Interpretation." *Syracuse Journal of International Law and Commerce* 3 (2): 369–412.

———. (1985). *OPEC in a Changing World Economy*. Baltimore: Johns Hopkins University Press.

———. (1991). *Arab Nationalism, Oil and the Political Economy of Dependency*. New York: Greenwood Press.

———. (1994). *The Economy of Iraq: Oil, Wars, Destruction of Development and Prospects, 1950–2010*. Westport, Conn.: Greenwood Press.

———. (1999). "Oil Resources in Iraq: Economic Growth and Development Until the Mid-1990's." In *Development Policies in Natural Resource Economies*, ed. Gorg Mayer, Brian Chambers, and Ayisha Faroog. Cheltenham, U.K.: Edward Elgar.

———. (2000). "Iraq: Economic Embargo and Predatory Rule." In *War, Hunger and Displacement: The Origins of Humanitarian Emergencies*, ed. E. Wayne Nafziger, Frances Stewart, and Raimo Vayrynen. Oxford: Oxford University Press.

———. (2001). "Iraq: Economic Sanctions and Consequences, 1990–2000." *Third World Quarterly* 22 (2): 205–218.

Al-Pachachi, N. (1968). "The Development of Concession Arrangements and Taxation in the Middle East." *Middle East Economic Survey* (supplement), March 29, pp. 1–11.

Al-Shabibi, S. (1991) "Iraq's Financial Obligations Could Cripple Economic Prospects." *Middle East Economic Survey*, November 4, pp. B1–B2.

Amuzegar, J. (1999). *Managing the Oil Wealth: OPEC's Windfalls and Pitfalls*. London: I. B. Tauris.

Arab Monetary Fund, League of Arab States, and Arab Fund for Economic and Social Development. (1992). *Unified Arab Economic Report*. Abu Dhabi, United Arab Emirates: Arab Monetary Fund.

Batatu, H. (1982). *The Old Social Classes and the Revolutionary Movements of Iraq: A Study of Iraq's Old Landed and Commercial Classes and of Its Communists, Ba'thists, and Free Officers*. Princeton, N.J.: Princeton University Press.

Beblawi, H. (1987). "The Rentier State in the Arab World." *Arab Studies Quarterly* 9 (4): 383–398.

Blair, J. H. (1976). *The Control of Oil*. New York: Pantheon Books.

Bradsher, K. (1991). "War Damages and Old Debts Could Exhaust Iraq's Assets." *The New York Times*, March 1.

Chalabi, F. J. (2000). "Iraq and the Future of World Oil." *Middle East Policy* 7 (4): 163–173.

Chipaux, F. (1991). "Saddam Sits Pretty as Iraqi People Suffer." *Manchester Guardian Weekly*, August 11.

Clark, R. (1994). *The Fire This Time: U.S. War Crimes in the Gulf*. New York: Thunder's Mouth Press.

Development Board. (1956). *Development of Iraq* (in Arabic). Baghdad: Development Board.

———. (1957). *Annual Report 1954–1955* (in Arabic). Baghdad: Development Board.

———. (1958). *Annual Report 1956–1957* (in Arabic). Baghdad: Development Board.

Dos Santos, Theotonio. (1970). "The Structure of Dependence." *American Economic Review* 60 (2): 231–236.

Dreze, J., and Gazdar, H. (1992). "Hunger and Poverty in Iraq." *World Development* 20 (7): 921–945.

Economist Intelligence Unit. (1989). *Country Report, Iraq 4*. London: Economist Intelligence Unit.

———. (1996). *Country Report, Iraq*. No. 1. London: Economist Intelligence Unit.

Elali, W. (2000). "Note: Dealing with Iraq's Foreign Indebtedness." *Thunderbird International Business Review* 42 (1): 65–83.

El Azhary, M. S., ed. (1984). *Iran–Iraq War: An Historical Analysis*. New York: St. Martin's Press.

El-Naggar, S., ed. (1989). *Privatization and Structural Adjustment in the Arab Countries*. Washington, D.C.: International Monetary Fund.

Engler, Robert. (1961). *The Politics of Oil: A Study of the Private Power and Democratic Directions*. Chicago: University of Chicago Press.

Farouk-Sluglett, M., and Sluglett, P. (1987). *Iraq Since 1958: From Revolution to Dictatorship*. London: KPI.

Food and Agriculture Organization. (1959). *Iraq, Country Report*. Rome: Food and Agriculture Organization.

———. (1995). *Evaluation of Food and Nutrition Situation in Iraq*. Rome: Food and Agriculture Organization.

———. (2000). *Assessment of the Food and Nutrition Situation: IRAQ*. Rome: Food and Agriculture Organization.

Food and Agriculture Organization, and World Food Program. (1993). *FAO/WFP Crop and Food Supply Assessment Mission to Iraq*. Rome: Food and Agriculture Organization.

Frank, H. J. (1966) *Crude Oil Prices in the Middle East: A Study in Oligopolistic Price Behavior*. New York: Praeger.

Freedman, L., and Karsh, F. (1993). *The Gulf Conflict, 1990–1991*. Princeton, N.J.: Princeton University Press.

Garfield, R. (2000). "Changes in Health and Well-Being in Iraq during the 1990s: What Do We Know and How Do We Know It." In Campaign Against Sanctions on Iraq. *Sanctions on Iraq: Background, Consequences and Strategies* (pp. 32–51). Cambridge: Campaign Against Sanctions on Iraq.

Gellman, B. (1991). "Allied Air War Struck Broadly in Iraq: Officials Acknowledge Strategy Went Beyond Purely Military Targets." *The Washington Post*, June 23, p. A1.

General Accounting Office. (1982). *The Changing Structure of the International Oil Market*. Washington, D.C.: U.S. Government Printing Office.

"General Attack on the Citizens' Livelihood and Numerous Privileges to the Followers." June (in Arabic). (1996). *Tareeq Al-Shaab*.

Gordon, J. (2001). "Chokehold on the World: Are Sanctions Ethical—or an Ill-Used Weapon of Mass Destruction?" *The Nation*, January 1, pp. 27–32.

Government of Iraq. (1950). *Law No. 23* (in Arabic). Baghdad: Government of Iraq.

———. (1955). *Law No. 43* (in Arabic). Baghdad: Government of Iraq.

———. (1958). *Law No. 30* (in Arabic). Baghdad: Government of Iraq.

———. (1959). *The July 14 Revolution in Its First Year* (in Arabic). Baghdad: Government of Iraq.

———. (1960). *The July 14 Revolution in its Second Year* (in Arabic). Baghdad: Government of Iraq.

Graham-Brown, S. (1999). *Sanctioning Saddam: The Politics of Intervention in Iraq*. London: I. B. Tauris.

Harik, I., and Sullivan, D. J., eds. (1992). *Privatization and Liberalization in the Middle East*. Bloomington: Indiana University Press.

Harvard Study Team. (1991). *Public Health in Iraq after the Gulf War*. Washington, D.C.: Wagner Communications.

Hasan, S. (1966). *Studies in the Iraqi Economy* (in Arabic). Beirut: Dar Al Taliaa.

Haub, C. (1991). "A Demographic Disaster." *Manchester Guardian Weekly*, March 10.

Helms, C. M. (1984). *Iraq: The Eastern Flank of the Arab World*. Washington, D.C.: The Brookings Institution.

Hiro, D. (1991). *The Longest War: The Iran–Iraq Military Conflict*. New York: Routledge.

———. (1992). *Desert Shield to Desert Storm: The Second Gulf War*. New York: Routledge.

Holsti, K. J. (2000). "Political Causes of Humanitarian Emergencies." In *War, Hunger, and Displacement: The Origins of Humanitarian Emergencies*, ed. E. Wayne Nafziger, Frances Stewart, and Raimo Vayrynen. Oxford, U.K.: Oxford University Press.

Ibrahim, I., ed. (1992). *The Gulf Crisis: Background and Consequences*. Washington, D.C.: Georgetown University.

Ibrahim, Y. M. (1990). "OPEC Members Close to Raising Output Ceiling." *The New York Times*, August 20, p. 1.

International Bank for Reconstruction and Development. (1952). *The Economic Development of Iraq*. Baltimore: Johns Hopkins University Press.

International Study Team. (1991). *Health and Welfare in Iraq after the Gulf Crisis: An In-Depth Assessment*. Washington, D.C.: Wagner Communications.

Iraq Ministry of Planning. (1969). *The Detailed Framework of the Five-Year Economic Plan, 1965–1969* (in Arabic). Baghdad: Ministry of Planning.

———. (1970). *Analysis of the Iraqi Economy to the Base Year 1969* (in Arabic). Baghdad: Ministry of Planning.

———. (1971). *Detailed Objectives of the Components of the National Development Plan, 1970–1974* (in Arabic). Baghdad: Ministry of Planning.

———. (1971). *Evaluation of the Five-Year Economic Plan, 1965–1969* (in Arabic). Baghdad: Ministry of Planning.

———. (1971). *Guide to the National Development Plan, 1970–1974* (in Arabic). Baghdad: Ministry of Planning.

———. (1971). *Law of National Development Plan 1970–1974 and the General Objectives of the Plan* (in Arabic). Baghdad: Ministry of Planning.

———. (1971). *National Income Accounts and Sectoral Accounts of Capital Formation and Its Financing, 1969 and 1974* (in Arabic). Baghdad: Ministry of Planning.

Iraq National Oil Company. (1973a). *Iraq National Oil Company and Direct Exploitation of Oil in Iraq*. Baghdad: Iraq National Oil Company.

———. (1973b). *Oil in Iraq: From Concessions to Direct National Investment, 1912–1972* (in Arabic). Baghdad: Iraq National Oil Company.

Issawi, C. (1982). *An Economic History of the Middle East and North Africa*. New York: Columbia University Press.

Issawi, C., and Yeganeh, M. (1962). *The Economics of Middle Eastern Oil*. New York: Frederick A. Praeger.

Jacoby, N. H. (1974). *Multinational Oil*. New York: Macmillan.

Jiyad, A. M. (2001). "An Economy in a Debt Trap: Iraqi Debt 1980–2020." *Arab Studies Quarterly* 23 (4): 15–58.

Kainker, L. (1991). "Desert Sin: A Post-War Journey Through Iraq." In *Beyond the Storm: A Gulf Crisis Reader*, ed. P. Bennis and M. Moushabeck. New York: Olive Branch Press.

Khadduri, W. (1993). "The Politics of Iraqi Oil Exports." *Middle East Economic Survey*, May 24.

Kubba, I. (1969). *This Is the Path of July 14 Defense Before the Revolution's Court* (in Arabic). Beirut: Dar al Taliaa.

Leeman, W. A. (1962). *The Price of Middle East Oil: An Essay in Political Economy.* Ithaca: Cornell University Press.

Middle East Economic Digest (weekly).

Middle East Economic Survey (weekly).

Mofid, K. (1990). *The Economic Consequences of the Gulf War.* London: Routledge.

Murphy, C. (1991). "Iraqi Death Toll Remains Clouded." *The Washington Post*, June 23.

Niblock, T. (2001). "The Regional and Domestic Political Consequences of Sanctions Imposed on Iraq, Libya and Sudan." *Arab Studies Quarterly* 23 (4): 59–68.

OPEC. (1969). *Annual Review and Record, 1968.* Vienna: OPEC.

———. (1990). *OPEC Official Resolutions and Press Releases 1960–1990.* Vienna: OPEC.

———. (1996). *OPEC Official Resolutions and Press Releases 1990–1996.* Vienna: OPEC.

———. *Annual Bulletin of Statistics.*

———. *Annual Report.*

———. *OPEC Bulletin* (monthly).

Owen, R. (1981). *The Middle East in the World Economy, 1800–1914.* New York: Methuen.

Pellet, P. (2000). "Sanctions, Food, Nutrition, and Health in Iraq." In *Iraq under Siege: The Deadly Impact of Sanctions and War*, ed. A. Arnov. Cambridge, Mass.: South End Press.

Penrose, E. (1968). *The Large International Firm in Developing Countries: The International Petroleum Industry.* London: Allen & Unwin.

———. (1971). *The Growth of Firms, Middle East Oil and Other Essays.* London: Frank Cass & Co.

Petroleum Intelligence Weekly.

Provost, R. (1992). "Starvation as a Weapon: Legal Implications of the United Nations Food Blockade Against Iraq and Kuwait." *Columbia Journal of Transnational Law* 30 (3): 577–639.

Rouhani, F. (1971). *A History of O.P.E.C.* New York: Praeger.

Sadowski, Y. M. (1987). "Patronage and the Ba'th: Corruption and Control in Contemporary Syria." *Arab Studies Quarterly* 9 (4): 442–461.

———. (1993). *Scuds or Butter: The Political Economy of Arms Control.* Washington, D.C.: The Brookings Institution.

Salinger, P., and Laurant, E. (1991). *Secret Dossier: The Hidden Agenda Behind the Gulf War.* London: Penguin Books.

Salman, R. (1990). "Iraq's Oil Policy." *Middle East Economic Survey*, March 12, pp. D1–D6.

Sayigh, Y. A. (1991). *Elusive Development: From Dependence to Self-Reliance in the Arab Region.* London: Routledge.

Sayigh, Y. (1992). *Arab Military Industry* (in Arabic). Beirut: Centre for Arab Unity Studies.

Sevan, B. V. (2000). Introductory Statement by Benon V. Sevan, *Report of the Secretary-General Pursuant to Paragraph 5 of Security Council Resolution 1302 (2000) of 8 June 2000.* New York: United Nations.

Seymour, I. (1996). "Can OPEC Handle A Resumption of Iraq Oil Exports?" *Middle East Economic Survey*, February 12, pp. A3–A5.

Sifry, M. L., and Cerf, C., eds. (1991). *The Gulf War Reader: History, Documents, Opinions*. New York: Random House.

Simons, G. (1998). *The Scourging of Iraq: Sanctions, Law and Natural Justice*, 2d ed. New York: St. Martin's Press.

Smithies, A. (1949). "Economic Consequences of the Basing Point Decisions." *Harvard Law Review* 62 (2): 308–318.

Springborg, R. (1986). "Infitah, Agrarian Transformation, and the Elite Consolidation in Contemporary Iraq." *The Middle East Journal* 40 (1).

Stauffer, T. (2001). "Compensation to Kuwait: Multi-Billion Dollar Miscalculation." *Middle East International*, February 9, pp. 20–23.

Stivers, W. (1982). *Supremacy and Oil: Iraq, Turkey, and the Anglo-American World Order, 1918–1930*. Ithaca: Cornell University Press.

Stocking, G. W. (1970). *Middle East Oil: A Study in Political and Economic Controversy*. Nashville: Vanderbilt University Press.

Tibi, B. (1981). *Arab Nationalism: A Critical Enquiry*. New York: St. Martin's Press.

Townsend, D. (2000a). "A State of Disrepair." *Petroleum Economist*, May, pp. 64–65.

———. (2000b). "Hope Springs Eternal." *Petroleum Economist*, August, pp. 3–4.

Tripp, C. (2000). *A History of Iraq*. Cambridge: Cambridge University Press.

UNICEF. (1999). *Child and Maternal Mortality Survey 1999: Preliminary Report*. New York: UNICEF.

United Nations. (1996). *The United Nations and the Iraq–Kuwait Conflict*. New York: United Nations.

———. (1998). *Report of the Secretary-General Pursuant to Paragraph 7 of Resolution 1143 (1997)*. New York: United Nations.

———. (1998). *Report of the Secretary-General Pursuant to Paragraph 10 of Security Council 1153 (1998)*. New York: United Nations.

———. (1999). *Report of the second panel established pursuant to the note by the president of the Security Council of 30 January 1999 (S1999/100), concerning the current humanitarian situation in Iraq, Annex II of S/1999/356—30 March 1999*. New York: United Nations.

———. (1999). *Report of the Secretary-General Pursuant to Paragraph 6 of Security Council Resolution 1242 (1999)*. New York: United Nations.

———. (1999). *Review and Assessment of the Implementation of the Humanitarian Programme Established Pursuant to Security Council Resolution 986 (1995) (December 1996–November 1998)*. New York: United Nations.

———. (2000). *Report of the Group of United Nations Experts Established Pursuant to Paragraph 30 of the Security Council Resolution 1284 (1999)*. New York: United Nations.

———. (2000). *Report of the Secretary-General Pursuant to Paragraph 5 of Resolution 1302 (2000)*. New York: United Nations.

———. (2001). *Report of the Secretary-General Pursuant to Paragraph 5 of Resolution 1330 (2000)*. New York: United Nations.

———. (2001). *Report of the Secretary-General Pursuant to Paragraph 5 of Resolution 1360 (2001)*. New York: United Nations.

U.N. Economic Commission for Europe. (1955). *The Price of Oil in Western Europe*. Geneva: United Nations.

U.N. Office of the Iraq Programme. (2001). *Basic Figures.* New York: United Nations. January 19, pp. 1–3.

———. (2001). *Basic Figures.* New York: United Nations. March 21, pp. 1–3.

———. (2001). *Basic Figures.* New York: United Nations. December 14, pp. 1–2.

U.N. Security Council Panel on Humanitarian Issues. (1999). *Special Topics on Social Conditions in Iraq.* New York: United Nations.

U.S. House. (1992). Armed Services Committee, 103d Congress, 1st Session. *A Defense for a New Era: Lessons of the Persian Gulf War.* Washington, D.C.: U.S. Government Printing Office.

U.S. Senate. (1952). Select Committee on Small Business, 82d Congress, 2d Session. *The International Petroleum Cartel.* Washington, D.C.: U.S. Government Printing Office.

———. (1975). Committee on Foreign Relations, 93d Congress, 2d Session. Subcommittee on Multinational Corporations. *Multinational Oil Corporations and U.S. Foreign Policy.* Washington, D.C.: U.S. Government Printing Office.

———. (1977). Committee on Energy and Natural Resources, 95th Congress, 1st Session. *The Geopolitics of Energy.* Washington, D.C.: U.S. Government Printing Office.

Uqaili, T. (2000). "Economics of Investments in Developing New Oilfields in Iraq." *Middle East Economic Survey*, December 18, pp. D1–D7.

Vernon, R., ed. (1988). *The Promise of Privatization: A Challenge for American Policy.* New York: Council on Foreign Relations.

Vickers, J., and Yarrow, G. (1988). *Privatization: An Economic Analysis.* Cambridge, Mass.: MIT Press.

Warriner, D. (1957). *Land Reform and Development in the Middle East: A Study of Egypt, Syria and Iraq.* London: Royal Institute of International Affairs.

World Bank. (1985). *World Development Report, 1985.* Washington, D.C.: World Bank.

World Health Organization. (1996). *The Health Conditions of the People in Iraq Since the Gulf Crisis.* Geneva: World Health Organization.

Index

ABOUT THE AUTHOR

Abbas Alnasrawi is the John H. Converse Professor of Economics, the University of Vermont. He is the author of *The Economy of Iraq: Oil, Wars, Destruction of Development and Prospects* (Greenwood Press, 1994) and *Arab Nationalism, Oil, and the Political Economy of Dependency* (Greenwood Press, 1991).